"This truly is film school, a m
all in one fantastic book!!! In
we, as indie film producers, can take charge, distribute our own films
and make a profit. It will take an entrepreneurial mindset he says, and he
makes it all sound so easy. Get our audience involved at the script stage,
build our data base along the way... get smart about crowdsourcing and
crowdfunding at every stage... get our community involved and our
local government onboard. Make filmmaking a win/win for everyone.
Marty is a genius and this book is a goldmine... an indispensable tool
and blueprint for success!"

Suzanne Lyons, *producer/author*

The Self-Sustaining Filmmaker

This book provides guidance on how to build an independent, financially sustainable filmmaking career through channels such as crowdsourcing, crowdfunding, and community filmmaking concepts.

Through real-life experiences, Marty Lang provides insight on how to use these key concepts through every stage of a film's lifecycle – from distribution (the stage that should be figured out first), through development, screenwriting, prep, production, and post, all the way through marketing and the film's release. By thinking of filmmaking as a start-up company, and looking at how businesses make money, Lang creates a completely independent financial model for films, turning filmmakers into businesspeople, conscious of the needs of their audiences, and empowered to use their creative work to make their living. Using interviews with leaders in the field, case studies, and practical experience gained from 20 years of community filmmaking, this book unveils an exciting, new way to make films that prioritizes a collaborative, entrepreneurial mindset at every stage.

This is an essential guide for aspiring and seasoned filmmakers alike looking to understand and apply crowdsourcing as an effective tool in their career.

Marty Lang is Director of the MFA in Film, Television, and Digital Media at the University of Georgia. He has written and directed two feature films, and his producing credits include *Chompy & The Girls*, featuring Udo Kier, *Being Michael Madsen*, starring Michael Madsen and Virginia Madsen, and the 2020 Sundance world premiere Web series *The Ride*. He holds MFA degrees in Film Production from Florida State University and Screenwriting from California State University, Northridge.

The Self-Sustaining Filmmaker

Creating Crowdsourced, Crowdfunded and Community-Supported Independent Film

Marty Lang

Routledge
Taylor & Francis Group
NEW YORK AND LONDON

Designed cover image: © Getty Images

First published 2024
by Routledge
605 Third Avenue, New York, NY 10158

and by Routledge
4 Park Square, Milton Park, Abingdon, Oxon, OX14 4RN

Routledge is an imprint of the Taylor & Francis Group, an informa business

© 2024 Marty Lang

The right of Marty Lang to be identified as author of this work has been asserted in accordance with sections 77 and 78 of the Copyright, Designs and Patents Act 1988.

All rights reserved. No part of this book may be reprinted or reproduced or utilised in any form or by any electronic, mechanical, or other means, now known or hereafter invented, including photocopying and recording, or in any information storage or retrieval system, without permission in writing from the publishers.

Trademark notice: Product or corporate names may be trademarks or registered trademarks, and are used only for identification and explanation without intent to infringe.

Library of Congress Cataloging-in-Publication Data
Names: Lang, Marty, 1977- author.
Title: The self-sustaining filmmaker : creating crowdsourced, crowdfunded & community-supported independent film / Marty Lang.
Description: New York, NY : Routledge, 2024. |
Identifiers: LCCN 2024001511 (print) |
LCCN 2024001512 (ebook) | ISBN 9781032282114 (hardback) |
ISBN 9781032282022 (paperback) | ISBN 9781003295754 (ebook)
Subjects: LCSH: Independent films--Production and direction--United States. | Motion picture industry--United States--Finance. | Motion pictures--Vocational guidance--United States.
Classification: LCC PN1995.9.I457 L36 2024 (print) |
LCC PN1995.9.I457 (ebook) | DDC 791.4302/32--dc23/eng/20240301
LC record available at https://lccn.loc.gov/2024001511
LC ebook record available at https://lccn.loc.gov/2024001512

ISBN: 978-1-032-28211-4 (hbk)
ISBN: 978-1-032-28202-2 (pbk)
ISBN: 978-1-003-29575-4 (ebk)

DOI: 10.4324/9781003295754

Typeset in Times New Roman
by MPS Limited, Dehradun

To Rhett, Lindsay and Luke
You can build a life you love. And I can't wait to help you guys do it.

Contents

Foreword	*xii*
Acknowledgments	*xiv*

1 A New Paradigm   1
Film Education Is Outdated 3
Studio Filmmaking Is Broken 5
Independent Film Is Broken 6
The Pillars of the New Way 7
Hedging Your Bets 10

2 From Filmmaker to Entrepreneur   11
Creating an Entrepreneurial Mindset ... Not a Business One 12
Answering the Business Questions 13
Translating the Mindset into Filmmaking 24
Your Film Is a Startup ... And It Isn't 30
Business in the Real World 31

3 Development   38
What Is Crowdsourcing? 39
Crowdsourcing Your Story 40
Who Is Your Audience? 46
Publicity and Teambuilding Begins Now 50
The Importance of Scheduling 51
Development for DEADBRAINS 52

4 Screenwriting — 60
Carding, the Shelf, and the Well 61
Crowdsourcing Your Writing 63
Writing Like a Production Manager 66
Screenwriting for DEADBRAINS 68

5 The Context of Crowdfunding — 78
Crowdfunding Is Networking 79
The Two Stories of Every Film 81
Crowdfunding Holistically 82
Conflicting Emotions 84

6 Crowdfundamentals — 88
Prepping Your Campaign 89
Leadup to Launch 97
Pushing the Button 102
What Happens Afterwards? 104
Crowdfunding DEADBRAINS 105

7 Pre-Production — 113
The Power of the Open Call 113
Thinking in Symbiotic Relationships 115
What You Can Offer Other than Money 117
Getting the Community Involved 123
Getting Your Government Involved 124
Know Your Tax Credits! 125
Planning Far Ahead 127
Pre-Production for DEADBRAINS 129

8 Production and Post-Production — 136
The BLRTS Process 136
The Story of Your Shoot 138
Transparency in Post 139
The Incredible Opportunities of Focus Groups 140
Creating Film-Adjacent Content 144
Production and Post for DEADBRAINS 145

9 Marketing 153
Re-engaging the Engaged 154
Expanding Your Digital Footprint 155
Always Be Tracking 156
Creating Relevant Content 156
Marketing for DEADBRAINS 175

10 Distribution 182
The Dried-up Waterfall 183
Golden Elevators and Free-range Films 184
Tay Leads the Way 185
Digital Distribution 188
Hire Your Crowd! 189
Distribution for DEADBRAINS 190

11 You're Done. Now What? 198
The Loop of Kindness 198
Building Your Ecosystem 199
Bridging the Indie Gap 200
You Can Build Anywhere 201

Index *203*

Foreword

Mark Duplass, Emmy and Golden Globe-nominated actor/writer/director/producer, and owner of Duplass Brothers Productions

"Beware the volunteer."

I was once given this piece of advice from an experienced indie film producer. Their point was that anyone willing to give you 12 free hours of labor on an indie film set is most likely the same person who wants something from you that you may not want (or be able) to give. And while I found this wisdom a bit jaded for my personal taste, it did stick in the back of my mind.

Cut to:

It's 2011 and I'm on the set of my wife Katie Aselton's latest indie feature BLACK ROCK. As usual, we are underfunded, understaffed, and wondering why we thought we could make this film with such limited resources. I am the film's co-writer and executive producer, and also the primary caregiver of our three-year-old daughter while Katie stars in and directs this incredibly complicated movie which she also co-wrote. In short? We're in the shit.

Our producer, Adele Romanski, quickly realized we could use some extra hands, so she mentioned she had a friend who lived nearby who might be willing to help out on a few of our more difficult shoot days. A volunteer! Of course, that little voice in the back of my head told me to be skeptical of this supposed good Samaritan and his potential motivations, but we were in no position to say no. Enter the gentlest giant of them all... the great Marty Lang.

He came to set with his trademark towering grin and enthusiasm. And he got to work immediately. Hauling cables, carrying gear through the sand, extra hands on set decoration, etc. You name it, he did it. And he seemed genuinely happy and excited just to be on set. Just to be helping. And that is what I've seen him continue to do in various shapes and forms since that day. He has never tried to "cash in" on his favors. He has never asked for anything in return. He has merely showed up to help, support, and be a part of independent film in whatever ways he can.

This spirit is becoming more and more unique in the increasingly Dionysian world of indie film. Everyone wants what's theirs. It all feels like a bleak, zero-sum game of decreasing opportunities. And it generally makes everyone feel scared, and a lot less generous.

But not Marty.

I've spoken a lot about the things we should be doing to keep independent film sustainable. How to make things at the right price so that they can be economically sustainable, not only for the filmmakers and crew making them, but also for the smaller companies that often buy them and release them. How we need to curate a trusting community of collaborators whose help we can depend on as much as they can depend on ours.

But at the core of it all is something basic that Marty seemed to understand from the first time I met him. In a time when most people are reaching their hands up to see who can grab hold of them and help bring them up to the next level, Marty simply looked around and asked who needed his help.

And that's what I love most about this book. It's not about "How can I get what's mine?" It's about how to build a community of like-minded collaborators, wherever you are, and build something sustainable and impenetrable together.

Acknowledgments

To my wife Mary Beth, who dealt with my attention being split in multiple directions the whole time writing this, and who took care of our son the majority of that time. You're my best friend. I love you so much.

To my in-laws, Dale and Lynn Helms, and my brothers-in-law Patrick and Reece Helms, for spending as much time with my son as I have, and giving me the gift of quiet, focused time at my computer to create this book. I love you guys.

To Katherine Lowe, thank you for replying to me on Twitter/X, guiding me through the proposal process, and giving me confidence that the idea for this book had merit.

To Mark Duplass, whose generosity is matched only by his ability to inspire everyone he meets in the independent film world. Thank you for all the inspiration you've given me. I'm proud to call you a friend. (And thanks again for the cookies.)

To Matt Giovannucci, my producing partner, attorney, and friend, thank you for motivating me to move to California, and start the journey that's led to our company – and this book.

To Lauren Shields, author of *The Beauty Suit: How My Year of Religious Modesty Made Me a Better Feminist*, thank you for showing me a narrative filmmaker could be a nonfiction author.

To Brian Trent, author of *Redspace Rising* among so many wonderful stories, thank you for planting the thought in my head 25 years ago that I could write my own book one day.

To Patrick "Klokwize" O'Sullivan, the brilliant hip-hop musician, thank you for showing me an artist can be completely independent, successful, and happy, and for being the sonic heartbeat of RISING STAR.

To Caleb Suggs, Allie Phillips, Tarrin McGhee, and Kristen Hill, thank you for all your hard work in creating the plan for ReelLife Entertainment, and showing me that if the theatrical moviegoing experience can be disrupted, maybe the entire process of filmmaking can be, too.

To Michael Hoffmeyer, Lisa Threadgill, Dawn Kimball, and the University of Memphis Crews Center for Entrepreneurship, thank you for your kindness, and for bringing me into your world.

To Daniel Kershaw, Alyss Barraza, Tarana Parveen, and the teams at Taylor & Francis and MPS Limited, thank you for all your help in the copy editing and publishing process. It's only through your hard work and expertise that this book exists in the professional way it does.

To Nic LaRue, interviewee and fellow debut author, thank you for keeping me accountable. I hope I helped you half as much as you've helped me.

To Leaf Maiman, thank you for being the energy behind STAY WITH ME, and the reason I was able to get myself back to creating films again. I'll always be grateful for that.

To Sarah de Leon and Pete Van der Pluym, producers extraordinaire, thank you for your help shepherding STAY WITH ME into existence. I'm so lucky to work with talents like you.

To my incredible interviewees, Emily Best, Brandi Nicole, Craig Brewer, Bri Castellini, Hannah Black, Megan Peterson, Noam Kroll, and Dan Mirvish, thank you for sharing your lives, your wisdom, and your stories with me. This book wouldn't be what it is without you.

And most importantly, to every person who's ever supported an independent film production I was involved in, whether as writer/director, producer, or actor, thank you so much for believing in me and giving me your support. You not only supported a filmmaker ... he's turned into an author, too.

1 A New Paradigm

Hello, filmmaker! I'm so glad you've decided to spend some time reading this book. Thank you so much for buying it. My name's Marty Lang, and I'm a college film professor, independent filmmaker, actor, crowdfunder – and now, apparently, author. If you've found this book, it's probably because you've got dreams of making your own movies, but have questions about what the process is like (or you've gone through the process, and are looking for new ways to approach it).

You've come to the right place.

You're also far from alone in those dreams. As of December 2023, there were 667,381 feature-length films listed on the Internet Movie Database, and a whopping 969,800 short films on there.[1] That's a lot of dreams – along with a lot of money, time and resources.

I've worked as a film professor since 2005, and I've taught a version of just about every film production-oriented class a college offers. As I've taught, I've also made my own movies and learned how to improve my process along the way. I always tried to incorporate what I learned in the field in the classroom, but there's one thing that I've never had the chance to teach:

How to successfully create your first professional film project.

That could be a feature film, and for many, it is, but it could also be your first short film with a bigger crew, your first project with a union actor, maybe even the first project you shoot that isn't set at your house. And with that effort, you're going to need lots of help from lots of people. You'll need to find actors who'll bring your story to life on screen. Crew members who are great at their jobs, and supportive of your energy and passion. Equipment to make the film look, and sound, as good as possible.

But there are many other elements you'll need to make this first project, elements that will help you in ways you're probably not thinking about yet. And you're going to need that help as your career progresses. Because if you have dreams of making your living as a filmmaker, there's something

DOI: 10.4324/9781003295754-1

you need to get past. Something that has stood in the way of every feature filmmaker who's ever existed, since the first film was ever made.

I call it the Indie Gap.

No matter how big a filmmaker you are, or eventually become, no matter what glitzy festivals your films play at, no matter how much money they make at the box office, or how much they're watched in theaters or on streaming, every filmmaker has a point in their career where they're making films, but they're not getting paid for making them. They make movies simply for the love of making them, with the hope (or goal) that one day, they could consider it their career. Each project is their next attempt to find the missing piece – an agent or manager, an A-list actor, a distribution deal, a financier – to bridge the Indie Gap, and get them to the other side, so that they're making money as a filmmaker.

Now there are as many paths to filmmaking success as there are successful filmmakers, so there's no set amount of time someone will have to stay in the Indie Gap. Depending on the filmmaker's career, it can vary widely:

- SHAZAM and ANNABELLE: CREATION director David F. Sandberg spent ten years in the Indie Gap, directing 14 short films that ran the gamut from horror films, live-action comedies and animated comedies from 2006 to 2016. But it was his tenth short film in 2013, the viral horror sensation LIGHTS OUT, which led to his bridging the Indie Gap, a feature adaptation of the short, produced by SAW director James Wan. The film went on to gross over $140 million worldwide.
- Writer/director Gillian Robespierre made a short comedy film about abortion called OBVIOUS CHILD and used the momentum from that to crowdfund a feature version of that story, starring Jenny Slate. The feature world premiered at the Sundance Film Festival and was picked up for distribution by A24. She was then hired to co-write and direct the dramedy LANDLINE for Amazon, starring Edie Falco and John Turturro, so she was able to bridge the Indie Gap quickly after her first feature.
- Before winning Best Picture and Best Screenplay Oscars with MOONLIGHT, director Barry Jenkins attended film school at Florida State University, where he made a number of short films before writing and directing his first microbudget feature, MEDICINE FOR MELANCHOLY, in 2008. That movie received three Independent Spirit Award nominations, and got him an agent, and screenwriting work, but not a second film. After nine long years, A24 hired him to co-write and direct his second film. Barry's time in the Indie Gap was much longer than Gillian's or Kevin's, but he made the most use of his first paid filmmaking opportunity.

In each of these cases, the filmmakers made the jump to directing a studio movie. (There are also scores of filmmakers who've made films on their own, and then got hired to work in television, but for this book, we'll be focusing on films.) The three of them, though, all share something that, frankly, is rare: they were eventually able to bridge the Indie Gap.

The harsh reality of this business is that most filmmakers never do.

So if the majority of filmmakers never get to the point where they get hired to make movies, should they just give up? If you pour your blood, sweat and tears into a first microbudget feature that doesn't get you that big break, should you just quit and never make movies again?

I say hell no.

And that question is the reason I've written this book.

If the odds are that you won't get the big break that will catapult you into the world of professional, for-hire filmmakers, there has to be another way to generate the people, resources and money you need to keep making films, while still living in the Indie Gap. And to take it a step further, there has to be a way for those filmmakers to generate revenue with their films, which can help finance future work. It sounds unthinkable. And I'll be honest, it will take a good amount of work. But it's possible. A filmmaker can make films, procure everything they need to make those films, and use the revenue from them to help finance more films, all as they work to find their way out of the Indie Gap.

They can be self-sustaining filmmakers.

Once they learn the skills that filmmakers are usually never taught. Because ...

Film Education Is Outdated

I started teaching college film courses in spring 2005, after graduating from Florida State University's film school the summer before. My first class was Introduction to Film, a class where you watch a movie each week, and talk about a specific filmmaking craft, or aesthetic idea, after watching it. I was nervous before my teaching debut, so I asked a faculty mentor if they had any advice for me. This professor said something I've never forgotten:

"You know more than they do. Just keep talking."

Not exactly what I was looking for.

This was my introduction to college-level film education, and it revealed something I've seen to be true at other universities I've worked at. Professors who teach filmmaking tend to subscribe to a one-way conversation. There's only a single way to do things, and it's the professor's job to teach students that one way, while the student's job is to dutifully transcribe all that precious information, and then follow it to the letter when making their own films.

And nowhere is that one-way conversation more evident than when film professors talk about film distribution.

Every narrative filmmaking professor I've ever worked with, as a student, staff member or faculty colleague, has banked on the assumption that they would raise private money, produce their film, and sell that film to a distributor, which would pay their investors back, and finance their next film. It's an assumption they also teach to their students, either because it's worked for them in the past, or because "that's how it's always been done."

Problem is, that's not how it's being done now. Mia Galuppo of the Hollywood Reporter explained that the 2022 Sundance Film Festival, generally regarded as the biggest independent film market in the USA, "saw a possible market correction," where no film generated a record sale. Galuppo also noted that "the pace of deal-making notably slowed, a product of the practicalities of the virtual market, among other factors."[2]

Not the best news if you're making a film for ten million dollars, with A-list acting talent. And really bad news if you're trying to make a microbudget movie.

Looking at how film is taught, there's always a need to be current. Cameras and lights are becoming smaller, faster, and more intuitive, so in addition to teaching fundamentals of composition and lighting, cinematography and production teachers need to know how to work with the latest gear. Post-production software is evolving constantly, so in addition to teaching story, pacing and building multilayered soundscapes, editing and sound design teachers need to know how to work with those programs, and how different media workflows affect them.

Yet for some reason, the business side of filmmaking hasn't evolved at the same rate as the production side. The vast majority of programs focus their "business" or "producing" education on the same old system: find rich financiers who will bankroll your movie, spend that money to produce the movie, and then find a distributor who will pay those financiers back, making them blissfully happy and lining up to finance your next work of genius.

Now why is that? There's really no one answer. So many of today's film professors came up in the business when that was the way things were done, so it makes sense they'd teach that method to their students. That's what they know. I worked with a producing professor who was able to make multiple films by selling foreign rights and using that money to produce the film itself. But in the age of Netflix worldwide deals, those foreign rights deals are drying up like raisins in the sun. There are so many film programs that focus on creative, technical, and aesthetic elements of filmmaking, but very few give the business elements the teaching time they deserve. When I started teaching, I had a Producing the Narrative Film course, and it was the only film business course offered in the seven years I taught at that university. A top 25 American film school I know only offers one undergraduate course in producing, taught by a professor who's never produced a feature film. And at my last university, the Producing for Film course taught by my predecessor focused on the history of film producers and film studios. Definitely interesting material, but it offered nothing in how current filmmakers can produce and monetize their work.

Plus, let's be honest – students would rather be watching the latest cool movie in class than discussing the fine points of developing a budget.

So there's a big gap here. Today's film students, by and large, are graduating into a world of film where what they've been taught no longer applies. And they're woefully unprepared for the wild world that currently exists.

Why's it so wild? Glad you asked. It's partly because …

Studio Filmmaking Is Broken

Summer and fall 2023 was pretty much a ghost town for film and television production, due to the dual strikes of the Writers Guild of America (WGA) and the Screen Actors Guild-American Federation of Television & Radio Artists (SAG-AFTRA). This was the first time two Hollywood unions struck at the same time since 1960, which by itself speaks to the precariousness of Hollywood as a place for workers to make a living in filmed entertainment. Their standoff against the American Motion Picture & Television Producers (AMPTP) stemmed from a number of issues related to pay and working conditions.

From the WGA's point of view, the major problem was that AMPTP members were looking for any opportunity to cut financial corners, while still paying their CEOs exorbitant sums of money. For example, streaming companies, like Netflix, Amazon or Hulu, aren't contractually required to pay the same amount of residuals, or additional payments to writers, when a movie or show airs on their platform. This is different from when a show airs on a broadcast or cable network, as the WGA had previously negotiated residual payments on those platforms. AMPTP members are also producing television shows with smaller seasons, sometimes as few as 4 episodes, where season orders for broadcast network shows can be as high as 22 episodes.

The WGA was also grappling with the future of artificial intelligence (AI) on screenwriting. Writers were scared that producers could use AI to generate a first draft of a script instead of a human screenwriter. This is important because a producer doesn't have to pay an AI a fee to write that first draft. If they only had to hire human screenwriters to rewrite and polish the AI's script, loads of screenwriting jobs would vanish. So they wanted screenwriters to be defined as human beings.

Similarly, SAG-AFTRA was concerned about AI affecting the ability of their members to make a living as actors. And not without good reason; an AMPTP proposal included the creation and use of digital replicas of actors, or digital alterations of performances.[3] Union representatives worried that this could lead to studios obtaining the rights to actors' performances in perpetuity, with no further payment after the first performance.

When the strikes ended, both unions were able to create guidelines that addressed these issues, to the great joy of their memberships. And this rare show of coordinated strike activity by two sister unions suggests we might be in a time of existential change for the studio film and television industry. Which, honestly, might be what it needs. But studio filmmaking is far from the only area of motion picture production that's got issues. And that's because …

Independent Film Is Broken

I've got my own battle scars from trying to work in indie film's old model. I was taught by film professors who had been successful with it, so that's what they taught me. And I followed it when I directed my first feature film, a romantic dramedy called RISING STAR, in 2010. I raised money for production (even crowdfunding some of it on Kickstarter, one of the first indie films to do so), made the film, and assumed I'd be able to find a distributor to get it out into the world. I found a distributor, but they threw my film in with a handful of other small indies, and sold them as a bundle to exhibitors. And they had their "expenses" paid for before any money was applied to the 50/50 revenue split we had agreed on. The end result was a disaster: after over ten years working with my film, my distributor has not paid me back one cent in revenues.

This made me pretty radical when it came to independent film distribution. And honestly, I had a chip on my shoulder about it for a while. But as the 2010s progressed, I began to see more opportunities for filmmakers who were willing to take matters into their own hands. Crowdfunding became more popular, and where Kickstarter was the only game in town for a while, portals like Seed&Spark, IndieGoGo and Patreon came into existence, ready to work directly with creators. Self-distribution also became more possible, with aggregators providing an opportunity for indies to sell on Internet, streaming, and VOD platforms. Companies like Tugg and Gathr came on the scene, allowing filmmakers to sell tickets to their own theatrical screenings, creating the possibility of self-theatrical distribution.

So when crowdfunding became ubiquitous, and self-distribution became more possible, I realized incorporating these into filmmaking was the way forward. If a filmmaker can crowdsource elements of production, crowdfund to pay for everything else they need, produce their film as efficiently as possible, and distribute it themselves, they can utilize the crowds they cultivate to help become self-sustaining. Which means the ability to make whatever they want, whenever they want, with full creative control, and an audience they're directly connected to.

But this method of filmmaking is wildly different from the method that's been taught, both in class and in the larger independent film world. It requires a shift in thinking, in the way projects are conceived, how they're produced, and how they get into the world when they're done.

And I know that when someone proposes a change in thinking, especially to something that's been done a certain way for over a century, it tends to go over like a fart in church.

Thing is, that certain way isn't how it's always been. Between the decentralization of film production away from the bicoastal hubs of Los Angeles and New York City, labor disputes over AI and making screenwriting a gig economy, and cost of living increases, the industry's normal is under threat like never before.

Indie filmmakers have always stepped up and innovated in times like these. Becoming a self-sustaining filmmaker is just the latest step in the history of that innovation.

The Pillars of the New Way

Now that we've established a new way is necessary, there has to be a set of principles that will underscore it. There are three major themes that are intrinsic to all the strategies, tips and ideas this book will present. If you've spent time making films, you'll be familiar with them all, but the new wrinkle here will be the focus you'll need to put on them throughout making your work. The three main themes in this book will be radical collaboration, an entrepreneurial mindset, and holistic filmmaking.

Radical Collaboration

If you've ever worked on a movie, you know that collaboration is vital in creating anything. No matter how strong a director's vision might be, they need the cooperation of their actors and crew, and it's a given that they would have ideas at each point of the production process. So that level of collaboration is pretty much assumed.

But our new way requires us to recontextualize collaboration. For starters, the idea of film authorship needs to be rethought. I believe that in a business where dozens, if not hundreds, of cast and crew members make films, the authorial stamp should be divided among all those who work so hard on them. (On my second feature film as director, a drama called STAY WITH ME, there's a possessory credit of "A Film Made By 59 Filmmakers," instead of "A Film by Marty Lang.") As such, this will be a very "anti-auteur" book. I think that idea runs counter to the concept of radical collaboration; while the director is undoubtedly the leader of a filmmaking team, they are far from the only contributor to the film they ultimately make.

In addition to filmmaking teams, though, collaboration must also be considered in every other part of a movie's life cycle. You can't think of the locations you'll be shooting at as services your production will pay for; you'll need to think of them as collaborators on your filmmaking team. Instead of considering your possible audience as passive consumers of your story, you'll need to bring them into your process, and make them cheerleaders who will bring their own friends and family into the fold. (Or even set up screenings of the movie on their own!) Every step of making your movie is an opportunity to bring more people onto your team, even if their role might seem small or unnecessary. That's a level of collaboration many filmmakers don't reach, but it's a critical part of being successful making films this way.

An Entrepreneurial Mindset

In so many areas of business, you'll find companies control the entire life cycle of their product. From research and development, to production, to distribution, it's the normal way of life for businesses to control every step of the process, and to iterate that process so that it's as efficient as possible. That way, they hold their financial fates completely in their own hands.

Yet, for some reason, film and television isn't like that.

For an independent film, producers often hand off the responsibility of distributing, and therefore monetizing, their work to outside companies. And sometimes (like in my case with RISING STAR), they even hand off the responsibility of finding a distributor to sales agents. Each of those entities takes a percentage of the revenue of the film, a process that always results in the producer (and their investors) being paid last.

That's not the most efficient way to maximize the financial potential of a movie.

This has been a spirited conversation in the film world for a long time, but my personal opinion is that if you're going to make a microbudget film, and your goal is a financial return, you need to take the responsibility of distributing and monetizing it yourself. We'll explore more of this in future chapters, but the key idea is that no one cares more about your movie than you do. So why would you do all the work of building an audience, only to pass off the majority of your possible revenues to companies that don't have your film top of mind? It is a lot more work – I'm not going to lie to you – but given the work you put in to find the people who'll love your movie, you deserve to reap all the rewards.

Holistic Filmmaking

This theme might be the newest for many filmmakers. Holistic filmmaking is the idea that you need to consider every other step of filmmaking as you work in the step you're currently on. So, for example, if you're writing a microbudget horror film, and the only location you have access to is a farm, you don't write the film to take place on the moon. You write it on a farm, because that will make things easiest for you when you get into production – you have that location, so you build your movie around what you have.

But there are many other considerations you should be thinking about as you go through making your movie. When you're in pre-production, the decisions you make when you're scheduling the movie could have an effect on your marketing, because the more days you shoot, the more it could potentially cost, and therefore, the less you would have to pay for advertising and possible theater rental. Similarly, the decisions you make casting your actors could affect how much rehearsal time you would need with them, depending on whether they know each other or not, and already have existing relationships. And believe it or not, the locations you film at don't only affect how you write your movie – they could also double as distribution venues for your movie once you complete it.

This type of thinking isn't very common, and I believe that's because the way film is often taught, with a focus on specialization, keeps filmmakers from becoming cross-trained, and able to make connections between different jobs and production phases. (This isn't done everywhere, of course; any film school that prescribes to the conservatory model, I believe, does their students a wonderful service.) Hopefully, this book can help you to understand how intimately connected every phase of filmmaking is to the others and learn how you can maximize the benefit of every decision you make.

This thinking also helps answer a question I'm sure will be asked: is this book a producing book? I say yes and no. Yes, because it deals with making a product (your film), as efficiently as possible, that can be monetized. But also no, because everyone is a producer now! Directors can't just hand off the producer's responsibilities to someone else anymore. Of course, teaming up with people who understand business, marketing, advertising and distribution is a huge help, but if you're a filmmaker, you need to know the whole process – and that includes the producing process.

A big part of the book will be case studies from movies that I've made; some I've directed, some I've produced, almost all I've crowdfunded. I've been crowdfunding since 2010, and I've incorporated more of the three main themes in my projects as time's gone on. I've come up with a fictional film that I'll write about in most of the chapters, so you can get a sense of what the entire process would look like, from beginning to end. I've also been lucky enough to interview friends of mine in the industry, all of whom have thrived in the microbudget space, and who've all become self-sustaining filmmakers in their own right. Some of their names you know, some you don't, but I can't wait for you to read their stories. They've all found a home somewhere in the film industry, and you'll be inspired by the creativity and hard work they've all put into building and maintaining their careers.

Hedging Your Bets

The dream of making that one movie that leads to your big break, fame and fortune, is fuel for at least the hundreds of thousands of filmmakers listed on IMDb. But the brutal truth is that those big breaks are now harder and harder to find. And unless you've been living under a rock (or with a trust fund), money is tight for everyone these days. Working in independent film has never been more difficult.

If you have that dream, though, I believe there's a way for you to live in the Indie Gap, making one film after another, bringing your community in to support your work, crowdsourcing the elements you need, crowdfunding everything else, working as efficiently as possible, and distributing your work on your own. And even if you never get that lucky break, you'll be able to create a body of filmmaking work, all pieces of intellectual property you own, and can distribute and monetize, to fund new work.

In other words, you can become a self-sustaining filmmaker.

Ready to do it? Great! Let's get to work.

Notes

1 https://www.imdb.com/pressroom/stats/
2 https://www.hollywoodreporter.com/movies/movie-news/sundance-market-2022-film-sales-1235086264/
3 https://deadline.com/2023/07/actors-strike-studios-respond-sag-aftra-1235437389/

Reference List

Galuppo, Mia. "Sundance Dealmaking Adjusts to indie Film Market in Limbo." *The Hollywood Reporter*, 2022. https://www.hollywoodreporter.com/movies/movie-news/sundance-market-2022-film-sales-1235086264/

Internet Movie Database December 2023 film listing data. https://www.imdb.com/pressroom/stats/

Pederson, Eric. "AMPTP Responds To SAG-AFTRA Strike: 'Union Has Regrettably Chosen A Path That Will Lead To Financial Hardship For Countless Thousands,'" *Deadline Hollywood*, 2023. https://deadline.com/2023/07/actors-strike-studios-respond-sag-aftra-1235437389/

2 From Filmmaker to Entrepreneur

When I started the process of making RISING STAR, I didn't think of it as a money making exercise. I had been producing films for the previous ten years, and I had directed a number of short films, but I never took the jump into feature directing. My biggest reason for making the film was so that people would take me seriously as a filmmaker, not just as a producer. I carried that strategy into my casting – I wrote every role for an acting friend of mine who had worked with me on one of my shorts. Many of them were trying to make the jump in their own careers, so giving them meaty roles in a feature would help them get there. It bled into my hiring crew as well – I looked for people who were amazing in their jobs, but who were looking to take a step up into a department head role. Our sound designer, for example, was a sound mixer who had actually gotten an Oscar nomination, but had never been given the chance to oversee post-production sound on a feature before. When I asked him if he wanted to do post sound with me (and get paid dog food money to do it), he jumped at the opportunity. And he wasn't the only one. Our cinematographer had been a camera operator on films like THE OTHER GUYS, and TV shows like SMASH, but she had never been the director of photography on a feature film. I could offer her a tiny fee and a bedroom in my house, but she came on board because she wanted to be a cinematographer, and someone was giving her that opportunity. (I actually slept in my neighbor's trailer during the shoot, so I could house more of my crew members. You do what you gotta do.)

I even told people that the movie wasn't being made with the goal of making money. The number one goal of RISING STAR was to showcase the skills and talents of everyone working on it – especially me.

What a dumb move that was.

Because of my aversion to commerce, I missed so many opportunities to make money and to help the distribution of the film. And none of those

DOI: 10.4324/9781003295754-2

opportunities would have kept me from accomplishing my original goal, showing the world that my team and I were talented creatives.

So over time, I've amended my approach to the films I make. I always think of my films as a vehicle to showcase the talent of myself, and of my team. But there's a big change now. When I start the process of making a film, I also come to it with an entrepreneurial mindset.

Creating an Entrepreneurial Mindset ... Not a Business One

You might have a question after reading that last paragraph. Why didn't I just say I come to my films with a business mindset now? Obviously, we're in show BUSINESS. It's all about the money. Right?

Not necessarily.

When people think of the word "entrepreneur," they think of someone who comes up with a great product or service, and then makes tons of money and runs a business where they can make all the decisions. Even bigger than entrepreneur, isn't that the definition of capitalism? The opportunity to make as much money as you can with what you create?

Billionaire and serial entrepreneur Mark Cuban would disagree with you. He did an interview with Adam Grant on his podcast Re:Thinking, and he gave a definition of capitalism that opens up a slew of other possibilities of how to run a business:

People don't fully understand the definition of capitalism.

Capitalism isn't just about trying to make as much money as you can. Capitalism is the opportunity to get the outcomes that you want, that give you personal reward. It could be making as much money as possible. Having the greatest amount of impact in one way or another. You get to make that choice.

That's what makes capitalism the best system, but sometimes people get caught up on the money.[1]

Now before you get into anything else, your business needs to provide a good or a service that addresses a need or problem people have. But while many businesses are created with the primary goal of making money by addressing those needs or problems, there are many other reasons why you could start one:

- Helping homeless folks find work
- Improving the climate, or life on Earth

- Setting yourself up to only do work you truly enjoy (even if that means your business isn't as profitable as it could be)
- Helping your community

And so many other possibilities. Since we're specifically interested in filmmaking, let's take a look at that particular type of business, and how an entrepreneurial mindset might affect your plans to make one.

Answering the Business Questions

In the business world, it's standard practice to put a plan together for your startup, something you can show to potential investors or collaborators. There are some specific questions you need to answer in order to convince an angel investor or venture capital firm that your idea is strong enough for them to write a check.

As a film professor at the University of Memphis, I worked with their center for entrepreneurship to create a startup film business, teaming up with four film students through a summer startup incubator. This company became a feature film distribution and exhibition company, called ReelLife Entertainment (Figure 2.1).

ReelLife aims to provide theatrical movie-going experiences, in any place that's not a movie theater. (That's how we came up with the tagline "Rethink Theatrical.") And as part of the incubator, we created a business plan that we pitched at the end of the summer. I'd like to show you that

Figure 2.1 Title slide of ReelLife Entertainment pitch deck.

14 *From Filmmaker to Entrepreneur*

business plan, and explain all the questions we needed to answer as we put our business together.

So without further ado, here's ReelLife Entertainment! (Figure 2.2).

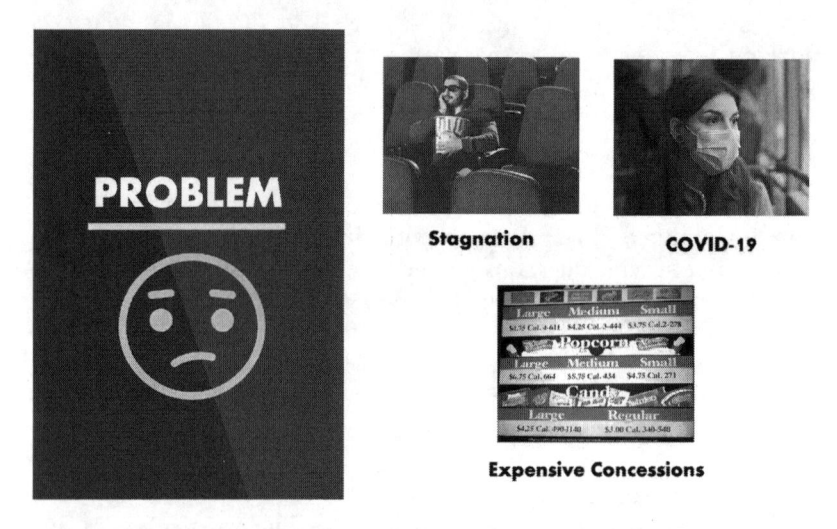

Figure 2.2 Problem slide of ReelLife Entertainment pitch deck.

Problem Solving

Whenever you're thinking of creating a business, you need to identify a problem. Solving that problem, then, becomes the reason your business exists. When you think of Amazon.com, for example, a problem that existed in retail was convenience. The only way to shop was to get in your car, drive to a store, buy the product you need (assuming the store had it), and then drive home, before you actually held the product in your hand. Amazon identified this problem, and created a business that would have products delivered to the customer, eliminating the need for them to spend the time obtaining it themselves. The product came to their door. (Safe to say, Amazon identified a problem that many people wanted solved.)

In this case, ReelLife thought consumers might want a different experience when they saw films. So to test their hypothesis, they went out and gathered customer feedback. They interviewed over 100 people who self-identified as theatrical moviegoers, diverse in age, background, and experience. And through that process, they identified three consistent problems with the current theatrical film-watching experience:

From Filmmaker to Entrepreneur 15

- STAGNATION: Watching a movie has been the exact same experience for over a century – you show up in a room, sit down in a chair (usually with popcorn or some other kind of food), the lights go down, you watch the movie, and when it's done, you get up and leave. The process has not changed at all. So ReelLife thought that could be an opportunity: disrupt the actual process by which people watch films, and moviegoers might be interested.
- COVID-19: When the pandemic began, the issue of air filtration and disease spread within indoor theaters became a major issue for moviegoers. Theater attendance dropped dramatically, tentpole releases suffered at the box office (just ask Christopher Nolan, with TENET), and streaming services instantly became the safe place to go to watch movies. ReelLife saw that if the locations for watching movies were opened up to include outdoor locations, that might present an option that moviegoers would feel comfortable with.
- EXPENSIVE CONCESSIONS: This one's pretty self-explanatory. The combination of food prices constantly rising, along with a policy by theaters to keep outside food from entering the theater, has made the moviegoing experience cost-prohibitive for many. (And has forced some to hide snacks in their back pockets.) Figuring out a way to bring down the cost of concessions, ReelLife found, would be a major attraction for moviegoers.

Once ReelLife identified the problems for the consumer, there was a long period of brainstorming to figure out how those problems could be solved. Which led to ... (Figure 2.3)

Figure 2.3 Solution slide of ReelLife Entertainment pitch deck.

Solutions

The business pedigree of my students came quickly, once we realized the problems consumers saw in moviegoing. Once they saw the process was an issue, they came up with the idea of bringing film screenings out of the theater. The ideas started flowing fast once we made that breakthrough. We thought of all kinds of different ways to watch different types of films:

- Watching JAWS outdoors on a blowup movie screen, at a pond, with audiences watching while sitting in inner tubes, snacks and popcorn being delivered by staff in a kayak, and a radio-controlled boat with a shark fin driving around them
- Watching any type of horror/slasher film in the middle of the woods, at night, with staff creating creepy sounds (breaking sticks, footsteps, screams) as the film plays
- Watching ELVIS in the front lawn of Graceland (the company's based in Memphis, after all)

All these different ideas, based in outdoor venues, created another benefit – breathing outdoor air is much safer than indoor air when it comes to COVID-19 prevention. These new venues, in addition to creating excitement, could help keep moviegoers healthier.

And if the concession costs could be lowered, all three issues identified by our customer base would be addressed. Hopefully leading to them all seeing films with us.

Once we identified these, we wanted to test our hypothesis about how an audience would react to this new kind of event. So we obtained more customer data by creating a test event. We partnered with the Memphis Museum of Science & History to host a prototype movie screening in their IMAX theater. The film was a feature I produced called CHOMPY & THE GIRLS, a horror/comedy about a woman who meets her birth father for the first time – and then goes on the run with him when they both witness a man swallow a young girl whole. (It's definitely more TUCKER & DALE VS. EVIL than CITIZEN KANE.) The poster for the movie is on the next page, so you can get a sense of the tone (Figure 2.4):

The choice of this film was important because it has an element of otherworldly creatures in it. That allowed us to create an event that wasn't just watching the movie. The IMAX theater was an indoor location, true, but the museum also has a planetarium, so in addition to watching the movie, we were able to give attendees a laser light show, too. We gave our audience an additional event to attend, along with the film, that was thematically related to it. This combination event was a huge hit with our audience; comments included that "It's not just a movie, it's an experience,"

Figure 2.4 Poster for the horror/comedy feature film CHOMPY & THE GIRLS.

18 *From Filmmaker to Entrepreneur*

and "I'd pay more than a movie for something like this." It also led to our other tagline for the company, "It's more than a movie, it's your whole night out" (Figure 2.5).

Figure 2.5 Benefits slide of ReelLife Entertainment pitch deck.

Benefits

Once we figure out the solutions to the problem, we can see the many advantages this type of moviegoing could have. Since the audience at the CHOMPY/laser light show event said they'd pay more for an experience like that, we could potentially bring down the costs of concessions, making them more affordable. The potential health benefits of outdoor screenings provide flexibility for a theatrical exhibition company; if you don't have to exclusively screen indoors, you'll be more likely to continue business if a pandemic-type event occurs. This flexibility would also allow ReelLife to screen films year-round, depending on weather. And perhaps most importantly, these events offer the promise of exciting experiences that you wouldn't normally associate with seeing a film. We really are rethinking theatrical (Figure 2.6).

Competition

One of the first questions a potential business investor will ask is "Who else is doing what you're doing?" A good entrepreneur should be able to not only answer that question, but compare and contrast your business idea with all the other ones in your space.

From Filmmaker to Entrepreneur 19

COMPETITION

	Traditional Theaters	Unconventional Theaters	Streaming Services	ReelLife Entertainment
Unique Venues	✗	✓	✓	✓
Mobility	✗	✗	✓	✓
Customization	✗	✗	✗	✓
Customer Interface	✗	✗	✗	✓
Community Engagement	✗	✗	✗	✓

Figure 2.6 Competition slide of ReelLife Entertainment pitch deck.

In the case of ReelLife, we found three major competitors: traditional theaters, unconventional theaters (ones that serve food in the theater, run a bar, that kind of thing), and streaming services. And this chart shows how it stacks up against each of them; ReelLife is the only one that combines unique venues (streaming services play on phones or home TVs), mobility (traditional and unconventional theaters own real estate), customization (events can be tailored to certain types of films), customer interface (screenings can take place based on customer suggestions), and community engagement (events can literally take place anywhere, so the company can become a part of local communities, creating brand awareness and potential repeat customers). Looking at this slide, it becomes clear that ReelLife is the superior option for theatrical film screening (Figure 2.7).

The Market

Creating an exciting business idea is only part of the job. Once you do, you also have to know exactly who would be interested in engaging with it, how you plan to reach them to let them know about it, and the partners that would help you accomplish your marketing as successfully as possible. When ReelLife decided on their market, they focused on three key groups:

- Film Enthusiasts/Casual Moviegoers – This is pretty self-explanatory. Folks who love films would be excited to try a new way of seeing them, and they're the ones engaging with competitors. The plan would be to

20 *From Filmmaker to Entrepreneur*

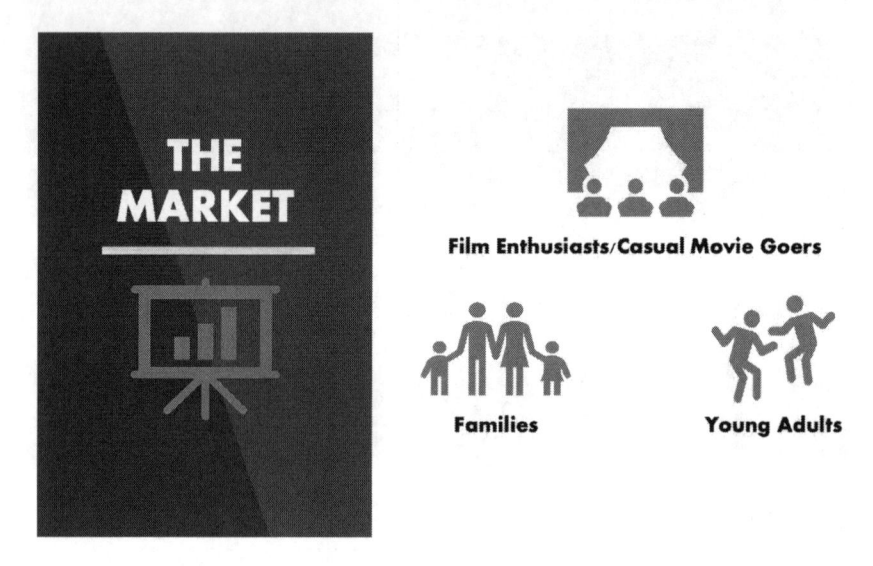

Figure 2.7 Market slide of ReelLife Entertainment pitch deck.

slowly pull people away from traditional and unconventional theaters, and get streaming service customers out of the house.
- Families – If parents have one mission throughout their kids' lives, it's finding fun things for them to do. And ReelLife can deliver to them, by screening family films (how cool would it be to see FINDING NEMO at an aquarium?), and giving kids a chance to do something unique.
- Young Adults – When you're in high school or college, you tend to have more free time than in other periods of your life. As a result, young adults are often looking for fun things to do (like young kids), and they can also attend events that combine a movie with more adult activities, like gourmet meals, alcohol, that kind of thing (Figure 2.8).

Their market identified, the next step was to determine the most effective way to reach them. They decided to employ the following methods:

- Partners – The structure of the product ReelLife offers requires the company partner with a number of different stakeholders to create their events. Since screenings will happen anywhere other than a traditional movie theater, they would have to partner with venues that would host screenings. If outside elements would need to be brought to the events, like food, they'd have to partner with vendors that would provide those elements. And in the case of screening independent films, they'd need to

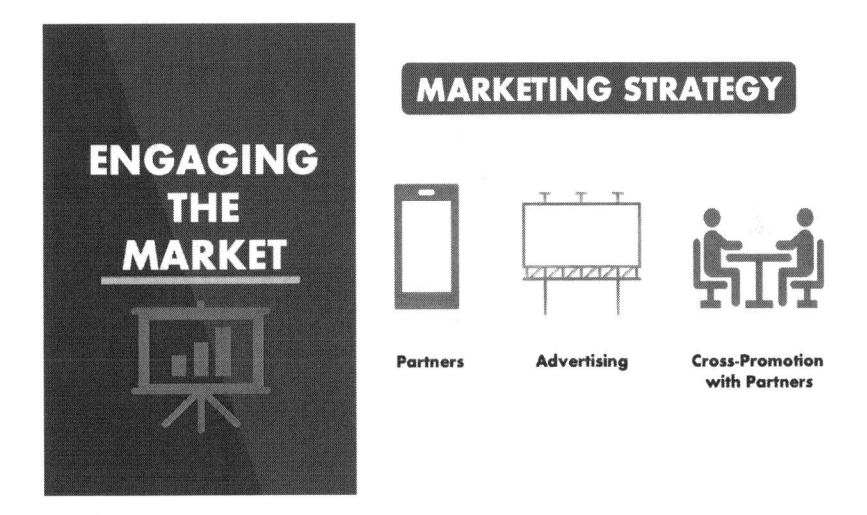

Figure 2.8 Engaging The Market slide of ReelLife Entertainment pitch deck.

partner with the filmmakers themselves, not only for the films they'd show, but if they're local, the filmmaker's audience as well.
- Advertising – The most common way for films to get the attention of moviegoers is through advertising, whether in newspapers, on social media platforms like Facebook or Instagram, or through more unconventional means. (Think of THE BLAIR WITCH PROJECT as an example of this; the film was about three documentary filmmakers who disappear while trying to find the urban legend, the Blair Witch. The Orlando, Florida-based filmmakers put missing posters up around the city, with the pictures of the three actors. People thought it was real, that the film was a real documentary. It became the most profitable independent film in history.) Since the company would work closely with the community, unconventional types of marketing would play a big role in engaging local moviegoers.
- Cross-promotion with Partners – Since ReelLife would have a close relationship with the venues, vendors, and filmmakers they'd partner with, it would make sense to use those event production partners as promotional partners as well. If you purchase a ticket to a ReelLife event that includes an Italian dinner at Joe's Italian Restaurant, it could come with a coupon for 10% off your next meal there. That would increase Joe's business and would encourage a strong relationship with ReelLife over time (and hopefully, a discount in what ReelLife would charge for their food!) (Figure 2.9).

22 *From Filmmaker to Entrepreneur*

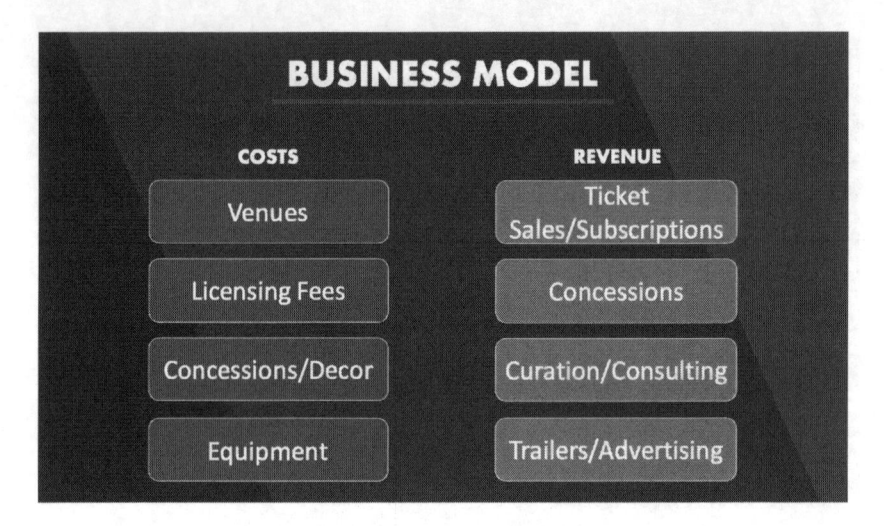

COSTS	REVENUE
Venues	Ticket Sales/Subscriptions
Licensing Fees	Concessions
Concessions/Decor	Curation/Consulting
Equipment	Trailers/Advertising

Figure 2.9 Business Model slide of ReelLife Entertainment pitch deck.

Business Model

This is really the biggest question of a business plan, and the one that could determine whether or not an investor will put their money into a project:

How will it make money?

This is a simple equation: it's costs versus revenues. If you make more than you spend, you have a business that makes money. And if you spend more than you make, you don't.

This seems simple, but in our business, it's shocking how many films are made for more than they could potentially recoup. So locking down a strong business model is incredibly important.

For ReelLife, they figured out four major costs they would need to pay out:

- Venues – Since there wouldn't be one central location for people to watch films at, finding locations would be a cost. If they wanted to host a FINDING NEMO screening at an aquarium with a movie theater, they must pay a rental fee to show the film, sell concessions, and collect ticket sales.
- Licensing fees – Whether it's a Hollywood blockbuster or an independent film, movies are pieces of intellectual property owned by someone. And that someone will need to be paid for the showing. Whether it's a flat fee, or a percentage of ticket sales, licensing fees provide the movies their audiences will actually watch.
- Concessions/Decor – Ever wonder how vending machines stay stocked? The people who own them go to the store, buy candy and chips, and stock them – while charging more for them than they paid. It's the same

situation here – ReelLife would need to buy popcorn, candy, and drinks at wholesale, and then upcharge customers at the events. (Keeping in mind, of course, that customers don't like how much concessions cost.)
- Equipment – Again, since there's no one central location for showing films, ReelLife would have to own and maintain its own projection and audio equipment, and bring it to each venue, along with paying staff to operate it.

That's a lot to pay out ... but the good news is that there are multiple opportunities for the company to bring in revenue as well. ReelLife also has four potential revenue streams:

- Ticket Sales/Subscriptions – This is the obvious one. Moviegoers will pay for the experience of seeing a film in a unique place, maybe with additional experiences to go along with it. There's also the possibility of subscriptions, which could create more revenue guaranteed up front, or offer customers VIP access to events that normal customers wouldn't get.
- Concessions – Another obvious one. Moviegoers will want popcorn, candy, and soda, so they'll pay ReelLife for it, at a price that's lower than their competitors.
- Curation/Consulting – One interesting thing about ReelLife is that since they can technically set up film screenings anywhere, that could lead to customers asking for their own events. A group of neighbors could decide to have a block party, for example, and they could request certain movies to play outdoors the night of the party (maybe the first three TOY STORY movies, or a popular movie that was filmed nearby to where they live). That curation would be something the company could charge for, effectively turning the company into an event management provider as well as a film exhibitor.
- Trailers/Advertising – Have you ever seen advertisements for local companies before a film plays? That's revenue for the theater. ReelLife could do similar work here, airing commercials and ads before films, as well as creating new forms of promotion because of the mobile nature of the company. Imagine seeing theater actors hired by a local car dealer to act out a commercial – live – for an audience gathered to watch a film outside. That type of creative promotion could really stick in the minds of moviegoers – and provide a nice revenue boost for ReelLife.

Many business plans also provide details on the profit potential of the company, assuming they receive a certain amount of seed investment, as a way of showing investors what the company could turn into. And, of course, they'll end the plan with the actual ask, the amount of money the company is looking for to get started. Here's what ReelLife asked for in their business plan (Figure 2.10).

24 *From Filmmaker to Entrepreneur*

Figure 2.10 Ask slide of ReelLife Entertainment pitch deck.

Their plan was to acquire all the necessary items they'd need to put events on – projection and audio equipment, venues, licensing fees for movies, and a catering contract (assuming they'd have food as part of a large number of their experiences). Then, once they started their "experiences," they'd hire more staff, beyond the four co-founders, to help run them. And if the first season was successful, and showed a profit, they would expand to premium experiences, which would include more things to do – and of course, would cost more.

Unfortunately, after putting this business plan together, ReelLife was unable to raise the $350,000 it hoped for to start the business, so the co-founders decided to move on to other projects. (In the startup world, this is very, very common.) But the work they did is a strong example of a well thought out business plan, that solves a problem, identifies a market of people who would be engaged, shows how they'd reach that market, and lays out a simple, clear business model.

So how does that all apply to the people who make the movies?

Namely, you?

Translating the Mindset into Filmmaking

I thought the ReelLife business plan was the best way to introduce these entrepreneurial concepts for a few reasons. First, like I said, the plan is very well thought out. But it's also a plan for a company that would work with filmmakers to distribute their own work – and that's not something filmmakers really think about. As you read through it, did you have any ideas pop in your head about a screening event you could hold with them, for a film you've made or are thinking about making? If you did, you're thinking entrepreneurially, thinking how you can get the outcomes you want (getting an engaged audience to see your film), with a positive financial result (making money on the screening). You might have other outcomes in mind, too – if you're making a film about climate change, for example, you might want to have a certain number of people sign up for your newsletter about politicians that are supporting pro-climate regulation – but the fact that you're in that mindset is the important thing.

Now that you've had a chance to digest that business plan, it's not too difficult to transpose the questions it answers to someone making a film. If you were to make a business plan for your film, you'd need to focus on the following:

The Problem

When you think about the problem your film will solve, you want to focus primarily on the experience of watching it. There might be a crossing of genres that no one has seen before, or a way of presenting characters that hasn't been tried. Any of those missing elements can be seen as a deficiency in the experience of watching a film – a deficiency that yours can fix.

Let's say you're a filmmaker who wants to make a zombie film. Maybe the problem with zombie films is that you've never seen a group of truly smart zombies. (Traditionally, they tend to focus on groaning and eating people.) So you could point to the fact that there's an opportunity in the zombie film world – zombies could actually be smarter than humans, but we'd never know it, based on almost all the zombie films we've seen. I can think of the zombie character Big Daddy in LAND OF THE DEAD, who could use tools and lead other zombies around, and all the zombies in I AM LEGEND, but zombies have been generally shown to be pretty inferior intellectually to us humanfolk.

This problem creates a "gap" that your film could fill in the marketplace. And it can be the first piece of your argument that your film is worthy of being made.

The Solution

This is where you can present your brilliant idea on how to "fix" the type of films that are currently being made. You've pointed out whatever element that's missing, so this is the point where you show how your film will provide it.

Back to our zombie movie. If the problem with those films is that we never see zombies that are truly intelligent, what's the best way to solve that?

Make a movie with zombies that can talk to each other!

Now there is the Jane Austen mashup PRIDE AND PREJUDICE AND ZOMBIES, where the zombies can talk to each other. There's also the romantic zombie comedy (zom-com?) WARM BODIES, where a zombie falls in love and slowly starts to communicate. But there's never been a movie where the zombies actually become smarter than humans. Faster, definitely (see 28 DAYS LATER and WORLD WAR Z), but the brainpower always heads in the other direction.

So the solution to the problem of dumb zombies is this:

Our zombie film is about zombies that become smarter than humans after they're bitten and they turn.

We can even come up with a title for our film based on our solution. Let's try out DEADBRAINS.

Benefits

This section can be where, as a filmmaker, you can talk about the experiences your audience will have that they wouldn't normally have in other, similar films. It can be in terms of subverting genre expectations, tone, type of humor/drama/scares, acting talent, location, or anything else to show that watching your film will give your audience something new.

Since DEADBRAINS will be about a group of zombies that are smarter than humans, that could lead to a story that wouldn't normally be thought of as zombie-adjacent:

- A courtroom drama (maybe the humans get captured trying to kill a group of zombies, and have to defend themselves on trial against zombies that successfully refute their arguments)
- A spy thriller (maybe the humans find out how smart the zombies are, and they try to infiltrate their ranks by using really good special effects makeup, only to find out the zombies were on to them the whole time)
- A war movie (maybe the zombies are led by a military mastermind – who might have been patient zero? – and they strategically attack humans in places where they know they're weak, forcing the humans to rethink their entire society before the zombies eradicate them)

Would I want to see any of these films? Honestly, I think the zombie war story would be pretty cool. And future chapters will break down how a zombie war film like that could potentially be made in this style. But whatever version you prefer, each of them offers something you've never seen in a zombie film before, as a result of the solution you've proposed.

Competition

Remember how I mentioned the other films comparable to DEADBRAINS in the problem and solution sections? Those films would be considered the competition to this one. If you've ever made a pitch deck for your film, this would be equivalent to the comps section, where you list comparable movies to yours. In this case, though, you can be very specific in how your film sets itself apart from the competition.

If we were going to make a competitors chart for DEADBRAINS, this is what it might look like (Table 2.1).

Table 2.1 Competitors chart for the zombie movie DEADBRAINS

	I AM LEGEND	*LAND OF THE DEAD*	*PRIDE & PREJUDICE & ZOMBIES*	*WARM BODIES*	*DEADBRAINS*
Higher Function	X	X	X	X	X
Talking Zombies			X	X	X
Romantic Love				X	X
Military Thinking		X			X
Outsmarting Humans					X

You could certainly incorporate visuals from these films as well, so that readers could get a better sense of what they are, but the key thing here is that you present your film as the superior one to its competitors.

The Market

You would think that this one would be pretty easy. Who's the market for movies? People who love movies! But this is an opportunity for you to really dig down and find out the people who would respond positively to your film – as well as figure out how to contact them directly.

Since DEADBRAINS is a zombie film, it's pretty clear that fans of zombie films could really be into it. You could also broaden out a little bit, and say that fans of horror films, slashers, and thrillers would enjoy it as well. But here's where you stop thinking surface level, and you ask yourself a very important question:

How can you reach these people directly?

Since you're making a film without the resources of a huge media conglomerate, you need to be strategic about how you'll build an audience. And this is the first point you can start looking for them.

I'll show you how.

Let's focus on the zombie film lovers as our main market. If you wanted to find large groups of people who love zombie films, where would you look? In person? On social media?

I say both. But for this conversation, let's look at social media first.

Finding online communities with lots of zombie lovers is a great way for you to find potential audience members. And if you go to Reddit, for example, you can see that at https://www.reddit.com/r/zombies/, there's over 101,000 members! If you got one percent of them, or 1,010 people, to buy **DEADBRAINS** online when it's distributed, at $5 per view, you just made $5,050. If you're trying to make a microbudget zombie movie, that could be a huge chunk of your production budget – or if you're really resourceful, the whole thing!

Doing this work up front, where you look for the people who would be likely to engage with your content, is the key to sustainable filmmaking. It'll show you how big of an audience you could have, which could also help you decide how much you want to spend on it, so that the film could be profitable. It will also give you a head start on connecting with them far before the film is distributed, so you can create a direct connection with them. (More on that soon.)

Once you find your market, the next step is figuring out how to let them know your film is out there. Again, since we're not working with a studio's marketing budget, social media outreach can be a wonderful way to let folks know about your film. You can use platforms like Facebook, Instagram, and/or TikTok for advertising (more on that soon, too), but as a microbudget filmmaker, you'll most likely be working with social media outreach, online advertising, and in-person hustling to get folks to see your stuff.

In terms of partnerships, you can think of all types of organizations, brands, and individuals that could help you promote your film. Imagine if **DAWN OF THE DEAD** director Zack Snyder agreed to send out social media posts, letting his fans know about your film! That's definitely ambitious, but even if you're local, you can find online communities (the same ones you might find figuring out who your market is) and in-person organizations, for profit and nonprofit, who could help.

For **DEADBRAINS**, since zombies are such a huge part of pop culture, it wouldn't be hard to find local groups who do in-person activities, who could potentially see your film as a group. In Memphis, Tennessee, for example, there's a Facebook group called Memphis Zombies (https://www.facebook.com/MemphisZombies/), and they have over 5,000 members! They run Zombie Walks each year in the city, and they head as a group to a local drive-in theater for a nighttime horror triple feature. They'd be an incredible group to reach out to, both when the film is released, and also when the film is shooting. What better group of people to play zombies than an actual zombie club?

The Business Model

This section is where a filmmaker might get antsy. Like I talked about in the first chapter, business isn't something that always comes easily to creatives. But for you to self-sustain, you need to have your projects at least break even financially – that way, you can slowly start to make bigger projects, if that's something you want, or continue making projects at the same scope. And like the ReelLife plan showed, that boils down to two things.

Revenue in, and costs out.

For films, the equation is actually backwards; you spend all the money up front creating the film and its marketing materials, and then you spend the rest of its life generating revenue from it, whether by theatrical screenings, licensing to TV, streaming, or online. This is actually a benefit for investors; you can tell them that once the movie is made, you'll never have to ask for more money, because the asset is created, and for the rest of its life, all it'll do is generate revenue (if you do your job and find those opportunities). For DEADBRAINS, a potential list of costs might look like this:

- Production/post-production costs (the actual making of the film)
- Marketing materials (poster, trailer, social media assets)
- Advertising costs (online, print media, TV media)

Once all the costs are accounted for, you can then come up with all the ways you'll be able to generate revenue from the film – and they don't always have to be from the film itself. A potential list of revenues, from a microbudget version of DEADBRAINS, could include:

- Theatrical screenings (self-distribution)
- Partnering with film festivals for theatrical screenings (you can access the film festival's audience by combining them with yours, and you each take half the ticket sales)
- Licensing to public television
- Sales on video on demand sites like Vimeo
- Merchandise related to the film (zombie brain hats, T-shirts, ties, etc.)

- Annual 21-and-over Halloween screenings as part of a Halloween night party, sponsored by the film (on top of ticket sales, you can make money on alcohol at the event, and also sell merch)

So even for a tiny film, you can create multiple avenues for making money.

Armed with all that information, you can then determine what a reasonable "ask" would be, the amount of money you would need to produce the film. This number would include everything you would potentially need to have, and it would assume you'd be paying cash for everything. It most likely won't work out that way – crowdsourcing will be a huge part of making any small film – but you want to know exactly what you'll need to make the film the way you want to. You might find that for DEADBRAINS, you'd need $100,000 to make the film by paying cash for everything you need (a zombie movie will need lots of makeup and special effects, you know). But you can start from that number, and then search for partners who could help you bring that number down, by offering in-kind services, locations, or donating money in a crowdfunding campaign. Don't let the size of the number worry you. It's just your starting point.

Your Film Is a Startup ... And It Isn't

You may have heard luminaries in the film business say that "every film is a startup business," and there's definitely some truth to that. You bring your collaborators together to make a film, no matter the size, and when it's done, you try to get it out into the world. So you always want to work with an entrepreneurial mindset, thinking of the questions we just reviewed, to make sure you're working efficiently, and that you have a plan for your film once it's completed.

But you also want to think of your film as something bigger. Yes, each film has its own closed loop of entrepreneurial activity, but you can also think of your films as pieces of a larger entity. You can think of each film as a product created by your filmmaking company, as an extension of your brand, as steps toward accomplishing long-term goals (awareness of an issue, community involvement), or as building blocks toward bigger-scope projects. But no matter how you think of them, you want each film you make to support something. You don't want to think of every film as starting from scratch. Once you make your first film, your second film will benefit from all the work you put into it. You're a better filmmaker on your second film than your first, because of everything you learned. Your audience is bigger starting your second film than your first, because of everywhere you played it. Your resources are still in place after your first film is finished. And with those benefits comes momentum. You want every possible advantage when you're working on small films – and thinking of your filmmaking in terms of a career instead of one film will allow you to best utilize them.

Business in the Real World

Now, the entrepreneurial process doesn't mean you can pocket every dollar you make in the process of monetizing your work. In addition to payments you make, you'll be responsible for tracking all you make and all you spend, along with paying taxes on any profits. The funds you bring in to make your film can be categorized in three ways:

- Investment: This is money you receive with the understanding that the person or entity investing will receive a financial interest in your film, or the company you create to make the film. If you are going to solicit investment for a film, you will need to create a limited liability company, or LLC, in order to receive it. (An LLC also protects you from being personally liable for accidents and claims against your film.) And if you plan on soliciting investment through equity crowdfunding, the Securities and Exchange Commission website states it must be solicited through an SEC-approved funding portal.[2]
- Gifts: This is money you receive with no expectation of a financial interest in your film, or in your company. Money raised through perks-based crowdfunding, which I'll explain in future chapters, is considered a gift to the filmmaker, with no strings attached. You can accept gifts through an LLC, or as an individual. If you accept through an LLC, you can spend that money, and it will not be considered income, if it's all spent in the same accounting period it's received. If you accept as an individual, however, you will have to report those gifts as personal income, and you'll be taxed on it accordingly.
- Donations: This is money you receive with the benefit of a tax write-off for the individual or entity who provides it. This tax write-off cannot be provided by an individual or by an LLC; it can only be provided through a fiscal sponsor, a nonprofit company that provides financial management and oversight for charitable projects. You can partner with a fiscal sponsor to offer tax write-offs for contributions.

Once your film is completed, you will also be responsible for tracking the revenues and expenses you process as you distribute it, along with paying taxes on any profits. If you have an LLC, those profits will be taxed separately from your personal income, but if you don't, they will be included with your own income, raising your personal tax liability.

You'll also want to look into securing insurance as you make your projects. There are many different types of insurance you could purchase, each protecting you from different things:

- Liability insurance, which protects you from financial liability due to accidents while filming (like if you drop a camera lens you've rented, and it breaks).
- Workers compensation insurance, which protects you from financial liability due to accidents involving workers you hire as cast and/or crew (like if a light falls on the foot of a grip, the grip breaks their toe and goes to the hospital).
- Errors and Omissions insurance (E&O), which protects you from financial liability due to your completed film showing items you don't have the right to show (like if a character wears a hat of a pro sports team, and you never obtained permission from the team).

Of course, any entrepreneurial venture requires that you seek the advice and counsel of financial, tax, and legal professionals. I strongly recommend you consult an accountant, a lawyer, and an insurance professional when you decide to begin your entrepreneurial journey. They'll guide you through the process of creating a business framework that will work best for you, and that will protect you from liability as much as possible.

Interview: Emily Best, Founder/CEO of Seed&Spark

Emily Best is the founder and CEO of Seed&Spark, a platform that makes entertainment more diverse, inclusive, connected, and essential. Seed&Spark's platform and national education program have helped thousands of bold storytellers raise millions to bring to life entirely new stories, and Seed&Spark delivers those stories into workplaces, replacing boring corporate training videos with cinematic learning experiences that drive innovation and inclusion.

Figure 2.11 Headshot for Seed&Spark Founder/CEO Emily Best.

Marty Lang: Tell me what being an entrepreneur means to you.

Emily Best: You know, what immediately comes to mind is Issa Rae. She said, "I'm an entrepreneur, which means I did it myself." But I don't actually think that's true. I mean, I like this theory of it. I think it does mean you have to be tremendously disciplined, as a self-starter. And you have to be willing to go from where there is nothing to something. And the something includes all the infrastructure to support the something, which is less fun to build. And an entrepreneur means you don't get out of making certain decisions, you don't get out of learning certain things.

But I think a successful entrepreneur is an incredibly skilled collaborator. This is somebody who can identify what he or she doesn't know. And is able to identify a process for discovering and uncovering, whether that is getting to the expert who can advise, or the collaborator who can come on board, or the set of tools and skills you need to solve a problem. And somebody who is not afraid to get into spreadsheets as much as they are unafraid to have a really collaborative visioning and brainstorming session.

And so far, in my experience, an entrepreneur is somebody who can hold a lot of duality. Right? You have to be a leader, and you also have to be an executor. Right? You have to be a visionary, and you have to be tactical. You have to be an employer and an employee. And you have to be able to see the two sides of all of it.

ML: We're obviously in a very unique time in the film industry. How do you think the industry can be disrupted by entrepreneurs now?

EB: I think it always has been. The original United Artists were like, "Hang on, the audiences care about us, and don't care about any of you. We can go get together and do our own thing." The challenge was at that time, the supply chain of film was still completely owned by the larger corporate interests. And that is still true, except that we all have access to the same tools they have access to now. We are on the same social media platforms where Netflix is putting their content. We have access to the same tools that allow us to deliver our content. However, that requires a lot from individuals and teams.

I think the greatest disruption comes from the unobstructed ability to reach one to many now. And those platforms all prefer really good storytellers. We've moved to a time of social media, where everyone is involved in authorship, everyone is involved in storytelling. So if you're good at it, these platforms are going to be much kinder to you than if you're not good at it.

I also think we're at a unique moment where the deal you're being handed by the industry at large, if you're able to get your foot in the door, is not a great deal. And it's a deal with the devil, no matter what. There's no getting into Hollywood and not shaking hands with a devil of some kind. And you have to decide if you're willing to make the tradeoffs that are necessary. For example, if you're gonna go to a Marvel movie, and you're gonna make that money, they own you for two years, and you are at every Comic Con. You must decide if the tradeoffs are worth it.

And I think, especially as everything is consolidated around streaming and digital creators, who usually like to be in community and like to galvanize people and see things in action, are really missing that in-person or community component. So while the Hollywood industry is going hard on digital and growth and global scale, it's creators who are building all the most interesting in-person experiences. And I think you can see just in terms of the economic value that can be generated from in-person experiences, whether it's concerts, like the Eras tour, or film experiences, like Naomi McDougall Jones' Joyful Vampire Tour of America. I think all the most interesting stuff, that is actually doing what storytelling is intending, which is to gather people, that's all creator driven. That's not price driven.

ML: For some reason, new filmmakers don't get into the industry with an understanding of how to generate revenue from their work. Why do you think that is?

EB: The first thing I would say is that, from an American standpoint, we don't treat the arts well at all. And every other developed nation massively funds the arts, so that they don't have to be commercial. And that includes film. Because commerciality is antithetical in many ways to the creative drive. So I don't think it's a problem of filmmakers.

    I think the problem is that film is probably the most commercial of all of the arts. Maybe music is close in a certain way, but it doesn't cost as much to make music. But art is not supposed to be a commercial endeavor. Full stop. And film schools do not really teach it as a commercial endeavor. They teach just like all other conservatories, they teach artists to be good artists. And you could argue that actually, the role at every conservatory should be to prepare you for the real world. I will tell you, our version of teaching crowdfunding is teaching entrepreneurship at universities. When we teach, the kids in the school come up to us afterwards and are like, "I cannot believe this is the first time we are hearing about this. This is the information we actually need." Because most people are going to school for this because they think it's the thing they're going to make a living at. But making a living as a filmmaker, and making the stuff that most creatively fulfills you, can be pretty far apart for a pretty long time. And I think number one, when you graduate arts conservatory, when you're at the peak of your artistic extension and expression, to be smacked in the face with that real world is really, really challenging. Number two, the commerciality necessarily asks us to make compromises all the time. So you're constantly teetering between these tradeoffs between your creative career, your creative energy, and your rent, and stuff like that.

The other issue is that nobody can tell me what the independent film business is. What does that business do? How does it work? How can you reliably replicate revenue film after film? And the answer is, you can't. So I think it's a little bit unfair, just to say that there's a film business that they can enter into. In technology, for example, if you have a good idea, there are replicable and scalable models for building a technology company. But it just isn't true in the independent film business, because there is a taste level that is required, there is a tremendous amount of resourcing required.

And you must be humble enough to make sure your first projects are really actually good, but do them at a small scale. Most creators have the $10 million, or $20 million, or $100 million picture in their head, and that's the thing they want to go out and make first. That's a terrible idea. You have to want to go out and make small things, and make them really successful. And I think that's not really taught. And then you have to have a way to pay your bills in the meantime.

Now some people are very interested in the insider business, and want to go do that at a production company, or at a studio. And it's really important to go learn from people who know how to make a production company successful. But I also don't think it's realistic for creators to try to build businesses that distribute at scale, as if they're not going to be partnered with distributors and platforms, and they won't need to know how those things work. They will.

The question is who holds the power in those negotiations. So if you as a creator, as a creative entrepreneur, have spent time building a deep relationship with an audience who cares about you, you hold the power in those negotiations. And that allows you a certain amount of independence. The Duplass Brothers, they own everything they make, and they license it to the big platforms who need their content. And that makes you way more money than if you were to produce it inside one of those studios. The TV series BLACK LOVE is another great example of that. They went out and produced BLACK LOVE on their own, and they licensed it to OWN, but it meant they got to build off of the popularity of BLACK LOVE, whatever they wanted. And now it's a national conference tour, it's a media brand, it's all these other things.

So there are ways of approaching creativity that give you more control than I would consider creative entrepreneurship. There's not really a way to scale yourself without working with the big platforms. But it's just a matter of who holds the power in those relationships. And that's based on how you build.

ML: How important is it to think of your films as pieces of a longer-term career, and not necessarily just one off projects?

EB: This is a really interesting question, because I think branding is less important than taste. Which is to say, I think artists should be able to make all sorts of shit. I don't think any artists should ever be constrained by an image or a persona that they choose early in their career. I think it's being focused on what you're making and who you're making it for. And connecting it really directly to those people, so that then they will come with you. I think it's more about caring about who's going to see this, and why they will care about it. If I were to build a brand that's really going to pay off, that would be the brand. Super audience focused.

There are people out there like Jennifer Reeder, whose films you can count on to be a certain kind of way. She's got a very specific aesthetic, right? And then you have a Greta Gerwig, she's everywhere. Those are strong storytelling brands. But I know what I can count on from Jennifer Reeder, who's just a brilliant horror storyteller, women's storyteller. And Greta Gerwig. I don't know what I'm gonna get, but I know I'm gonna be really interested. And I think they are very clear about who they make for. And that allows an artist like Greta to go kind of anywhere she wants to go.

I think the only thing that future-proofs your career is a direct connection to your audience. Much more so than any of the other kinds of trappings of success. And so being audience focused, really caring about who you're making for. I think that is the branding piece that early career filmmakers really need to think about.

ML: What's the best advice that you can give someone who wants to become a creative entrepreneur?

EB: Build deep and lasting relationships with people whose creative tastes you profoundly respect. I was just listening to a TikTok, about these five people who worked together at a Sears call center in the early 80s. And they all wanted to be in music. They all said, "If any of us make it, then we all make it." There were six people, and one of them was a terrible rapper. So he got left to the side at first, and one of them was a producer, and he started working with these two women and they would release a B-side. They thought nobody would ever gonna listen to it, but the producer was like, "No, we got to make this track." The women were Salt 'n Pepa, and the track was Push It. Their other two friends, Chris and Chris, would go on to work with the same producer and become

Kid 'n Play. When Salt 'n Pepa started touring, Martin, the one who didn't know how to rap, was Martin Lawrence. He would come and open for them on their tours. They all came up together, and then when Kid 'n Play got those movie deals, Martin Lawrence was in those movies. You know what I mean?

You find your tribe of people. You want to have people who have an honest assessment of taste. Think about Ira Glass's gap, that terrible gap between the tastes that you have and what you're able to produce early in your career. Your friends will also help you not, not make those things. You must make those things, you have to put them out and share them, but you want to share them with people who will give you an honest assessment of how to make them better next time. And that's how you come up together.

Notes

1 https://www.inc.com/jeff-haden/with-1-sentence-mark-cuban-just-provided-perfect-definition-of-capitalism.html
2 https://www.sec.gov/education/smallbusiness/exemptofferings/regcrowdfunding

Reference List

Haden, Jeff. "With 1 Sentence, Mark Cuban Just Provided the Perfect Definition of Capitalism." *Inc.com*, 2022. https://www.inc.com/jeff-haden/with-1-sentence-mark-cuban-just-provided-perfect-definition-of-capitalism.html

U.S. Securities and Exchange Commission Regulation Crowdfunding. https://www.sec.gov/education/smallbusiness/exemptofferings/regcrowdfunding

3 Development

Now that you've gotten a taste of an entrepreneurial mindset, it's time to start thinking about your story.

And who's going to watch your film. And how you're going to reach them. And where they'll actually watch it. So it's not really just about your story. Don't worry. I'll explain.

When you're in the phase where you're coming up with your story (not actually writing it – we'll get to that soon), it's vital that you're also thinking of the other steps in your film's life cycle. Because this is the point where your story is the most malleable. Since you haven't written scenes or dialogue yet, you're most ready to change the plan for your story, based on how you could write it, fund it, shoot it, even distribute it.

Holistic filmmaking.

Now you've already dipped your toe in that pool by coming up with your business plan. You've figured out the basic story you want to tell, you know why it's special, you've got a general sense of where people are who would enjoy it, and a basic idea of how you could get it out into the world.

This is the point where you'll get really specific about those things. You want to put your film in the best possible position to be successful all the way through its creation and distribution. So you'll actually review those phases, plugging in your story to see if it fits well, and adjusting it if it's not. By starting with a focus on those things, you'll find ways to tweak your story that would improve your odds. You might think of this as putting the cart before the horse, but I'd call it something else:

Beginning with the end in mind.

So in this chapter, we'll take a look at each of the phases you can analyze during development. And we'll also define one of the three terms you read in the title of this book:

Crowdsourcing.

DOI: 10.4324/9781003295754-3

What Is Crowdsourcing?

Whenever I teach a class in screenwriting or producing, I make sure to focus on the value of social media in creating and developing relationships. I've been able to befriend all kinds of folks in the film and television industry by establishing relationships with them on Facebook, Twitter/X, Instagram, and others. One of those relationships is with Richard "R.B." Botto, the CEO of Stage 32, a worldwide online community of creatives that's over one million people strong. I met R.B. for the first time on Twitter/X, and then met him in person at the Austin Film Festival, where Stage 32 hosts an incredible party every year. We became fast friends, and we've collaborated in a number of ways since. I taught a webinar on Stage 32 about place-based filmmaking, which actually planted the seed for this book, and he's interviewed me for Stage 32 as well.

R.B. wrote a book that I use when I teach crowdsourcing, called CROWDSOURCING FOR FILMMAKERS: INDIE FILM AND THE POWER OF THE CROWD. It's pretty much the Bible of crowdsourcing for motion pictures, and I recommend you read it soon as you finish this book. (Full disclosure: my film RISING STAR is one of the book's case studies.) In his book, he defines crowdsourcing pretty simply:

> Crowdsourcing is a people game. It's a relationship game. It's a trust game. It's about commonality. It's about loyalty. But, at its most base, crowdsourcing is simply this: Identifying, engaging and moving an audience (Botto, 2018).

Pretty simple, right? Thankfully, R.B. goes into more detail about exactly what each step practically entails. When you're working to identify a crowd, he says you need to be identifying two things. The first is, who is the audience for this film? And the second is, what individuals, groups, or organizations might have a vested interest in the project? This is the point where you will start doing that work, and I'll explain more of how to do that in a moment.

Once you identify them, the next step is to engage them. And as R.B. says, this step is all about approach. If you want someone to become a part of your journey in making a film, you must connect with them, whether in person or online. It's all about creating relationships with the people you want to bring along with you. And R.B.'s advice here is a paragraph to live by:

> You must take an interest in the people you want to take an interest in you. How do you do that? By being gracious, generous, and most of all *selfless*. You do it by showing concern, empathy and by *asking questions*. You take the time to respect people's time.

And once you've done all that work, connected with all the people you want to be a part of your film, once you have connections with these people that are both honest and germane to the subject matter of your story …

THAT'S when you move them.

Not after sending them one message on social media. Not after shaking their hand the first time you meet them.

Once you've established a relationship with them.

And then, you make an ask. Not a demand, a humble, personalized ask, to this person, to help you out somehow in the making of the film.

Now you'll notice I said help you out somehow, not specifically with money. That's because there are a million different things that could help you in the making of your film that are not money. Need a location? You can approach someone who owns it. Need a meal for your crew? You can connect with a restaurant owner to donate one. Need a herd of goats? Someone could provide that.

Seriously. On RISING STAR, we created a Google form so that anyone who had anything they thought could help us could contact us and offer it up. And we had 159 people respond! We found a still photographer in that group, a family that let us shoot in their house, a classical violinist who offered to play music for us, a tradesman who offered us welding and excavation services (seriously), and a farmer, offering us his herd of goats to be in the movie. I tried SO HARD to find a way to incorporate them into the movie, but I couldn't make it work. But you can bet I've got that person's contact information in case I ever need goats for a film.

This is why crowdsourcing needs to happen as early as possible in the storytelling process. That way, you can learn what you have access to, and can develop a story that best takes advantage of the unique audience and resources you've been able to cultivate.

Crowdsourcing Your Story

If you're a screenwriter, you've had the moment when you write a great scene, and you can see it playing out in your head. The location is perfect, and you can hear the world's greatest actors and actresses performing your words. It's almost a rite of passage for a writer, that moment where you imagine your work in its perfect form.

Problem is, it takes moving heaven and earth to get your work to that magical place. And the bigger your story is in scope, the harder it becomes – assuming you can get it made in the first place. If you're looking to get a film of yours made, I propose you try something I bet you haven't done before:

Create your story in reverse.

I don't mean actually write it from the end to the beginning – watch Christopher Nolan's amazing film MEMENTO to see how to do that – but rather, create your story based on elements you have access to, and bend it to fit those elements. It sounds strange, I know, but it can significantly improve your chances of getting your film produced and can actually help you infuse some energy into it.

Make Your Story Personal

We've all heard the phrase "write what you know," but when it comes to reverse engineering a story it becomes an imperative. If you have family or friends that inspire your storytelling, focus your story around them. Having those people around will help you stay focused on developing your story, since you'll be able to observe them and ask them questions. This can also help you on a more practical level, too – they might become part of the making of the film as well.

For a perfect example of this, look at the Independent Spirit Award-winning film KRISHA. Writer/director Trey Edward Shults built a story around his own family, and the struggles they had with addiction. His aunt was addicted to drugs and estranged from her family. She would visit them on Thanksgiving sometimes, and one year, she showed up drunk. That incident became the spark for the story of the film. When he actually made the film, he got many of his family members to act in it – and he shot the film in his own house.

"As soon as I started writing, I started planning out all the shots and the structure and how we would do this," Shults said in a New York Times interview. "It was the only house I would make the movie at" (Rapold, 2016).[1]

Build Your Story Around Your Community

When I was thinking about making RISING STAR, I knew the story had to be something I was familiar with and passionate about. And one thing I always thought about was my work/life balance. When I started developing the film, I had been laid off four separate times. I knew no employment was forever, and my company was laying people off while I was working there, so the threat of losing my job was always over my head. That stress led me to working three jobs, for fear of having somewhere to land if I lost one. My work/life balance was completely tilted toward work. So I decided to focus on that.

Once I knew what I would examine in the script, I started looking around to see if my community could help influence my story. I lived a few minutes from Hartford, Connecticut, nicknamed the "Insurance Capital of the World," so I decided to make my lead character, Chris, an insurance adjuster, a buttoned-up, conservative fellow who is a slave to his job. He would meet his polar opposite, Alyza, in the film, a Bohemian, free spirited woman who follows all her desires. (This worked well because Hartford also has a thriving underground music scene.) They would be total opposites on the work/life spectrum, and through their interaction, they would both come closer to finding a balance.

Once I decided the film would take place in Hartford, I drove around the city, looking for places that would make compelling locations, and that would support the story. I wanted the film to include cultural landmarks, so I visited the Mark Twain House and Harriet Beecher Stowe House, homes to two world-renowned authors. I also visited the grave of Pulitzer Prize-winning poet Wallace Stevens, who is buried in Hartford – and who was also a Vice President of The Hartford Insurance Company.

Going to these locations helped me firm up the story – and Wallace Stevens actually became the story's key. When I visited his grave, I learned he had written all his work while holding down a day job. He was the epitome of someone with their work/life balance in equilibrium. I could build around that location, as it spoke to the central conflict in the story. And it ultimately became the location for the film's midpoint scene, where Chris realizes his work/life balance is tilted too much in one direction. Visiting the Mark Twain House also inspired some scenes, and after talking with the museum director, we eventually got permission to film inside!

This pre-writing location scouting can also do something very interesting – it can help you visualize what your scenes will look like before you actually write them. The opposite way it's normally done, sure, but it can help you infuse specificity in your writing when you already know where scenes will take place.

Consider Your Local Celebrities

No matter where you live, there are people in your community who people look up to – they could be media personalities, thought leaders, political folks, even popular teachers. Those are people who know the story of your community, and they can be a great resource for material.

When I was developing RISING STAR, I was also doing movie reviews for a local television station on their Sunday morning broadcast. I worked with the weekend anchor on-air for these reviews, and through talking with her, I got a lot of ideas for places to research, and people to talk with, in the Hartford area. (It also didn't hurt that when the film was done, we were able to do segments about it to help bring people to local screenings.)

In some cases, you can include them in the production of your film. One of the most popular media figures in the Hartford area was a morning DJ named Gary Craig, and he's also an actor, having appeared on films and TV shows like CURB YOUR ENTHUSIASM and AMERICAN HUSTLE. After seeing his work, I knew he'd be perfect for a role in RISING STAR. So after writing it for him, I met with him and he jumped on board. We had a great time filming, our cast and crew had a blast meeting him, and when the film was done, Gary was kind enough to talk about it on his radio show, which was great publicity for us. Everybody wins.

Whenever I've taken a screenwriting course, I was always told to let my imagination run free and think up locations that would perfectly fit the stories I was telling. But reverse engineering your story with elements you can see and touch could bring a whole new dimension to it.

How Pizza Turned into a Microbudget Feature

My second feature film as director, STAY WITH ME, is a drama about mental illness. And the development of the story was a perfect example of reverse engineering to fit the elements that we had at our disposal.

My co-writer and producer, Leaf Maiman, and I met while we were film students at California State University, Northridge. I was a graduate screenwriting student, as well as the manager of the school's script library, and Leaf was an undergraduate screenwriting student – and my script library intern. Leaf and I talked all the time about independent film and he was driven to make his first feature film once he got out of school.

One day, he invited me out for lunch, and convinced me that we should make something together. We laid out a reverse-engineering plan over pizza that day, which led to us eventually making the movie.

The first thing I asked him was what he had access to, and he told me we would be able to shoot in his parent's house, a gorgeous three-bedroom, two-story home in nearby Woodland Hills. He also said he had a network of family and friends in town, who were interested in helping him make his first film.

At the time, I had met a number of other CSUN film students who were interested in working on a feature film and would do so for much less money than the going crew rate. I met different students who wanted to work as director of photography, production manager, and assistant director on a feature, so those major positions would be covered. (I actually met our production designer tutoring him in screenwriting, in the script library.) I also had a 1080p camera that I used for corporate and documentary shoots, so we had a camera as well.

At first glance, we had all the gear we would need, the probability of a small crew that would work for peanuts, and a location that could provide a number of different rooms to shoot in, in a beautiful Southern California neighborhood.

Now we just needed a story!

I'll let Leaf take it from here – I asked him to give me his experience of how STAY WITH ME was developed:

After we knew what we had to work with, the next big question was, 'What movie are we going to make?' Knowing that film shoots could easily get very complicated, we put two major constraints on ourselves. First, we were going to shoot the whole film in one location, likely a house. Second, we would have three actors, two women, one man, all in their early 20's, because these were some of the actors we had easy access to.

'What themes do you want to tackle?' After a bit of back and forth, we agreed the film should center around the issue of mental health. I was fascinated by the idea of unanswerable questions and how to live with them. I had struggled with fairly severe depression and anxiety for most of my life. On top of this, psychology has always been a special interest of mine, which is not completely surprising when you consider I'm the child of two retired therapists. But no matter how much I seemed to know about psychology, none of it seemed to help me figure out why I was constantly miserable, and more importantly, how not to be constantly miserable.

At the age of 25, I was diagnosed with Level 1 Autism Spectrum Disorder and ADHD, which suddenly gave me a lot of answers to my unanswerable mental health questions. The revelation really altered the way I saw my past, and that includes the way I saw STAY WITH ME. We shot the film when I was 22 and undiagnosed. In the opening monologue of the film, Katie says, 'Bipolar, borderline, PTSD. A different doctor. A different diagnosis.' STAY WITH ME was about my experiences as an undiagnosed person – at least partially.

The interesting thing was that I actually wanted to tell a story about grief; my mother had passed away a year earlier, so that was a topic heavy on my mind. And since I'm 20 years older than Leaf, I thought I would be able to bring a different viewpoint to the story, as someone who's lived through the death of loved ones.

Leaf also said something interesting; he wanted to tell a story in two timelines. He was very interested in non-linear storytelling. As he explained,

Usually, films have a point of view, often because the film will have a protagonist whom the story focuses on. I was a fan of GAME OF THRONES, which does not center around a singular protagonist, and traditional media's preoccupation with protagonists has always bothered me. Life doesn't have a protagonist. Everyone is just a person; they have their own perspective, and they justify their own stance. When tackling the complications of navigating relationships with mental illness, it felt wrong to give the film a central character. The film isn't about any one of them. It's about all of them navigating a situation that none of them are prepared for. I didn't want the film to take sides. They all had their reasons and their faults. I didn't need the story to judge them.

After some pizza-filled discussion, I also contributed a structural guideline: I wanted to tell a big story in one location. Since we were going to be all in one location, I thought of following characters at two different points of their lives, before and after a major event, and that the wardrobe and production design of the house would be changed to reflect the time they were in.

So now we had a little better idea of how the film would look, and how it would be structured, but still, no real story had been developed.

That's when Leaf figured out the idea that would pull everything together.

The film would be about a young woman who committed suicide because of her undiagnosed mental illness, and we would follow her loved ones in the time before and after that moment.

When I heard that, I jumped in and suggested the loved ones we could follow could be her best friend, and a new boyfriend the young woman had. And once the young woman passed away, her best friend and boyfriend would be responsible for picking up the pieces of her life, and dealing with their own grief. So in a sense, the story would be about how two people, connected by their love of this young woman, struggle to become her mental health advocates, and come to terms with what they did right – and wrong – over the last part of her life. This also fits into the idea of a microbudget production because we only had three main characters. It would not be hard to cast (and as it turned out, Leaf and I also had small roles in the film, along with the three leads. Working in multiple roles.)

It was a dramatic story, to be sure, but it felt like something that we had the resources to create. Leaf and I have both spent lots of time in therapy, and both of Leaf's parents were psychologists, so in addition to physical production resources, we had mental health professionals who could vet our story as we created it.

Once we finished our pizza, we had a solid plan to begin writing our film, and it would be a project that would best take advantage of the limited resources we had access to.

Who Is Your Audience?

As you're figuring out your story, there's another piece of the puzzle you need to be giving time and thought to – who's going to watch your film.

Now your reaction to this might be "Isn't that kind of early?" And for a long time, that's what I thought, too. But if you're taking on the responsibility of distributing your film yourself, you need to be thinking about who'll be watching it right from the get-go.

This process consists of breaking the world up into groups of people you can contact directly, **through email, through media, and/or in person.** Each group has a specific connection, either to you or to the story of the film. These groups could involve:

- Your friends and family (this is usually the easiest group to assemble)
- People who have a specific connection to you
- People who are passionate about the subject matter of the movie
- People who have a geographic connection to the movie (it takes place where they live)
- People who are part of a group or organization that has something to do with the story of the film, or to a member of your filmmaking team

Again, this might seem really early to be doing this work, but these are the folks who could have access to something that could take your story to the next level.

My First Audience

As I was coming up with RISING STAR's story, my team and I knew we would need to crowdfund a sizable portion of the film's budget. So, we started to identify the groups of people we thought would be interested in seeing the film. And as it turned out, we put an audience together where some groups had very little to do with others. But they all had one thing in common: they had a connection to our story.

It took over a year for us to come up with this audience, but it meant everything when we got to our crowdfunding campaign, when we got to production, and all the way through post.

So who were they?

People Struggling with Work/Life Balance

When I was coming up with this story, work was the most important thing in my life. I was working three jobs at once, I had huge student loans to pay, and I was having a hard time finding any time to spend doing things I enjoyed. Turns out, I was far from the only person feeling that way.

Between the dot-com implosion and the 2008 financial crisis, there were so many of my friends suffering in a similar way. (And now that we're in a post-COVID economy, I would bet folks are suffering similarly nowadays, too.) So my team and I started to collect their information, and we eventually ended up with a list of about 100 people – and their email addresses. Since they were all friends with someone on the production team, these people were also candidates for in-person interactions as well.

Total Audience: 100 Via Email

People Who Live in Connecticut

Since Connecticut was the focus of the story (specifically, the capital city of Hartford), and because I grew up there, I knew people who lived in the state would be interested in the film, regardless of what the actual story content was.

But Connecticut also has a unique status among states: it's had its heart broken by not one, but two major sports franchises. In 1997, the National Hockey League's Hartford Whalers left town for North Carolina, where they became the Carolina Panthers. And two years later, the National Football League's New England Patriots backed out of a deal that would have built them a new stadium in Hartford, instead staying in Massachusetts.

With these back-to-back heartbreaks, Connecticut needed something to rally around. And we thought the film could do that.

Now did I have the email address of all three million people in Connecticut? No. But there were plenty of newspapers, TV news stations, radio shows, and blogs with a Connecticut focus. We felt confident they'd be interested in getting the word out about us. And since it's a small state, the chances were really good that if we held in-person events, we'd be able to reach out and meet a good amount of those folks, shake their hands, and tell them about what we were doing.

Total Audience, 100 Via Email, 3,000,000 Via Media

The Connecticut Film Scene

Generally, Connecticut has a supportive independent film scene; there were groups in certain parts of the state that produced short films, like the Southeastern Connecticut Filmmakers, and multiple state universities, public and private, had filmmaking or media production majors.

The state also had a very specific film-related education initiative, one that I created. It was a workforce development program, called the

Connecticut Film Industry Training Program (FITP), where state residents could take classes to learn how to work in crew positions. The program ran from 2008 to 2012, and we were able to train 520 residents in that time, who ended up working over 19,000 days on film, television and digital media projects. When we started developing RISING STAR, we were in the third year of the program, so we had 350 people who were either FITP students or alumni in the program – and we had their emails. And since I had a personal connection with every one of them, the chances were high that they'd attend any in-person events we would hold.

Total Audience: 450 Via Email, 3,000,000 Via Media

The Florida State University Film School Community

Why would a film community in Florida have any interest in a film being made in Connecticut? Because I'm a graduate of FSU's Graduate Film Conservatory! I had learned about other FSU filmmakers making projects through their alumni newsletter, which goes out to over 800 very engaged alumni each week, and had supported them through crowdfunding campaigns. I was hopeful that if I posted in the newsletter, those same grads would come around to help me on my film. And since the newsletter is delivered each week via email, I automatically had access to all those alumni, without even knowing their email addresses! Since they're literally based all over the world, it was less likely we'd be able to connect with them in person (unless we went to industry hubs like Los Angeles or New York City), but we knew we could reach them directly.

Total Audience: 1,250 Via Email, 3,000,000 Via Media

The Kinsella School for Performing Arts

One thing our team prioritized while putting this film together was the importance of engaging with the community we'd be filming in. One of the ways we did that was to partner with a performing arts middle school in Hartford, the Kinsella School for Performing Arts, and we teamed up with their eighth-grade media arts class. We showed them all the different crafts in making a movie – and then we actually made a move ourselves! This was a great way to spend time in person with our audience; we met some of the parents of the students we taught, and they loved what we were doing. The students had a good time, and we were able to build some goodwill in the community. Kinsella also had a school email list for their 400 students, which we would be able to access as we made the film.

Total Audience: 1,650 Via Email, 3,000,000 Via Media

Everyone the Director Knows

This category is sometimes the entirety of a filmmaker's crowdsourcing work – friends and family. It's essential that you look far beyond who you know to build your audience, but don't forget the people that you already do know. I had been working in independent film for about ten years by the time we started making RISING STAR, so my family and friends knew I was trying to become a feature writer/director. And whenever a friend came to me asking for help on their projects, whether by giving a crowdfunding donation or physically helping them make the thing, I always said yes. This built up lots of goodwill. And, most importantly, I try to be a good person. That goes a long way. So when I listed out all the emails I had in my Gmail account, it came out to about 800 friends and family members, most of whom lived within a drive from my house, who knew about my dream and would hopefully help make it a reality.

Total Audience: 2,450 Via Email, 3,000,000 Via Media

Everyone Our Producer/Lead Actor Knows

I was smart to team up with our lead actor and producer early in the process, since he knew so much more about social media than I did, and also had a completely different circle of people than me. At the time, he worked at a college in Instructional Technology, and was also an MFA Theater student, so he had the worlds of storytelling and tech covered. He ran his own Web site, so he understood how to navigate the Web. He's also a Connecticut native and grew up in a different part of the state than I did, so we had two different areas covered with our friends and family. (That's an important thing to remember; you want as little crossover between audiences as possible. That way, you reach a larger number.) Through all his connections, friends, and family, he had about 500 email addresses he could contact and could reach another 4,000 students, staff, and faculty at his school through social media. And his college is in Yonkers, New York, so his audience was close enough that we could reach them in person as well.

Total Audience: 2,950 Via Email, 3,004,000 Via Media

Everyone Our Other Producer Knows

Thanks to the FITP, I was able to work with Matt Giovannucci, a recent college graduate who wanted to become a film producer. (He's now my producing partner – as well as my attorney!) I asked him if he wanted to produce RISING STAR with us, and he immediately jumped on board. You'll see that Giovannucci is an Italian name, and his family was active in UNICO, the largest Italian-American service organization in the United States. They had a national media apparatus and could contact their 100,000 members through their magazine. Matt was able to round up 50 email addresses, along with the huge media reach of UNICO. Matt's family and friends were close enough to reach in person, but since UNICO is nationwide, it would be less likely we'd be able to meet those members at a public event.

Total Audience: 3,000 Via Email, 3,104,000 Via Media

So once we locked down the story for RISING STAR, we were also able to put together a list of three thousand email addresses, and a possible audience of over 3.1 million people! With this list, we had a first place to look in order to find online support; however, we defined it.

Publicity and Team Building Begins Now

Even though your crowdsourcing work will help you identify the people who could be interested in your film, you need to put in the work to let them know that it exists.

That's publicity.

This is the first opportunity to engage the audience you've identified, and it can be audio, photo, video, polls, suggestions of content they'd like, really anything that can get these people to connect with you and allow you to begin building a relationship.

While developing RISING STAR, our first publicity attempt was our lead actor and I making a YouTube video, asking to hear stories from our audience about frustrations they've had in the workplace. When we posted it on social media, people started writing short posts, talking about bosses they struggled with, long commutes, snotty coworkers, all kinds of things. But the most important thing was that we created a dialogue with folks. We made sure to respond to every one of them, and they became the first of our audience members to engage with us. Fortunately, that number would grow over time, but this is where it began.

The other thing you should be doing at this stage is looking for the people who'll be the key members of your filmmaking team.

Yes, this early.

And I don't just mean production team. Now having key production team members, like your producer(s), cinematographer, production designer, editor, sound designer, and composer, on board as you're developing your story can be a huge help in identifying problems and addressing them, before they become more expensive. But crew members shouldn't be the only team members you should be thinking about at this stage. If you find there are people in your community who are huge movie fans or have spent their life wishing they could be a part of one, recruit them now! What they might lack in experience, they will more than make up for in excitement, engagement and good vibes. You're at the start of a long, hard journey; the more people you can have on your team who are thrilled to be on the journey with you, the better.

The Importance of Scheduling

One other element of crowdsourcing that isn't talked about very much is the vital importance of laying out your deadlines. This is where "beginning with the end in mind" becomes literal. Making any film involves a myriad of deadlines you must meet in order to get your completed project done when you want, so laying them out at the beginning of the process gives you a roadmap to follow as your film comes to life. If your goal is premiering at a certain film festival, for example, you'll need to have all of the following scheduled and planned for:

- The film festival submission deadline, two years out from starting the process of creating the film, for that film festival (so you'll know when the entire film must be finished)
- The completion of color correction, a year and ten months out from starting
- The completion of sound editing, a year and nine months out
- The completion of music/score creation, a year and nine months out
- The completion of picture editing, a year and six months out
- The completion of principal photography, a year and two months out
- The completion of pre-production, a year out
- The completion of the film's crowdfunding campaign, nine months out
- Each of the crowdfunding campaign events, during month eight
- The completion of audience building, six months out
- The completion of writing the script, four months out

And even within each of those major steps, there can be multiple deadlines. Just for writing the script, you might have:

- Final draft completed four months out
- Peer feedback completed three months out
- Second draft completed two months out
- First draft completed one month out

Of course, no two films are alike, each project will have specific steps that are unique to itself, and deadlines can always change as you go. (And it would be incredibly fast for a writer to complete a first draft of a movie in four weeks.) But you can see the number of deadlines that present themselves throughout. By scheduling everything out, you can have a holistic (remember that word?) look at the making of your film, and you can see where you need to be, and the work you need to have done, at any particular point in the process.

Development for DEADBRAINS

Last chapter, we put together our business plan for DEADBRAINS and figured out what made this zombie movie different from all the others. We also thought a little bit about who might like to watch the movie, so we're actually a little ahead of the game when it comes to crowdsourcing. This is the point where we figure out what we have access to, that we could potentially use for the movie.

Crowdsourcing the Story

Let's assume we'll be making the film in Memphis, Tennessee. And let's move forward with the idea that it will be a war film, like we talked about the last chapter:

   A war movie (maybe the zombies are led by a military mastermind – who might have been patient zero? – and they strategically attack humans in places where they know they're weak, forcing the humans to rethink their entire society before the zombies eradicate them)

   A war movie would potentially need open locations to have battles in. After a quick look around Memphis, I unearthed Paintball Park, a huge, open paintball facility that has jungle, residential and Old West sets. It's quite possible that talking to the folks there could open up the possibility of using those sets as film locations, potentially in exchange for special thanks credit in the film. (I haven't actually contacted these folks, so this is all hypothetical.)

   Zombie movies need tons of makeup, so a quick search found HowardArtSPFX, a group of special effects makeup artists in Memphis. They offer zombie makeovers for $25 per person, so we could make a deal with them: if they cut the cost down to the cost of materials, the film could give a percentage of the film's profits to the group. (Again, hypothetical.)

   And of course, a zombie film would need lots of folks who could play zombie extras, in addition to the actual speaking (or grunting?) actors cast in the film. This ties in nicely to Memphis Zombies, the 5,000-member Facebook group we found in the last chapter, that does zombie walks and drive-in zombie movie trips. I would bet a number of them would love to be zombies in the film (and could potentially do their own makeup, too, cutting down the cost of the materials HowardArtSPFX would need).

Audience Identification

Here, again, our work has been started by discovering the Zombie Memphis group, and their 5,000 members, who you could potentially contact directly, through Facebook direct message. (This isn't exactly the same as an email address, but direct contact is the ideal, and this method can work.) We also have the Zombies subreddit, who gives us potentially 101,000 people we can reach via media. But we want to get much more specific about who we can reach. So we can look for other online groups with Memphis and zombie connections, like these?

- There's a Memphis Zombie Hunt, a zombie paintball hayride, at a local park in Memphis, and there's an email address on its Web site that could allow you to connect with the people in charge. That could open you up to dozens, or hundreds, of emails of local zombie lovers.
- Memphis has a Creative Works Conference, where artists of every type gather for a three-day conference of networking, education and networking. They have an email list you can sign up for, and they could be an ideal partner to reach a critical mass of Memphis-area creatives, some of whom I'd bet would be zombie lovers.
- Since 2009, there's been a Memphis Zombie Walk, where residents dress up in zombie makeup, walk through the city, and raise money and donations for a local food bank. Connecting with their director could lead to teaming up with the walkers, all obvious zombie fans.

Publicity and Teambuilding

All the crowdsourcing work you do seamlessly transitions into the publicity work you'll do for the film. Each of the groups we identified can be groups you can advertise to, whether on social media (asking them what their favorite zombie movies are, for example), or in real life (perhaps by hosting a "Best Memphis Zombie Makeup Artist" competition, giving a cash prize – and scouting for the best makeup talent at the same time). So long as you're building community, and getting people to know you're a good person and truly interested in the subject matter, you're in great shape.

This work can also help you start building your team. Specifically for zombie films, the production design team will play a huge role in the quest to make zombies who look "real." So you might find people through your crowdsourcing who could work in makeup, wardrobe, or set dressing. You'll also need to have a good set of assistant directors and production assistants on a film like this, because of the large amount of extras you'll be using as zombies; if there's no one corralling them on set, they could float away and disappear when you need them to be on camera. So you might find those people through this work, too.

Interview: Screenwriter/Filmmaker Brandi Nicole

Brandi Nicole is a writer, performer, and artivist whose work centers on women fighting to return to themselves. While she started off as an actor, she fell in love with the storytelling process after writing and producing MUTED, a short film about media discrepancy when a child of color goes missing, that was acquired by HBO and to date has just over 172k views on YouTube via Issa Rae's #ShortFilmSundays. She followed that up by making ALOHA, a short film about one mother's quest to honor a difficult birth experience, which was awarded the Emergence Filmmaker Grant. And her latest short, SPIN, co-directed by Jen West, highlights intimate partner violence and serves as a prelude to what they hope will be their first feature.

Figure 3.1 Headshot of filmmaker/artivist Brandi Nicole.

After working as a staff writer and recurring character on season two of Showtime's YOUR HONOR, Brandi is currently writing on an Untitled BOSCH spin-off.

Marty Lang:	Your career has been so interesting, in that you've worked in independent film production, television production, and in crowdfunding. So you have a unique viewpoint on the intermingling of story and production. How did you start your career?
Brandi Nicole:	I started with a web series when that was what everybody was doing. And then I made a short film. That was the calling card. Then I got into a television writers program, where I really did try to buckle down and focus on television, because I saw that being an independent filmmaker was going to be a hard road financially. And I knew I needed to make money. So short films were sort of the launching point. But once I started writing television pilots, then I was like, "Oh, this is definitely the thing for me." And when I can make films, I will just because I want to artistically, but in terms of it being a career, I don't see myself as a filmmaker, as a career filmmaker. I see myself as an artistic filmmaker, because I just see how hard of a road that can be.
ML:	How did you approach the production of your projects at the beginning, relative to your story? Were you thinking about locations when you were writing? Were you thinking about other phases in the process as you were putting the story together?
BN:	So the first web series, I just wrote whatever. And then very quickly realized, "Oh, no, I don't have that kind of money."

And that was in 2009. So the web series was my first foray into crowdfunding, and I failed. So that didn't work. But for the short film, I learned how much work, time, and effort it takes. And we raised about $18,000 on Kickstarter. The short film was my calling card. But that was the first time that I really saw how much goes into making things, even at a short film level. Because it wasn't a skeleton crew. So even though we were paying people significantly lower than their normal rate, everyone did still get paid. So we raised $18,000, and then I'm sure we spent another five to seven thousand afterwards. Just trying to send it to film festivals and things like that. That experience set the tone for approaching it in the future because on that one, I was the writer/producer, but I wasn't the director, I hired a director. And then for the two after that I was writer/director.

For me, I started by writing whatever it is that I want to say. And then I really look at okay, now how can I make this? And what do I need to change to make this? Finding locations always seems to be one of the most important things. And once I can get my location as affordable as possible, then I can figure everything else out. As a short filmmaker, I've always only made things over a weekend. And I've just done a one weekend thing. No reshoots or anything like that because I don't have my own equipment. Having to rent those things or hire crew that had those things, it was always like, we have to get it during this time. And that is it.

I have also always worked with a casting director. I think that's very important.

ML: That's unusual for beginning filmmakers.

BN: I think casting directors, number one, they save you time, because there are so many actors willing to submit. They also sometimes see things in your script, they see choices that you wouldn't necessarily see. And then when they bring those choices, sometimes you end up with something that you never saw. And it's beautiful, and it works out really, really well. So that's also a position that doesn't get paid as much as I would like to pay them. But they still get paid something. And they've always elevated every project that I've done.

I've realized now after making two different films, that when you have people who have powerful name recognition, that's less power that you have to make a decision. And there are some stories where that's totally fine. Because I just want the story to be made in any sort of way. And it's just a fun story that I want to do. So you want this, you want to change that line? That's fine. But then there are other stories like this one particular feature that I want to make that I've made as a short (the drama SPIN). That story is so personal, I must be the final say on these matters, point blank, period. So if that means this will now must be a $200,000 feature, as opposed to a $2 million feature, I am okay with that. Because of how protective I am. It is also because of the sort of summer camp experience I want to have with my actors that you don't necessarily get when you're on a bigger set. Both are good experiences, but they're just very, very different.

ML: You went from writer/producer on your first short to writer/director after that. What made you want to do that? And what did you learn in that process?

BN: Well, with the first film where I was writer/producer, I realized that if you are going to hire a director, you guys really have to be on the same page. Because otherwise, it can make that working relationship strained. And that was a situation where the director is very talented. But in terms of even our work process, the way that we work, we didn't really fit very well, as opposed to me and my co-producer, where our work processes are very complementary. We're very different people. But our work processes are super complementary. So I realized that for any future project, if I was going to only produce, I would need to find a director that I felt could be like another half of my brain. And if I couldn't do that, then I was gonna just have to direct myself.

So you know, to that end, there are definitely some stories that I will write that I will have no desire to direct whatsoever. But if it's a story that is personal to me, either I'm going to be directing it or I've got to find somebody who I feel like I can leave it in their hands, and trust that they're going to carry out a vision in a way that feels right. And that can be a challenging thing to do. I wish I knew who said this, but it's a quote I'll never forget that some director told an actor and then that actor said on a podcast, which is, "The job of the director is to make sure everyone's making the same movie." And that is exactly it.

ML: You worked at the crowdfunding portal Seed&Spark from 2018 to 2020. Did your experience working in crowdfunding give you any insight as to your own creative process?

BN: I think the only thing that I took away from it, working there that I use as a creative is how important audience building is. Because I recommend crowdfunding even when you have the money. And the reason why I do that is because it's an opportunity to expand your audience. There are people who know about projects I've worked on specifically just from the crowdfunding campaign, who would have never come across them any other way. But they donated because they thought it was a cool project. And now they are familiar with our work. So that is probably the biggest thing is that it's such an incredible audience building tool, even if you're raising a small dollar amount.

And it's such a great way to stay in touch with your audience to continue to give them updates. It can be a launching pad for future relationships, too. With my first campaign, there was a woman who saw the campaign after it ended, so she couldn't donate. But she reached out to us directly to donate, and she has been a funder of everything I've done since then. She wanted to go into producing, to work on projects that had something to say that resonated with what she believes in. And so that's what she's been doing. Then I was able to introduce her to someone who she then supported their projects. So it's a really good tool for building your audience and connecting with them and engaging with them. And just clarifying the message of your work.

ML: After Seed&Spark, you got started working in television. What has that process been like for you as a creative, in terms of how you create your own stories?

BN: Yeah, I mean, because I work in TV, I am reminded that none of this is made in a vacuum. And that even shows, like for example, SCANDAL, a huge, popular show, we always would be like Shonda, Shonda, Shonda (Rhimes, the showrunner), but some of those episodes are not just the genius Shonda. The contributions of everyone helps. It's almost like making a gumbo, where you can't remove one thing because it all melts together. And if you take one thing out, it changes everything. That's probably the biggest thing that I've learned. Even if it's your baby, it's your brainchild, it's your vision. But your team puts their stamp on it.

It always starts with leadership, good, bad or otherwise. So that's also something that I've definitely been watching as a lower-level writer, what I want to do when I have my own show versus the ways that I don't want to do it, you know, setting the tone so everyone is heard, even though of course you are the ultimate decision maker. There are ways to make people still feel heard, and still feel like their voice has value. And there are ways to not, and that will just shut people down. And that is not the sort of environment that makes for good art.

ML: Let's talk a little bit more about that. What are the most important things when you're the leader of a creative team?

BN: Certainly, understanding that good ideas come from everywhere, and giving credit when those ideas come from places that you don't expect. And not feeling threatened by that. Instead of being threatened, being grateful that this person who you weren't expecting to come with the key just gave you a gift. I think that's a very big one. Understanding that everyone has a different perspective. And while everyone's perspective is valid, theory should never be held in a higher regard than lived experience. Now if you make a choice where "I hear what you're saying, as the person who has lived this experience, and I am just choosing to make an artistic choice to go another way," make sure you say that and own that. But disregarding someone's lived experience because of research that you've done, never goes well. I mean, never in every possible way. So understanding that your research may have shown you XYZ, but if someone is, and I don't mean like they had this anecdotal thing, but they have lived as a woman, they've lived as a person of color, they lived as someone incarcerated, they lived as whatever, listen to them, listen to them, Take it in.

And understand that you have blind spots because we all do. If you're a leader, instead of feeling like you're being challenged on your blind spots, you're actually being given a gift to see outside of those things in the mirror. And good leaders get it, see that and value that and use that. And then they end up creating something that makes all the people who work for and with them want to do a great job. They will want to call them in as opposed to call them out. Because I've done both. I've called people in, and I've called people out. And I've only called people out when they refuse to be called in. When you refuse to be called in, and you keep exhibiting this behavior that is a detriment to the working environment and is a detriment to the story because it's not giving an authentic story, then you're gonna get called out.

So I would say in terms of being a leader, understand that if people are challenging beliefs that you have, take a moment to sit with it before immediately becoming defensive. Because there may be something to it. Maybe not always, but there may be something to it.

ML: What would your biggest piece of advice be for people who are at this development stage? How can someone best merge the processes of storytelling with the processes of production?

BN: The very first thing that I think is key, because when I think about every project I've done, it was to figure out who your partner is.

And partner doesn't necessarily mean a 50/50 partner. I don't even necessarily mean that. With ALOHA, it took me a while to find someone to help me make that. Had I had someone right from the beginning, it would have been so much smoother. Whether that's your producer, your director, if you're the writer, whoever. But having someone who believes in the project as strongly as you, I cannot tell you how valuable that is. Someone who's going to work on the project, who believes in the project as much as you. Two heads are better than one. Brainstorming sessions become instantly fruitful, you guys are both dividing and conquering. You're feeding off of each other. And then when one of you starts to get depressed and discouraged, the other person is like, "No, no, no, we're gonna do this." And then it flips. And then this person is frustrated. The other person's like, okay, you can be frustrated for an hour, let's get a drink. Let's go get ice cream. Let's figure this out. I think that is absolutely key.

There's a TED Talk about how the greatest predictor for a woman's success in business was her partner, and whether that partner was supportive. That made me think of a lot of ambitious women I know, who don't necessarily have partners who are supportive, versus the ones I know who do and the difference it made. And even though that's a different type of relationship, when you have that person who can give you that support on something that is as fulfilling and rewarding, but also as difficult as trying to birth a creative project, they help sustain you. And you're going to need that. You need to find your person who is going to be in the trenches with you. Because you cannot do this alone. I mean, you can – but I wouldn't recommend it.

Note

1 https://www.nytimes.com/2016/03/13/movies/with-krisha-a-director-finds-a-cast-he-can-relate-to.html

Reference List

Botto, Richard. "Crowdsourcing for Filmmakers: Indie Film and the Power of the Crowd," *Focal Press*, 2018.

Rapold, Nicolas. "With KRISHA, a Director Finds a Cast He Can Relate To," *New York Times*, 2016. https://www.nytimes.com/2016/03/13/movies/with-krisha-a-director-finds-a-cast-he-can-relate-to.html

4 Screenwriting

Of all the classes I teach, Screenwriting is my favorite. I was a journalist before I got into filmmaking, so writing is something that's deep in my bones. My first academic exposure to filmmaking was through screenwriting, too, via a course I took when I was an undergraduate. My professor was a produced screenwriter, and the class focused on character, story, description, and creating an experience for the reader. All vital and important things.

What that professor didn't teach me, though, something I learned over my time in indie film, is that a screenplay isn't a finished creative work. Sure, you want to create an emotional roller coaster for the reader – that's what gets people interested in the story in the first place. But once you get those people interested, that screenplay turns into a blueprint, a document that will guide the work of every other person that works on your film, as they create a visual story from it. And I don't just mean people who work in physical production; this blueprint will also guide the work of the folks who market and distribute your film, and quite possibly the people who will help finance your work through crowdfunding.

So you need to be thinking of all those people as you write your script. And that's a big shift for a screenwriter to make, since they've most likely been trained to focus solely on story. Plus, honestly, many filmmakers think of their scripts as sacrosanct, a divine communication straight from their soul. Considering commerce in the process of communicating their feelings would feel dirty. (A student actually told me that once. My eyes hurt because I rolled them so hard.)

A good filmmaker understands how every phase affects every other phase. And creating a blueprint that considers every other phase will allow them to execute the most efficient shoot possible, proceed smoothly through post-production, and allow for the most successful marketing and distribution of it as well.

Holistic filmmaking.

DOI: 10.4324/9781003295754-4

There are some easy ways to incorporate the work of all those other people when you write. Let's talk about a few of them.

Carding, the Shelf, and the Well

Once you have the basic spine of your story nailed down, filmmakers have a variety of ways to prepare how they'll actually write the screenplay. This usually involves breaking their story down into scenes (check out Blake Snyder's SAVE THE CAT! if you're a newer screenwriter for a great explanation of how to do this), sometimes involves writing out an actual outline (read Eric Edson's THE STORY SOLUTION for an incredible method of writing story outlines), and a Google search can give you a stack of images that show how act and scene structure work in screenplays. But this step is an opportunity to develop more than just your writing, and a very well-known filmmaker has a method that will allow you to do just that.

Writer/director Craig Brewer, who's made films like COMING 2 AMERICA, DOLEMITE IS MY NAME, and HUSTLE AND FLOW, is a Memphis resident, and a leader in the local film and arts scene. He's also incredibly generous with his time, and he has spoken in my Screenwriting class multiple times to talk about his work, his process, and the state of the film and television business. It was in my class that he explained his process for screenwriting, and it's fascinating.

When Craig decides he's hit on an idea he wants to write into a screenplay, he starts to put pen to paper. In actuality, the papers are index cards. This is his first step, what he calls "carding." And in this step, he takes index cards and lays them out, so that one card equals two minutes of screen time. He organizes them so that five cards sit in a row, equaling ten minutes of screen time, and once he's done, he'll have twelve rows of five cards each, roughly equal to a two-hour film. (This can, of course, be altered for different script lengths.) This allows him to pull back and look at the entire story from an arm's length distance, instead of being locked in on one particular scene or sequence. Carding can give you a view of your three-act structure (15 cards for Act 1, 30 for Act 2, and 15 for Act 3).

Once they're set up, he starts writing one scene on one card, not a full scene, but a little description of what will happen in it. And as he works, he'll be able to see his full story – and perhaps more importantly, the parts of his story that he hasn't figured out yet.

Once he has all his cards figured out, and a path for his story, he does something he calls "the shelf." He explained to me the way he came up with the shelf:

> What happens is that you kind of know, certain moments of a movie idea that you have, but you just don't know the whole thing. So I developed

this method that I call the shelf. This was back in the previously viewed VHS tape days of Blockbuster Video, where film nerds such as myself would, every Tuesday, run around to all the different Blockbusters, and you literally are diving into these bins, trying to find like, used Truffaut movies that they're trying to get rid of out of their rental catalog. We would buy them all, and they would leave out their black cases that they had too much. And I would get those black cases. And that was my movie collection, right? But I started to think: What would my movie look like in one of those cases? You know, because you'd walk into a Blockbuster and everybody would pick up their movie. And they would look at the back of it, and they'd look at the pictures, they'd see who's in it, they would read what it was about. And I started thinking 'Okay, well, what would my movie be in one of those previously viewed black boxes from Blockbuster?' But then I started thinking, what would be the two movies on either side of it, if it were on a shelf, and if there was a theme to the shelf? So you'd see a director section, or it's a horror section or something like that. But what if you had 80s musicals, or 70s musicals. So you could put up SATURDAY NIGHT FEVER, you could put up PURPLE RAIN if you were doing 80s. And then that got me thinking. When I got the idea for HUSTLE AND FLOW, I felt like I needed to study some other movies that were kind of in its spirit. So my four movies were Alan Parker's THE COMMITMENTS, SATURDAY NIGHT FEVER, ROCKY, and PURPLE RAIN. So I could see those four movies with HUSTLE AND FLOW, kind of sandwiched between those.

We'll hear more from Craig about his screenwriting process at the end of this chapter.

Once he finds those shelf films, he watches them. Trying to crack the structure of the film, pinpointing its major turning points and character moments. And he does that by watching the films ten minutes at a time. Once he's done, he looks at the events that happen in those ten minutes.

And then he cards those films.

So he's doing structural research on these films – and that leads to questions about his own. When he was shelving for HUSTLE AND FLOW, he watched THE COMMITMENTS, and saw that there was a rehearsal that was really raw, but at the end, the musical group in the film sounds really polished. So he thought: What would that look like in my world? That moment became the creation of "Whoop That Trick," the rap song that would be the first attempt by his lead character D-Jay (Terrance Howard) to create music. As he said, "It's kind of raw, but kind of exciting. Like, hey, we did it. We're starting. You know, it wasn't perfect, but it sure was exciting." When he's finished shelving, and he's figured out the bones of each of the four stories, that's when he starts a new set of cards. For his own movie. Based on all the research he's done deconstructing those four films on his shelf.

Once that second set of cards is completed, only then will he start the actual writing of the screenplay. And he'll do so with a well thought out, visual outline of how the story would be told. But even then, he's not really writing a "first draft," per se, of his story. Here, he starts writing what he calls "the well." This is essentially a first draft ... but he overwrites. He promises himself he'll write at least three cards a day, the new set of cards for his movie he's written after shelving. Once he gets to the end, he'll have a document that could be 150–160 pages. And that will be the point where he starts writing his proper first draft, only now with a "well" of information that he can go back to if, after cutting something, he decides he can use it somewhere else if it's retooled. And it's at this point that he starts to focus on elements like dialogue, only after he's done the work to fine-tune his story.

From a story construction standpoint, I think Craig's method is genius. By the time he sits down to write his actual first draft, you could argue that he's done seven other story drafts, of both his film and his shelf films, before writing something the outside world would see. But what's interesting about this method is that it also allows you to continue your crowdsourcing. When you determine what four films inspire your film in the shelving phase, you have just figured out four different groups of people who'd be interested in your movie, because the films you pick will be the DNA of the film you create. Once you identify them, you can look for places online where fans of those films congregate, theaters where those films might play, or real-life events where fans of those films meet up.

If the film THE BIG LEBOWSKI is an inspiration of yours, for example, you're in luck – there are events all over the country called Lebowski Fests, where local Lebowski fans take over bowling alleys. They screen the film, have costume contests, and sell White Russians at the bar. If your film has Lebowski in its DNA, you'll have a golden opportunity to find your audience at those events.

Carding, shelving and the well is a great way to lay out your story before you begin screenwriting, and it can also give you additional directions to research to find your audience. And it's done by an incredibly successful studio filmmaker. It's worth a look.

Crowdsourcing Your Writing

Writing your screenplay can also be an opportunity to recruit people to the cause of making your film. For so long, the image of the screenwriter bent over a computer screen, typing away in solitude, has been their assumed existence. But by embracing technology, it's possible for today's screenwriter to create opportunities to bring others into the writing of the script – not as co-writers, but as an active audience – and excite them about your story.

The screenplay is still an analog document, even though we live in a digital age. And Southern Oregon University Digital Cinema professor Andrew Kenneth Gay agrees. In his article "Screenwriting 2.0 in the Classroom? Teaching the Digital Screenplay,"[1] he argues that if a Hollywood screenwriter from 1950 time-traveled to today, all they would need to do is learn how to use a computer, and they'd be able to pick right up writing screenplays. There hasn't been any evolution in the creation of screenplays in all that time (Gay, 2012).

But since writing now happens in the digital world, we can create new screenwriting practices that don't focus on print. Things like websites, blogs, wikis, and interactive media can now be incorporated into the actual creation of scripts.

How, you might ask? Gay called this new style "Screenwriting 2.0," and explained its structure in terms of "Web 2.0," a phrase coined by web designer Nancy Dinucci in 1999 that envisioned the web as a "transport mechanism, the ether through which interactivity happens." Gay took five core principles of Web 2.0, and applied them to what he thinks Screenwriting 2.0 could become:

Harnessing Collective Intelligence

This is just another term for crowdsourcing. Think of Wikipedia, or the stream of personal information you and others post on Facebook or Twitter/X. Web 2.0 allows multiple users to contribute information to a completed whole.

If you transfer this to screenwriting, the obvious example would be collaborating with a co-writer in another physical area, to write a script together. But what if you expanded your pool of creative collaborators? Say you want to write a script with six main characters. Each of the actors playing those characters can become writers on the project and can tailor their own dialogue and action based on how they interpret their characters. This would make a collaborative screenplay possible, without losing the narrative cohesion that sometimes lessens when films are improvised.

Perpetual Beta

This deals with the ending of software release cycles. Web-based applications, on desktops, laptops, and mobile, constantly evolve with upgrades; those who have them always have access to the latest version.

A screenwriting equivalent of this would be a cloud-based wiki script, where revisions could easily be tracked. This way, everyone involved in a project (both writers and production folks) would have immediate access to every revision of the script, in real time. This would eliminate the need for the multi-colored script revision pages so common on professional sets. It would allow those same people to have access to the revision history of a script as well.

Rich User Experience

When you think of a website today, there are all sorts of interactive and dynamic elements that the site can provide. Gay mentions seven facets of user experience-focused design, saying an interface should be useful, usable, desirable, findable, accessible, credible, and valuable. Audio, video, animation, and even VR/AR elements are common.

Thinking of how to apply this to screenwriting, if you're writing a cloud-based wiki script, there's no limit to the kinds of interactivity you can embed into that script. Have a story that takes place in Boston? Embed a Google map of the city, with your locations highlighted. Hyperlink dialogue in your script to the research you did when figuring out how to come up with a character's voice.

There's no limit to the kinds of additional elements you can add to this type of screenplay. When Zach Braff wrote the script for his first film GARDEN STATE, he included a CD of the songs he wanted for the soundtrack when he sent it to producers. He also added notations in the script, for when the reader should listen to each song. Now anyone can do the same – or better – by creating the script online. Gay called it a "living pre-visualization of the film to come."

Software Above the Level of a Single Device

Likewise with screenwriting, this idea translates to writing above the level of a single medium; that is, to write in transmedia. Have backstory in your script that doesn't make sense to include in your narrative? Branch it off and create a graphic novel to tell that piece. Is there a conversation you really wish you could include, but time constraints won't allow it? Add them as a text message conversation. Are there side characters you think would be perfect for their own stories? Write a web series or television series that focuses on them, and their own stories. Gay suggests Screenwriting 2.0 might eventually involve focusing on story-world creation as opposed to the traditional three-act script design.

Leveraging the Long Tail

WIRED editor Chris Anderson first described the "Long Tail," a graphical representation of how many of today's Internet-based businesses work. He explained the theory of the Long Tail as "that our culture and economy is increasingly shifting away from a focus on a relatively small number of 'hits' (mainstream products and markets) at the head of the demand curve and toward a huge number of niches in the tail. As the costs of production and distribution fall, especially online, there is now less need to lump products and consumers into one-size-fits-all containers. In an era without the constraints of physical shelf space and other bottlenecks of distribution, narrowly-targeted goods and services can be as economically attractive as mainstream fare" (Anderson, 2004).[2]

As screenwriters, this means that writing a mainstream, four-quadrant film is not the only way to become successful. By focusing on small, niche markets, screenwriters can target their work to specific audiences. Over time, those writers might be able to identify those audiences through email lists, social media, and crowdfunding campaigns and could even make the jump to becoming producers of their own material, with their own audience built in from the first typed sentence.

Understandably, this might be difficult for screenwriters to wrap their heads around at first glance, but incorporating technology into writing screenplays holds a lot of promise. As Gay says, Screenwriting 2.0 could "attempt to integrate conception and execution through an interactive digital text."

Write Like a Production Manager

Of the many positions on a film set, the production manager doesn't seem like the most creative. Some consider them nothing more than beancounters, who have little regard for the artistic process. As you get more into the industry, though, you quickly learn how vital production managers are in film and television production. They're responsible for making a film cost-effectively, and because of that, they look closely at some things you may not think about when you're writing. As you create your next script, thinking like a production manager may help it stand out among the pack.

Locations

A production manager is very worried about the locations a film is shot in, for two major reasons: how much they cost, and how much time they can take away from a shooting day. As a general rule, the more locations there are in a film, the more that film will cost to shoot. So as you write, keep that in mind, and see if there are opportunities to consolidate multiple locations into one.

You may have heard the term "contained" before – a producer may be looking for a contained thriller or horror script, for example. That means they want a film that is shot in one location. A writer might think that's just so the crew can have an easy shoot, but there are serious financial ramifications to making a film this way. The more locations a film has, the more "company moves" they will have to make. A company move is just what it sounds like – moving every truck, car, piece of equipment, and person from one location to another. If the film must do this during a shoot day, it can eat up hours of time – time the film should be shooting.

Schedules

Locations play a major role in the way a film is scheduled as well. And if you haven't been on a film set before, you might be surprised how many factors go into a shooting schedule. Day shoots, night shoots, interior and exterior locations, actor scheduling, location availability, and specialty equipment use are just some of the variables that can affect a film's schedule. It could be almost anything; I once acted in a short film where I had to have two different hair colors over the course of the film. (It was a comedy called TO DYE FOR.) That became the major scheduling issue of the film; all my scenes with my first hair color had to be shot first, I needed time to change hair color during the shooting week (when we filmed scenes with other actors), and then scenes in my second hair color were shot last.

So being mindful of your film's schedule can make your script much more attractive to a production manager – and a producer. As you write, try and limit, if possible, the amount of night exterior scenes you have. Night exteriors require much more lighting than interior scenes do, which costs money. Of course, if you have a script that takes place entirely outside at night, there isn't much you can do. But paying attention to what costs money can make your script more affordable – and therefore more attractive.

You also want to think about the page count of your film's shoot days. For independent films, I've found that a successful shooting day is when you film four or five script pages. Take a look at how many pages you shoot in each location; if you can, work it so each location shoots a number of pages that's a multiple of four or five. Why? If you can shoot full days at your location, you won't have to company move in the middle of a shooting day to another one. You'll just show up at the next location on the following shoot day. That will allow the production to spend the whole day shooting, instead of breaking the day up with a time-sucking company move.

Minor-Aged Actors

You might not know this, but labor laws limit the amount of hours child actors can work on set. If you have one, they can be limited to much less

68   *Screenwriting*

than the twelve hours in a standard film set work day. (That's why you often see twins working as the same character in a project; think the Olsen twins when they were younger, on the show FULL HOUSE.) If you have a minor as a major character in your script, know that it may take much longer for a producer to film that script, which will cost much more money, since the rest of the crew needs to be paid for the additional days it will take to film.

Clearance

Do you have a song in your head that just has to be in your movie? Keep in mind that the producer will be responsible for getting the rights to that song before it can be included. There are two types of rights they need to secure: the publishing rights (from the person who wrote the song) and the master rights (from the person who recorded it). To use a piece of music, you need permission from both people/entities, and they're not always the same.

This also holds true for any mention or usage of copyrighted material in your script. Any character wearing a New York Yankee hat, drinking a Pepsi, or riding an Uber must have those images cleared before they can be used in your movie. There are people on film sets whose entire jobs revolve around obtaining clearance for items in a film. If you don't present any clearance issues in your script, a producer might need to hire one less person – making your story that much more enticing.

Production managers handle many logistical issues that screenwriters may never think about. But by being cognizant of what they worry about, you can make your script much more producible. Which could give you the edge that might be the difference between being produced and ending in the slush pile.

Screenwriting for DEADBRAINS

Assuming we would go through the process of shelving and carding while writing DEADBRAINS, we'd already have some of the work done. If you think back to when we were putting our business plan together, there were a number of zombie movies we referenced, while coming up with the story:

- LAND OF THE DEAD
- I AM LEGEND
- WARM BODIES
- 28 DAYS LATER
- WORLD WAR Z
- PRIDE AND PREJUDICE AND ZOMBIES

Since DEADBRAINS will be a war movie, I'd say WORLD WAR Z can certainly be one of the four shelving films, since war is literally in the title, and it's about a zombie epidemic that we see in many parts of the world. I also love the idea of including this film because it's based on the book by Max Brooks. That means you could also engage everyone who loved the book, as well as the film.

I also think I AM LEGEND could be one of the four films, because of the organization and coordination the zombies exhibit in the movie. That would be magnified in DEADBRAINS, since the zombies would be smarter than the humans. And in this case, too, you'd be able to engage all the fans of the Richard Matheson novel that the film is based on.

I wouldn't use the other zombie films, though, because there are some other things the movie could focus on. Since it would be a war movie, I think a movie like SAVING PRIVATE RYAN would be a good pick, to emphasize the military-type scenes, and the relationship between the main characters stuck in this war, as they wrestle with a goal not everyone may agree with. Some humans may not think the zombies are smarter than they are, which could create conflict between them as they fight.

For the final film, I'd pick one you might not think would have anything to do with a zombie movie, THE USUAL SUSPECTS. In this film, crime kingpin Keyser Soze (Kevin Spacey) outsmarts the cop who interrogates him by making him think he's a low-level criminal. This could carry over into DEADBRAINS, where there could be a human infiltrator in the zombie military, who could exploit a weakness of the zombies (maybe they can't smell, so they can't tell the human is alive, or maybe they're able to stake out a zombie hideout and steal their plans).

So our shelving process for DEADBRAINS gives us a solid roadmap for us to find audience members, fans of the four films we've picked. Of course, we're not actually writing the screenplay for this book, but the process would be to watch all four films and break down the structure of all of them, thinking throughout about what moments of those films should be included in our film.

We could really have some fun applying Screenwriting 2.0 concepts to the writing of DEADBRAINS, because of the rabid (pardon the pun) world of zombie lovers. This type of film is the ideal situation to harness collective intelligence, as zombie fans have all kinds of films and TV shows to pull from, and their own ideas of what they'd do if the zombie apocalypse ever happened. This could all potentially influence the story of the movie. In addition to zombie fans, military aficionados could also provide insight on how a zombie war might take place. And if you had actor friends who you wanted to play the main zombie roles, they could be a part of creating their zombie characters, in collaboration with you, while you're writing. Reaching out to those audiences online, and inviting them into the writing of the script, would improve the story – and engage your audience.

You should also be thinking like a UPM while putting a script together like this. You may love seeing armies of zombies snarling across the screen, devouring human flesh – but your budget won't allow you to match up with the big-budget zombie flicks. You need to write smarter. You could think of things like:

- Setting scenes in interior locations, with characters talking to each other, with no windows (or windows blocked out with wood or furniture), while outside, you can hear zombies breathing, screaming, breaking things, etc. This allows the sense of lots of zombies closeby, but you don't have to worry about finding 100 people to dress up in zombie makeup.
- Shooting exterior scenes at night, with minimal lighting on purpose, and once again using sound to give a sense of lots of zombies in the area. This will make the scene feel like a zombie army is close, without having to find and make up those 100 people.
- Focusing most of the story on what led up to the zombies coming into existence. Those scenes wouldn't require zombie makeup at all; that would just be human beings interacting (and potentially doing dumb things that the zombies could take advantage of, once they come to be).

The screenwriting process could also provide a number of cool ways for you to get the word out about your movie and continue building your team for the film's eventual production. For DEADBRAINS, you could reach out to zombie groups, and ask them to create zombie characters for the movie. They could write out their own zombie backstory (what they did while they were human, before they were bitten, where they ended up after, what body part tastes best to them, whatever), and this could be submitted to the wiki script that was being developed. This could do a few interesting things:

- Every person who submits a backstory for a character could have the opportunity to play that zombie character in the movie! This would create a rich storytelling tapestry beyond the main story of the film, and every person who submits could then become an extra in the movie, with a character they created – and an engaged team member for crowdfunding and beyond.
- Talented writers who create really interesting zombie characters could be incorporated into the main story of the film! You might keep a zombie role open while you're writing, on the assumption that someone will write something so fantastic, they could be plugged in as a small supporting character in the movie. (The person who writes this backstory will feel like they won the lottery.)

- It's possible all the writers who submit those backstories could begin writing fan fiction with those characters, possibly creating an entirely original companion story, taking place in the world of DEADBRAINS, but completely separate. Every person who contributes to this fan fiction is automatically bought into the world of the movie.

Interview: Writer/Director Craig Brewer

Figure 4.1 Headshot of writer/director Craig Brewer.

Craig Brewer is a writer, director, and producer who's worked with some of the world's biggest actors in film and television. His feature HUSTLE AND FLOW won an Oscar for Three 6 Mafia for their original song "It's Hard Out Here for a Pimp," and an Oscar nomination for lead actor Terrance Howard. He reteamed with Howard and fellow HUSTLE alum Taraji P. Henson on the Fox drama series EMPIRE as a writer, director, and producer. His feature credits include FOOTLOOSE, DOLEMITE IS MY NAME, and COMING 2 AMERICA.

Marty Lang: Your first three films are very specific to Memphis and Tennessee. In those films, the locations almost serve as characters. What is it that those locations bring to you in the writing process? What does that specificity bring to your stories?

Craig Brewer: I think that it's the one thing a lot of young writers or filmmakers don't think about that they should, which is that their location is kind of a special effect in their story, when you don't have a lot of money. Look at Spike Lee's early films, look at Martin Scorsese's early films. Brooklyn, Hell's Kitchen, they're part of what you're experiencing in a big way. And you can say that, well, of course they are. The characters are from there. But there's a rhythm, there's a soundtrack, there's an attitude, a language.

And for me, what I found when I was living here in Memphis and experiencing, I don't even want to call it street culture, but it was definitely a culture where black and white below a certain economic line were existing together, and not in some sort of, like, token way. It felt real. It felt like everybody was just trying to get by and earn a dollar. And it wasn't as polarizing as I'd seen in movies.

But I think I realized that the region itself was not represented the way I was seeing it, in Memphis. I could look at A TIME TO KILL or MISSISSIPPI BURNING, and I'm not saying that those elements aren't here, however, how many times are we going to tell that story? I mean, I'm sure there's people that say it can't be told enough. But I'm not the only one. It's not the only story and it's definitely not the story that I'm seeing.

And I found that even with something as complex for a city to get behind as HUSTLE AND FLOW, it's not like the visitors bureau was saying, "Oh, let's have a movie about a pimp trying to rap on the streets of Memphis, while he's moving his hookers from strip club to street corners." It's a complex movie for certain elements in the city, and the people in charge of the city coffers. But go to any Memphis Grizzlies game and 20,000 people are going to be chanting "Whoop that trick," because the attitude of the city is one of being an underdog, and being dismissed and being like, "Well, okay, we may have problems with crime and car theft, but we're interesting. We're aware of it. We're not afraid of it."

There was an attitude with that, just like there was an attitude in SHE'S GOTTA HAVE IT. Just like there was an attitude in MEAN STREETS. And just like there was an intellectual point of view with Christopher Nolan's FOLLOWING, right? The location, the subways, the city informed that attitude. And you can utilize that. My movie THE POOR AND HUNGRY, which I shot for $20,000, ran for eight weeks in a theater here in Memphis, it was their biggest hit. It ran for eight weeks! That's awesome. Making money that whole time. And it's because people wanted to see their home and see themselves. And if you're true to it, if you somehow imbue the movie with the feeling and the language and the attitude of the region, the region feels heard. They feel seen. They feel like, "Oh, look, one of ours just made something that's of us."

And I love not even explaining things. My favorite thing, whenever I watch HUSTLE AND FLOW, is D-Jay is being carried away by police officers, and he's yelling at Nola about trying to get his music on the radio. And he goes, "I want you to get my music up on the radio. I want to hear my shit in the yard at 201." I've heard so many people that are not from Memphis saying, "Is that like a radio station?" I say, "No. 201 is an address, 201 Poplar, the address for our prison. And we call it 201." If you're not from Memphis, you don't know that. And I was like, precisely. It's not for you. It's for us to go "We know it," and it's now sparking a conversation where you say what is 201. So even people outside who can't understand it, it's providing a fun, cool badge of honor for people who do know.

To make regional movies, one reason why I love to remain here in Memphis is that I felt like the city assisted me in making my career. Also, there's an element that they did it with me, and that any success I may have is theirs, too.

ML: Have you ever been in a situation where a location or a region sparks the inspiration for a story?

CB: My career got started with THE POOR AND HUNGRY, and I was in this bar called the P&H Cafe. And there was this glorious older woman named Wanda Wilson who wore these big curly wigs, almost like a New Orleans madam, you know, big hats and big jewelry and everything. And she had a husky voice from years of smoking cigarettes and working as a long haul trucker. But now she worked at this bar, and I loved the characters that came into it. I loved the way she treated everybody.

One day when I was writing the script about car thieves in Memphis, I said, by the way, what does P&H stand for? And she goes, well, it's short for The Poor and Hungry. And I was like, that's what I'm calling my movie.

So that whole movie was inspired by like, I think I'm just going to do a movie that would take place in here. And then all these characters can exist in this bar.

I mean, even with HUSTLE AND FLOW, having gone to people's homes and seeing how they would put quilts on the walls to deaden the sound. And I was like, "Oh, I haven't seen this."

Like I've seen, people going into studios, big studios or something like that to make music.

But I haven't seen this makeshift shit. This seems more noble to me.

ML: You mentioned you spend time at coffee shops writing. P&H sounds like an example of where you can just sort of soak in the world around and have that help you.

CB: Well, definitely the P&H did that. And I get that question a lot. Because I think, for obvious reasons, I think there's a lot of times that people could look at the dialogue that I have in BLACK SNAKE MOAN and HUSTLE AND FLOW, and even the movies that I'm writing right now, and they kind of go like, what gives? You're this middle-aged white guy. What is it that you really are doing in terms of trying to get this ear or get this language?

And my answer is always the same. It's a cultural question.

And once you start thinking about cultures, there's so many. You're not just dealing with racial cultures, you know. For me to listen to my uncles and grandparents say something as simple as, "Look it." Some people go, "What's a look it?" And I say I guess it's "Listen to me" or "Look at what I'm saying." Over the years, my relatives, when they really want me to hear what they're saying, they start off by saying, "Look it."

"Look it, if you're going to go outside and expect not to get rain on your head in a thunderstorm, then you know you're a fool, right?"

And so you hear it and you go what is that? And when I write it, does it make sense? Maybe not. Maybe someone will say, "What are you doing?" But I just know that it's the language that I'm hearing and it feels real. So it's really having an ear and an eye.

I'll never forget this moment where in Memphis it was really cold and we didn't have central heat and air. We had one of these floor furnaces and it was on the fritz. But we could still cook in our oven. And I went over to somebody else's house and they had the same problem, but they had their oven open.

I was like, oh, I didn't even think about that. Just open the oven. So I'm sitting there doing it, but I've moved my TV in my kitchen and now we have some warmth until our heater gets fixed.

I was like, this feels like if I put this in a movie that my neighbor who showed me how to do this is going to go "Hey, I do that too." Or like, "Oh yeah, my grandmother used to do that."

That's what having your ears open and your eyes open are for. And whether or not you're in a location, I definitely feel it on a regional level. You know, rhythms of the way people talk, what economic level are they in and, you know, how can I have flourishes in there so that people go "Oh, this is honest because that's real in my life," and they're now recognizing things that they see on the screen.

When I was filming DOLEMITE IS MY NAME, I came into the set that we had at this bar, and it was this moment where Eddie Murphy's character, Rudy Ray Moore, was on the Chitlin circuit.

He was going club to club doing his comedy routine.

I came in and I had a great production designer, Clay Griffin, and I come up to this peanut warming machine, this vintage peanut warming machine, you know, with the bulbs.

And I go, "Look at this peanut warmer."

And he's like, "I thought you would like that."

And I go, "Okay, okay, wait a minute." I turn to props, I go, "We got peanuts?"

He's like, "We got peanuts."

And I go, "All right, all right. I know what I'm doing."

So Eddie's up on stage and we're about to do a rehearsal, and all the extras come in. I was like, "Hello everybody." And I start handing them all bags of peanuts. I go, "Okay, you and you and you," I'm pointing to extras. "When the camera's going by, I want you to just take these peanut shells and throw them on the floor and eat the peanuts, just throw them on the floor."

I remember Eddie just looking confused, like, why are they all throwing the peanut shells on the floor? And I was like, this is how it's done. You know, it may not be how it's done here in Hollywood, but you know, in certain places in the South, you've got these peanuts and you just throw the shells right there on the floor. They'll sweep them up later.

But now this beauty, you know, I look at a prop, I don't know what I'm going to do, but now it gives me the idea like, no, I've seen this. Let's film it. I don't care if everybody doesn't know what's happening. I know what's happening and the people who've seen it know what's happening. You know, it's real.

ML: What advice would you give to filmmakers that are looking to do regional cinema? What are the things that they should focus on?

CB: Well, I can only give advice on what I had to learn the hard way, which is, you know, really make a movie that you can get your arms around.

THE POOR AND HUNGRY really was something that came to me with a collision of two things.

My sister-in-law's car got stolen. I watched her cry over it while a cop was telling me there's a scam that's going around. If car thieves steal your car, they chop it down, they take off all the doors and the wheels and the wheel wells and the steering columns and the seats and the engine and everything. Then, when they dump it at the impound and you come to pick it up, much like my sister-in-law, who was crying, did, they ultimately leave it there.

And when they leave it there, every Wednesday they have an auction, and then the car thieves, who have all the parts to that car, send someone in to buy the shell of a car, and then they put the whole car back together, and then they own your car, legally, for about $90.

And I thought, that is a fantastic scam.

But I'm also seeing the human element of it. There's my sister-in-law over there crying. And I was like, that's a good story. I don't know what I'm gonna do with it.

Then there was a news story where a young man and a young woman went in a restaurant, desperate for money, and they went in there with a child's baseball bat wrapped in a flannel shirt and tried to rob the place. They got some money, and when they were running out, I believe the owner shot at them and hit the guy. They were driving away, and then he collapsed and died.

Now you get your fair share of people going like, hey, if you're gonna rob a place, you're gonna get shot. And people calling the guy a hero and everything. But I couldn't help but think, what if I made a movie where I got the audience to care about those two in the car?

Yeah, they were stealing, yeah, they were doing wrong, but what if I cared about them?

And then that married with the first idea of the car.

I was like, okay, we're really talking about a story with just three people, really. Whereas other stories, I got too sprawling with it. I wanted it to be larger because I wanted it to mimic movies that I'm seeing on the screen with big casts and everything.

But for a first-time filmmaker, I think what helped me with that was that then I had three collaborators that were all making the movie. It was easier for me to get them for a weekend here, a day here, a week there. And if I needed to, I could go out and reshoot a scene that I didn't feel like we really got there.

So for me, having the regional flourishes of a crime story in Memphis, that still was a love story that involved the regret that a car thief had by stealing this girl's car, by seeing his environment differently through the music, she was a cello player, but through her music, I felt like if I can just nail the performances and have it take place in a world where people, even in Memphis, would be like, "I don't know if I wanna hang out in that world with car thieves and strip clubs and chop shops and pawn shops, but I'm falling in love with these characters, and I'm worried for them."

For me, I think that is the best thing for a young filmmaker to concentrate on. Can you write this in a way, can you assist in the performances, can you direct a story or tell a story where people get emotionally involved?

There is not a better thing to hear in my first two movies, THE POOR AND HUNGRY and HUSTLE AND FLOW, then a gasp because they know something awful is about to happen.

In THE POOR AND HUNGRY, a man steals this girl's car, inside the car is the tape of all of her music. He starts listening to the music, then he finally gets together with the girl, the girl finds his Walkman, she starts listening to it, oh my God, that's her music, this is obviously the guy that stole her car. To see her pick up that Walkman and put it on and to hear the audience go "Oh God, no, don't play it, because you've begun to care about this guy and you see that he's earnest with his love and everything, but now it's all gonna go to shit."

The same thing happens to HUSTLE AND FLOW, when you've been working on this music and seeing them sweat and seeing them suffer to make this demo and then suddenly D-Jay, Terrence Howard's character, is reaching down into a toilet and picking up his demo out of this toilet. (The rapper Skinny Black, played by Ludacris, dropped it in the toilet.) And to hear people in the audience just like "Oh, he better kill that motherfucker for what he did to his demo tape."

You don't get that through fake guns with blanks. You get it through a series of scenes where you get glimpses into their hearts and their dreams, and then you feel a connection. If these characters could aspire for things and they get things in the movie, then maybe the audience can too ... and then suddenly something awful is about to happen. They're like "Oh, no!" and they can't help but feel the emotions themselves.

That's the advice that I basically have. You can achieve that better with a tighter, smaller cast.

Notes

1 http://framescinemajournal.com/article/screenwriting-2-0-in-the-classroom/
2 https://www.wired.com/2004/10/tail/

Reference List

Anderson, Chris. "The Long Tail," *Wired Magazine*, 2004. https://www.wired.com/2004/10/tail/

Kenneth Gay, Andrew. "Screenwriting 2.0 in the Classroom? Teaching the Digital Screenplay," *Frames Cinema Journal*, 2012. http://framescinemajournal.com/article/screenwriting-2-0-in-the-classroom/

5 The Context of Crowdfunding

As I was gearing up to run the Kickstarter crowdfunding campaign for RISING STAR back in 2010, my producers and I knew this would be the catalyst for us to make all the money we needed to pay for the film. We would engage our audience, they would come out to support us in droves, and two weeks after its completion, we would begin production of the movie. After all, we were running the campaign as part of pre-production – it would be the perfect synthesis of fundraising, community building, and actual film work. When it actually started, we were confident we'd raise our budget and prep the film at the same time.

We ended up losing our minds.

That first campaign taught us so many lessons, but I think the biggest thing I learned through it was that crowdfunding has to exist as its own stage of production. The decision to combine it with pre-production was, to be honest, insane; not only were we trying to raise money all day, every day, we were also trying to secure all the elements we needed for the movie, hire crew, rehearse with our cast (one of whom was also a producer on the crowdfunding team), and scout every place we were shooting. What I thought would be efficiency actually turned out to be over 24 hours of work in a 24-hour day. Now back in 2010, we didn't have many other campaigns to compare ours to – RISING STAR was one of the first feature-length independent films to crowdfund on Kickstarter – so it was definitely trial and error. Thankfully, years later, we've got thousands of completed campaigns, good and bad, that we can analyze for best practices.

After spending way too much time studying Kickstarter, Indiegogo, Seed&Spark, Support Our Stories and GoFundMe, for short films, feature films, web series and documentaries, I've picked up a few things that I think you should know. These bits of wisdom aren't exactly magic bullets to crowdfunding a hundred grand for your next movie – but don't worry, crowdfunding fundamentals are in the next chapter – or shortcuts to building an audience of millions. They are items that put crowdfunding in its proper context: as an exercise in community, a unique phase of

DOI: 10.4324/9781003295754-5

filmmaking that ties in, holistically, with every other phase, and a time where you have to confront some emotions you may not be ready for.

(One point of clarification: when I say "crowdfunding," I mean perks-based crowdfunding, not equity crowdfunding, where backers become financial partners with the filmmaker. Equity crowdfunding could – and definitely should – be its own separate book.)

Once you understand that context, you'll see that all the work you've done up to this point has led you to this moment.

The moment where you push the launch button and make the ask.

Crowdfunding Is Networking

When you think of a crowdfunding campaign, it's easy to think about all the ways you can be helped financially – after all, funding is part of the word. But that's thinking too short-term for all the benefits it can provide. Like the Google form we put up for RISING STAR, asking for people to help us any way they can, the community you build through crowdfunding can help you far beyond the financial aspect of a campaign. And the benefits can work in both directions.

You may not believe this, but crowdfunding RISING STAR helped me get a job! We made sure to stay in contact with our backers throughout the process of making the film, and we learned one of our backers was a producer and production manager from New Mexico. It just so happened he got a job production managing a film (ironically called GOATS), which was filming in multiple states. And one of those states happened to be mine! He knew I'd worked in location management before, so he asked if I wanted to be a location scout. I said yes immediately, I scouted, and I actually got a promotion, eventually working as the Location Manager for the additional unit on the film. And it all came from him backing our little film.

Now what if you don't have a project you want to crowdfund? You can't be in constant crowdfunding mode forever, right? You can still get in on the fun – by backing someone else's. As part of researching for this book, I went back and counted the number of crowdfunding campaigns I've backed since I started back in 2010. It was kind of crazy: I've financially supported 81 Kickstarter campaigns, 35 IndieGoGo campaigns, and either financially supported or followed 99 Seed&Spark campaigns! That's over 200 campaigns, for feature films, short films, documentaries, web series, comic books, all kinds of creative endeavors. For years, I reserved a small amount of my monthly budget to supporting crowdfunding campaigns. I spent a lot of money, no matter what the perks were that I obtained for the contributions, but I can promise you all that support has paid off for me, in all kinds of ways.

There was a wonderful Kickstarter campaign I supported called A YEAR WITHOUT RENT, where creator Lucas McNelly wanted to travel the United States for a year, working for free on other people's independent films. I ended up backing his campaign and helping him complete an insane rally on its last day, where he raised almost $8,000 of his $12,000 goal in the last 24 hours.[1] Once Lucas reached his goal, he began traveling the country, and I was able to help him on his trip; he stayed at my house multiple times during his year, sometimes for over a week at a stretch. And in exchange for that, he spent a day with us during our focus group screening of RISING STAR. He took video of us finishing our edit for the screening, and the event itself, giving us plenty of great PR. And he helped us with our film festival strategy, too. During his year on the road, Lucas worked with Seattle filmmaker Wonder Russell on her short film CONNECT TO, and through Lucas, we all became friends. When RISING STAR was finished, Wonder suggested I submit the film to the Seattle True Independent Film Festival, a festival she had worked with. Making the film in Connecticut, I never thought a festival on the other side of the country would be interested in it. But I submitted, and the film got in! We world premiered the film there in 2012 – partially thanks to a film project I backed on Kickstarter.

Crowdfunding can also help you become part of a professional network. When A YEAR WITHOUT RENT was happening, many of the filmmakers involved went on to work on bigger things – and since we were all helping each other out starting out, we all became friends. Two of the AYWR filmmakers I met, Vancouver's Jen and Victoria Westcott, were crowdfunding their first feature film, LOCKED IN A GARAGE BAND, around the same time I was directing RISING STAR. I backed them, and we became friends as they got their film out into the world. The Westcott sisters went on to make an animated Christmas movie, called ELIOT: THE LITTLEST REINDEER, with an eight-figure budget! And since we all helped each other out when we started making movies, we're all part of a team. Think of it as a film school that costs way less.

So how can you take advantage of all the benefits of crowdfunding? Check out the most popular portals and browse through the films crowdfunding there. If you find a project you connect with, or a filmmaker local to you, back them. Doesn't have to be for a lot of money; even a few dollars can establish a connection. Then, talk with those filmmakers – find out what they want to do, see if there's other ways you can help them, and find out what their ambitions are for later in their careers. That introduction could lead to all kinds of positive things. Since you're reading this book to learn more about making your own films, you can use crowdfunding as a way to connect with filmmakers and film lovers who want to be a part of something creative. That's one thing so many people fail to realize about perks-based crowdfunding – the opportunity to be a part of a creative project is of great value to a lot of people who don't often do so. You're offering them a spot on the team – that can be really exciting. There's no telling how they could help.

The Two Stories of Every Film

One thing any crowdfunder needs to realize before getting started is that crowdfunding is an extension of your storytelling abilities. Successful campaigns understand that a film has two pieces to it: the story of the film, and the story of how the film is made. And it's the combination of these two stories that create strong campaigns.

Now what does that mean? Wherever you can find opportunities to allow the story of one to bleed into the story of the other, you'll have an opportunity for your audience to become a part of it. That can mean taking a part of your movie (a supporting character, a particular location) and building more story that becomes part of the crowdfunding campaign. You can also do the opposite; allow the audience to essentially dictate a part of the story of your film. It can work in either direction.

Sometimes, building a story based on a small character in your movie can give your audience a great way to get excited about it. I'm the producer of a feature film that crowdfunded doing just that, and we got all kinds of engagement from it. The film is a mockumentary comedy/drama called UNIBALL, and it's an autobiographical story about a 20-something man who learns he has testicular cancer and must have one of his testicles removed. (It's funny. I promise.)

When we crowdfunded on Seed&Spark[2] one of our social media strategies was to build a week-long Instagram/Twitter/X campaign called "Where's Balldo," a spoof on Where's Waldo, where viewers try to find a pair of poorly drawn testicles in a different picture each day. It started and ended with animated videos, too. It became a story that ran concurrently with the story of the feature film, with a "character" that doesn't speak in real life, but was brought to life by the magic of animation. It definitely wasn't G-rated, but it was a neat way to communicate the feeling of the movie, and give our audience a sense of what it would ultimately be (Figure 5.1).

The RISING STAR campaign was all about experimentation, and we were able to find some innovative ways to allow our audience to have a hand in shaping the story of the film. During the campaign, our producer suggested "The Alyza Challenge." He wanted to engage online with a new community, so he asked me if I would change our lead female character, Alyza, into a vegetarian or vegan. This would make the film's story eco-friendly, since eating those types of diets puts less strain on the environment,

Figure 5.1 An animated still frame from the "Where's Balldo" social media video campaign, during the "inconveniently Late Late Show" segment.

and it would allow us to reach out to the online veg community, a community we hadn't reached out to at that point. I said if our audience decided she should change, I would do it. We asked our fans to tweet #VeganVegRS or #OmnivoreRS to the movie's Twitter/X feed, depending on what they wanted Alyza to eat. The challenge caught fire online, being featured on ELEVEN vegan/vegetarian and eco-friendly blogs and news sites. We also had so many fans wanting Alyza to be vegan, I called the challenge off a week before it was supposed to end. I rewrote the script to make Alyza a vegan character. (This wasn't the type of change that altered any of the major storylines; it was simply changing the items she ate in some scenes, and her turning down non-vegetarian/vegan foods in others.) So in addition to helping the Earth, being green turned into great press for us, too, and revved up our fan base.

This concept is something I've thought a lot about, and I think it holds the key to the creation of some really unique, crowd-involved storytelling. Could you imagine a movie that's made during its crowdfunding campaign, where the audience gets to vote every day for where the story goes? That would be incredibly cool – but even if you don't combine your film's two stories to this extent, finding points of overlap is key to an engaged audience.

Crowdfunding Holistically

One thing a lot of filmmakers don't realize about crowdfunding is that you're not locked into running a campaign to just raise money for production. That's definitely the way most films did it starting out, but the point at which you crowdfund can have big benefits for you, depending on what you need in terms of audience and resources. This decision can help you not only in terms of the project you're crowdfunding, but future projects in your career. Not all platforms allow for crowdfunding at all points, so you'll have to check your particular platform to make sure it allows for what you want, but different stages allow for different strategies:

DEVELOPMENT: Did you know some platforms allow you to crowdfund before you even have a script? You could run a campaign to pay for things like research, travel costs, and interviews for a project you're in early stages on. Very few filmmakers take advantage of crowdfunding at this step, but it has a huge benefit for those that are new to crowdfunding: it can help you build your first small audience. Even if you run a campaign for $500, if you can reach that goal for a development campaign, you'll attract the first group of people who have an interest in your project. And here's the cool thing: those people can follow you throughout the lifecycle of the project, and potentially help you in a second crowdfunding campaign later on in the process! Remember, when you're thinking in terms of radical collaboration, you want as big a pool of audience members/collaborators as possible. If you're new, you want to take advantage of every opportunity to find them. A development campaign can be a huge help for just that.

PRE-PRODUCTION/PRODUCTION: Again, this is the most common point for crowdfunders to run their campaigns. There are definite benefits to it also – you can find the resources you need to actually shoot your movie! In addition, though, if a filmmaker has taken the time to build their audience before reaching this point (either through a development campaign, or by the crowdsourcing methods we talked about earlier), this is the phase where their audience can feel the most ownership of the film. Since their contribution, assistance, or cheerleading will be a key reason why the film will actually be shot, audience members can feel like they're part of the reason why it exists. That's a powerful draw for a lot of people – I've seen plenty of campaigns, including more than one of my own, where strangers team up with crowdfunded films by giving four-figure contributions. They want to have their name on the film, in a primary role (usually some sort of producer), and see how the production process goes, knowing that they're part of the reason it's happening.

POST-PRODUCTION: Post campaigns are interesting – because you've already gotten past the point of shooting the film, they have the huge benefit of being able to show actual footage to your audience. This will give them a very specific feel for what the final project will be. Another benefit is that this phase shows the most momentum of any other type of campaign. Since you've gotten past filming, post is the only thing left to do! There's no way this film isn't getting made, so join the team and get on the train! I think post campaigns are similar to development campaigns, in that you usually don't have as much to raise as you might in a production campaign. They also give an opportunity for filmmakers to focus more on audience development than a production campaign might; production campaigns almost always have the singular goal of getting those resources for shooting. But post campaigns can have another interesting benefit: if you're thinking long term, you can use a post campaign as momentum for your next project. If you're making zombie movies (like, say, DEADBRAINS), you could use a post campaign for that film to get the word out about your next zombie film. Maybe it's a tender love story about two zombies from the wrong side of town, who meet and fall in love while eating the same human ... or something like that. You could offer a trailer or mood reel for that film as part of the DEADBRAINS campaign, and get people interested in it before you even start. If your filmmaking has a common thread to it (similar genre, same actors, same geographic location, etc.) post campaigns can be a great way to tip your audience off to what's coming next.

DISTRIBUTION: Have you ever heard of a distribution crowdfunding campaign? Where backing the campaign ultimately unlocks the opportunity to immediately see a completed film? Now it's true that for many production and post campaigns, one perk is the ability to watch the movie when it's finished, but my friends David Branin, Karen Worden, and Gregor Collins made that the sole focus of the IndieGoGo campaign for their feature drama GOODBYE PROMISE. The campaign was simple: if you were one of the first hundred backers to contribute at least one dollar, you got a link to watch the film. After that, you just needed to contribute at least two dollars to get that link. And even though they made a micro-budget feature in Los Angeles, they were able to get 410 backers to contribute and see the movie. This is a simple, potentially lucrative way to earn money for your film's release, and you don't need any outside distribution help taking a cut. If you team a campaign like this with a solid public relations plan (which we'll talk about in a bit), it could really reach a large audience. I'm surprised that more films haven't done this.

Conflicting Emotions

It always fascinates me to see how my students react to crowdfunding, both the process of it and the emotions that bubble up as a result of the work. I thought students would always react positively to the idea of raising money and corralling resources for their films, but no group of students ever has the same reaction to it – and some of them are pretty skeptical. Some quotes from my students about how they feel about crowdfunding:

"I shouldn't need help. I'm a man."

"If people are giving money, they should be investors."

"It feels like a scam."

As a teacher, those feelings are things I always talk about, because they're valid – and they create an interesting dialogue about the role of patronage in our society. To some of my students, the idea of filmmakers holding their hat out feels like begging. To others, it's as normal a part of the filmmaking process as making their film. So we discuss this in class, the idea that "payment" could include things other than money. That emotional experiences are worth as much as a paycheck. It can be a hard conversation, and students can dig in on their positions, but discussing the elephant in the room makes everyone feel more comfortable with the idea.

Arts patronage has been around since the times of early Europe, but with the advent of social media, and companies like Patreon and crowdfunding portals, it's everywhere now. So we're seeing artists and projects that bring these questions to the forefront.

One of the most notable of these comes from the world of music, and a performer named Amanda Palmer. Palmer ran a Kickstarter campaign in 2011 for her first solo album, THEATRE IS EVIL, after her label, Roadrunner Records, had dropped her. She was able to raise a whopping $1.19 million for the record, an art book and a tour, raised from many of the same people who were fans of hers while on Roadrunner. And when she went on the tour to support the album, she invited musicians to perform with her on stage – but didn't pay them. She basically offered beer and hugs to those who wanted to be a part of her performances. And while many of the musicians loved the opportunity, many thought she was taking advantage of people. The press got in on the action; The New Yorker wrote a scathing article about her unusual payment system, calling her "the Internet's villain of the month" (Clover, 2012).[3]

Palmer, through her crowdfunding and subsequent touring, brought the question of art versus commerce to the fore. She did a TED Talk, called THE ART OF ASKING, where she explained her struggle to decide if her practices were fair, and she told fascinating stories about the emotional connection between the artist and the fan, and how crowdfunding and social media opened up new ways to express that relationship. She talked about her work as the Eight Foot Bride, a street performer who received donations by sharing a silent moment of eye contact with passersby on the sidewalk – and who received jeers of "Get a job!" from people driving by. And she explained how that work was the beginning of her education of working in the music industry. I believe that in this talk, she identifies the biggest advantage of crowdfunding – and the biggest challenge:

"The media asked, 'Amanda, the music business is tanking, and you encourage piracy, how did you make all these people pay for music?' And the real answer, I didn't make them, I asked them. And through the very act of asking people, I had connected with them. And when you connect with them, people want to help you. It's kind of counterintuitive for a lot of artists, they don't want to ask for things, but it's not easy, it's not easy to ask, and a lot of artists have a problem with this.

Asking makes you vulnerable. And I got a lot of criticism online after my Kickstarter went big for continuing my crazy crowdsourcing practices, specifically for asking musicians who are fans if they wanted to join us on stage for a few songs in exchange for love and tickets, and beer. [...]

And people are saying, you're not allowed anymore to ask for that kind of help really reminded me of the people in their cars yelling, 'Get a job.'

Because they weren't with us on the sidewalk, and they couldn't see the exchange that was happening between me and my crowd, an exchange that was very fair to us, but alien to them.

[...] For most of human history, musicians, artists, they've been part of the community, connectors, and openers, not untouchable stars.

Celebrity is about a lot of people loving you from a distance, but the Internet and the content that we're freely able to share on it are taking us back, it's about a few people loving you up close, and about those people being enough.

So, a lot of people are confused by the idea of no hard sticker price, they see it as an unpredictable risk, but the things I've done, the Kickstarter, the street, the doorbell, I don't see these things as risk, I see them as trust. Now, the online tools, to make the exchange as easy and as instinctive as the street, they're getting there, but the perfect tools aren't going to help us, if we can't face each other, and give and receive fearlessly, but more important, to ask without shame" (Palmer, 2013).

She's right. Asking makes us vulnerable. That can make some artists uncomfortable, myself included. That said, the benefit of that vulnerability is the connection you'll receive from people, and their desire to help you tell your stories.

Notes

1 https://filmmakermagazine.com/18224-a-come-from-behind-9th-inning-kickstarter-win/#.V2wY3usrJaQ
2 https://seedandspark.com/fund/uniball
3 https://www.newyorker.com/culture/culture-desk/amanda-palmers-accidental-experiment-with-real-communism

Reference List

Clover, Joshua. "Amanda Palmer's Accidental Experiment With Real Communism," *The New Yorker*, 2012. https://www.newyorker.com/culture/culture-desk/amanda-palmers-accidental-experiment-with-real-communism

Macauley, Scott. "A Come From Behind, 9th Inning Kickstarter Win," *Filmmaker Magazine*, 2011. https://filmmakermagazine.com/18224-a-come-from-behind-9th-inning-kickstarter-win/#.V2wY3usrJaQ

Palmer, Amanda. "The Art of Asking," *TED Talks*, 2013. https://www.ted.com/talks/amanda_palmer_the_art_of_asking

Seed and Spark. "Uniball" crowdfunding campaign, 2021. https://seedandspark.com/fund/uniball

6 Crowdfundamentals

I moved to New York City in the fall of 2013 after co-founding Catalyst Media, a video production and crowdfunding consulting startup. My two co-founders and I were working with some incredible clients, like Startup Weekend and the Yale Entrepreneurial Institute, and I thought it would be smart to expand our reach from New Haven, Connecticut (where our offices were) to the Big Apple.

Once I got there, I found something wonderful: the IFP Made in New York Center, in Brooklyn. This amazing place (now, sadly, closed down) was a meeting space and coworking facility for anyone working in film, video, and digital content creation. I fell in love with it immediately. I started working in their coworking space and attending events there that were hosted by local filmmakers and technology folks.

One of those events, in the winter of 2013, changed the trajectory of my independent film career. It was a workshop by a startup tech company called Seed&Spark, called "Crowdfunding to Build Independence." Over the course of 90 minutes, they walked through each step of a crowdfunding campaign, and laid out, in detail, how to handle all the mechanics of a campaign; finding audience members, pitch videos, incentives, campaign management, all the nuts and bolts you needed to successfully crowdfund. They showed multiple examples from campaigns run on their platform, helping to clarify each step.

They also talked about something else. Something that I had never gone over with my Catalyst Media consulting clients. They talked about data analysis, and how to evolve your campaign with it. Up until that point, portals provided almost no data to crowdfunders. But Seed&Spark was giving their filmmakers lots of data – where their backers were coming from, which websites they accessed the campaign through, all kinds of things. They also talked about how to obtain data from potential customers through interviews. And they showed how you could use that information to reach more potential backers.

It blew my mind.

DOI: 10.4324/9781003295754-6

That cold night in Brooklyn was the first time Seed&Spark showed the world "Crowdfunding to Build Independence," but they've presented it thousands of times since then, at film festivals, conferences and other events all over the world, refining and improving as they've gone. And they've been kind enough to let me pull from it in this chapter, along with my own experiences, to show you the best practices in prepping, running, and completing a successful film crowdfunding campaign.

So let's build some independence.

Prepping Your Campaign

Right from the beginning of their presentation, the main point is made crystal clear. It's a pretty declarative statement:

> "Can we get really real for a sec? Waiting to be picked is NOT independence. This is about your career. Independence comes with a direct connection to your audience" (Best, 2023).

Couldn't have said it better myself.

Like the rest of this book has preached, you can create those direct connections at every step of your filmmaking. They pose three questions as a place to start:

- Who the hell is your audience?
- Where the hell are they? (online or IRL)
- How the hell do you get their email addresses?

Thankfully, by this point, that's work we've already done! We've built a network of friends and family, as well as (hopefully) a bigger network of people who have some sort of connection to our work, who we're ready to engage now that the campaign is about to start.

A vital thing to remember here is that your demographics don't necessarily have to be wide. If you think of what a woman between 24 and 35 years old looks like, it could be anything:

- An urban hipster
- A member of the military
- Or a corporate go-getter

Similarly, a man between 24 and 35 could also be almost any type, like:

- A golf shirt-wearing preppie type

- A spiky-haired punk rocker
- Or a scarf-adorned intellectual

Each of those people are totally different, in terms of look, and in terms of the shorthand characteristics you might assign to them. The punk rocker gentleman might suggest a little more mischievous nature than his golf shirt-wearing peer – you'd think he would be much more conservative. So there are personality characteristics that aren't being accounted for in these broader demographics. The dominating variable you should be focusing on as you build audience is how someone specifically relates to your project. That might create some correlation (for example, if you're making a historical film, it's possible your audience might skew older), but correlation doesn't lead to causation. Keep the focus on the individual.

When you do that, they also offer a strong way to start collecting data that might be useful to continue building audience. They propose you interview five people who like your idea, and ask them questions about their Internet habits and entertainment consumption:

- Where/when do you hang out online?
- How do you get your news?
- Who do you follow on social media?
- Where do you spend free time in real life?
- What music and podcasts do you listen to? When?
- Where do you watch movies and TV shows?
- How often do you go to movies? Is there anywhere else you watch stuff?

Those answers can begin to map out a strategy for you to find more people to join up with you. (It's 100% recommended that you start this process as early as possible; you don't have to wait until your campaign is gearing up to do this, in addition to the other crowdsourcing/audience-building work you'll be doing.)

While you're doing this work, you'll also be answering the questions that will guide the creation and execution of your campaign. Questions like:

When Is the Right Time to Launch One?

The time of year you launch can allow you to take advantage of different holidays, as well as the natural ebb and flow of crowdfunding. Horror filmmakers can take advantage of the fun around Halloween by launching in October, and St. Patrick's Day films could do the same by launching in March. (Writer's note: I feel like we need more St. Patrick's Day films.) Generally, August and September can be a little slow, and November through the first week of January are not recommended times to launch, because of the holidays, and the immense amount of spending everyone does on their gifts. People are focused on their families and friends that time of year – you want to appeal to strangers as well when you crowdfund, so that's a time of year to avoid.

You can also time your launch to a certain day that can be advantageous – if you launch a campaign early in the morning on a Tuesday, people are still fresh, because it's early in the work week, but they're not going over so much of their post-weekend catchup work. You can reach them online at a point where they're not overwhelmed by either end of the week.

How Do You Build a Team?

One of the most important, and often ignored, aspects of crowdfunding is that you need a team. As the presentation cheekily advises, "Friends don't let friends crowdfund alone." And they're right. A campaign is 24/7 work, so having as many people as possible to help is vital.

Now it's rare that filmmakers are able to put a team together, specifically for a campaign, where every person fills an incredibly specific role. When you start out, the key thing is just to find people with beating hearts who will help you. Ideally, you can get people to whom you can delegate, and who can do things that you're not good at (for example, social media). One particularly important person to have is a graphics person, who can create visual incentives. Usually, a crowdfunding team is the creator and a small group of people helping them out.

You want to keep everyone happy and make sure everyone knows what's expected of them.

This is important because oftentimes, the team you build for crowdfunding is part of the team you'll have when you make your movie. And you want to be sure everyone feels valued, and that they're contributing equally. Brandi Nicole said she saw the flipside of that when she was working in crowdfunding:

> The campaigns where it's one person doing everything, or doing 80% of it, oftentimes they didn't make their goal. Or if they did, there'd be a lot of resentment. Because they have done it by themselves, and they have felt alone. That's not a good place to be going into production, feeling resentment of your team. And I've seen both sides. I've seen where creators feel resentment, because no one showed up to help them, and then I've also seen where no one helped the creator because they tried to do it all on their own. And when people tried to help, they didn't accept it. They wanted it done a certain way. This should be a collaborative process.

I can vouch for the value of a sizable team in campaigns. When RISING STAR was crowdfunded, our team was three people – me, our producer, and our lead actor/producer. And we struggled with the workload throughout the campaign, despite the fact that we really did a lot of work prepping. So years later, when I crowdfunded STAY WITH ME, I figured out a way to invite the students in my Producing class to be part of the campaign. Those 20 students were broken into 4 groups, and each of them ran a different element of the campaign each week it ran. We had a group doing crowdsourcing work, researching online communities who'd be interested in the movie, a group doing video production for our campaign updates, a group doing public relations work, researching media and organizations we could partner with, and a group managing our social media output. Each week, the groups switched, so that once the campaign was done, every group did a week in all four positions. Believe me when I tell you that having a team of 20 students to go along with you and your two producers is worlds better than a team of just three. The next time I crowdfund for a movie of mine, I want to find not only a new Producing class to help (I teach the course every year), but I also want to bring fans in of my other movies and make them part of the process. Maybe as social media evangelizers, maybe as crowdsourcing researchers, but I want to have an even bigger team next time.

How Much Should You Try and Raise?

This is always a controversial question, because the very nature of crowdfunding can have you seeing green, thinking of all the things you could potentially get for your film if you had unlimited funds. I think this question can be answered in two ways.

The first is, "How much do you need?" You need to figure out your costs to make the film, pre-production through post-production, and possibly include festivals, marketing, and distribution, along with costs to deliver incentives (more on that in a bit). If you create a budget for your film, you'll be able to come up with a number that will realistically get it to the finish line.

There's also another question you need to ask when it comes to the campaign. Because of the uncertainty this process is known for, you need to also ask "How much is the absolute least you need?" Some crowdfunding sites are all or nothing in their fundraising, others give you a greenlight when you reach a percentage of your goal, and still others allow for creators to keep everything they raise. Once you determine what platform you want to use, you can get a sense of how much money you'll keep of what you raise. You also need to have a number that is the absolute minimum that you'd feel ethical keeping.

Indie films are notorious for being made for next to nothing, but you need to know the budget number that is the absolute lowest you could possibly raise, and still finish some version of your project. That's being a good financial steward, but it's also being respectful of your backers. They'll be giving you financial support on the assumption that you'll be able to finish your film. Make sure you know what the lowest possible fundraise would be that could get you there.

The other element of figuring out how much to ask for is the size and makeup of your audience. It goes without saying that the larger your audience is, the more money you'd have the potential to raise. But your experience comes into play here as well; if someone is involved in the film world, or has some sort of celebrity, it's a very different budget discussion than for someone who's just graduated from film school. Age can also be a factor here; older crowdfunders may not have as high a number of audience members, as crowdfunding/social media use tends to be less in older people, but they can rely on a higher amount contributed per backer, because their older friends are in a more comfortable financial situation (they have houses, savings, etc.) Younger crowdfunders can have the opposite issue; they may have a million friends, but they're all broke.

What Should I Offer for Incentives?

Ah, incentives. The items you create so that your audience members can become your backers. I've probably spent more time thinking about incentives than any other part of my crowdfunding campaigns. I really try hard to create goods and experiences that tie into the content of my films, whether it's the subject matter, or the creation of the film itself. This is the most concrete interaction with you and your audience before the actual movie comes out. And it's a huge missed opportunity to create memorable things, to encourage the audience to pay attention, but not also direct their excitement toward getting additional people to support you. Fun incentives means fun crowdfunding. If someone likes and buys it, they can become liaisons for the campaign, not just backers. This is incredibly important while the campaign is going on.

A few guidelines:

- Six incentives are a good number to start with, and one or two should be specific to your project, especially perks that are below $100.
- Your $25 perk should be irresistible; it should be personal, visual, shareable, and digital. That way, backers will want to share it on their own social media, and it will grab the attention of their own friends and family, who might want one of their own! I backed the Seed&Spark campaign of Dan Mirvish's feature 18 1/2, a dark comedy about the

missing minutes from the Nixon tapes. When I backed, Dan sent me a picture of Elvis shaking hands with Nixon ... only my face was on there instead of Elvis's. Take a look (Figure 6.1):

Figure 6.1 The author Photoshopped into a picture of Nixon and Elvis, as a campaign perk for the Seed&Spark crowdfunding campaign 18½.

I laughed my head off when I got this perk, and I posted it everywhere I could on social media. The incentive turned me into a cheerleader. It was really smart.

- Humor works! (See above.)
- Hold at least two incentives back when the campaign begins, so you can add new energy into the campaign later on and get current backers to give a little bit more.
- Try to offer as many incentives as possible that you don't have to manufacture. The time and cost it takes to create items, pack them, weigh them, and ship them can be enormous ... and it can suck a big chunk of money out of what you crowdfund. After we finished crowdfunding RISING STAR, I had to create about 40 DVDs to mail out to backers

when the movie was finished. I won't tell you how much it cost to create and ship them, but here's a picture of me holding the receipt from the post office (Figure 6.2):

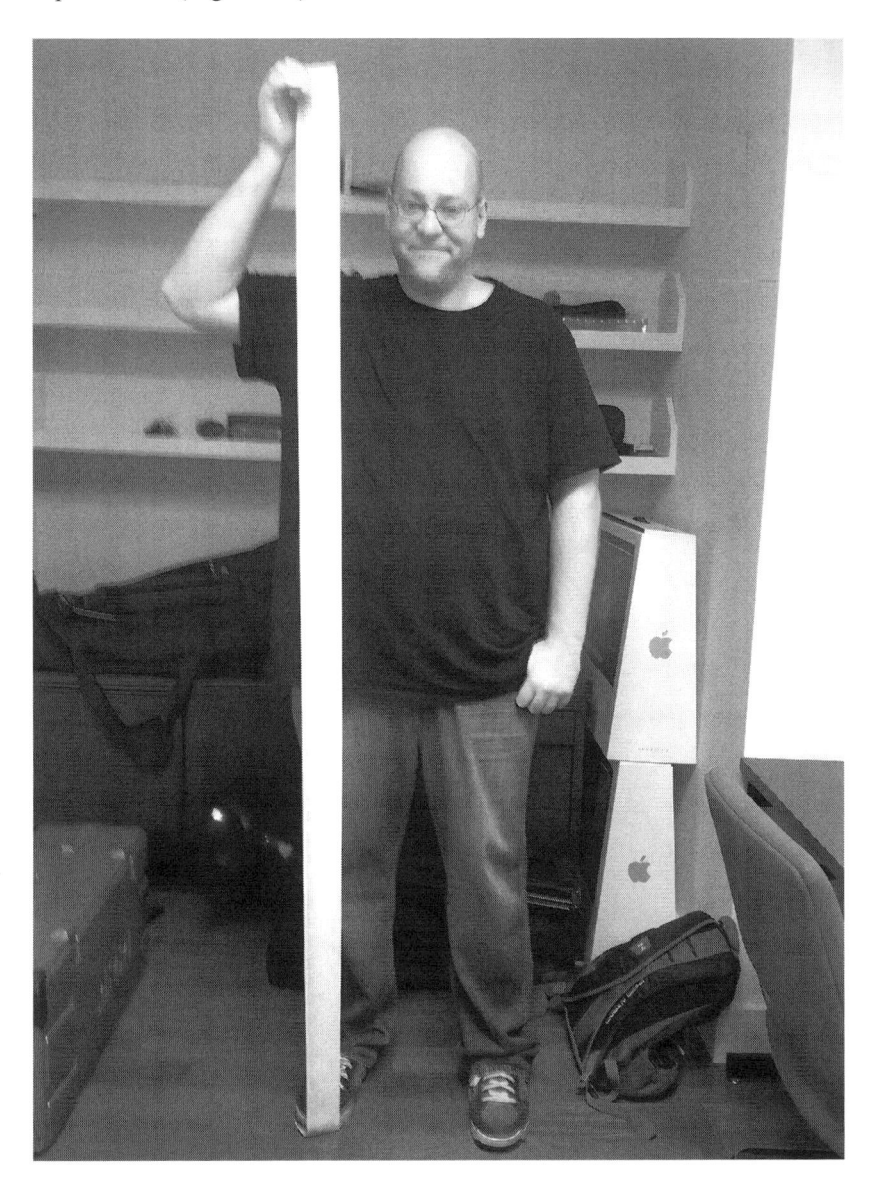

Figure 6.2 The author holding an unbelievably long post office receipt.

(And so you know, I'm six feet seven inches tall.)

How Do I Create a Pitch Video?

Your pitch video is your best chance to convey that you're a dynamite visual storyteller, and that your new project is an opportunity that can't be missed. The key thing for them, though, is that you don't fall into the trap of trying to cram everything into one.

Shorter is better.

I believe that 90 seconds to 3 minutes is a good length for a pitch video. You should think of it as an opening statement for backers, a way to get the most important or exciting details across for your project. It's the beginning of the conversation, not the whole conversation.

The first 15 seconds should also show that you can deliver on the type of film you'd like to make. Are you making a comedy? Make me laugh in the first 15 seconds. Making a thriller? Scare me right off the bat. (Horror filmmakers don't realize how many opportunities they have to make an incredible pitch video – they can use lots of visual elements.) If you can make it fun, but somehow match the topic and themes of the film, that's the best way to build a pitch video.

How Important Is It for the Filmmaker to Be the Face of Their Campaign?

This is a common question I hear. And my general answer is this:

It's essential that the filmmaker be either the face or the voice of their campaign.

If you're comfortable on camera, if you're an actor yourself, or if you just ooze enthusiasm for your project, I say you should be the face of the campaign. Remember, backers aren't just backing a film, they're backing a creator. And if your energy can come through in your pitch video, that's just another positive for your campaign.

But sometimes, filmmakers aren't as confident on camera. They might come off awkward or nervous, and that can actually be a negative for how people perceive them. So sometimes, it's worth evaluating strengths and weaknesses, and giving alternative options a thought.

One great example of a creator who wasn't seen in their pitch video was Kyle Edward Ball, the horror filmmaker who made the 2022 horror hit SKINAMARINK. Kyle has a dry, monotone voice, but he found a way of making the nature of the movie feel like the pitch video he made to promote it. This allowed him to not be on camera, while still providing the viewer an experience that would be very similar to the movie he'd later make. Some people are just not natural speakers, and it'll be more of a detriment by having them on camera. But creators should still make sure their presence is felt everywhere else in the campaign.

Leadup to Launch

Once you've figured out what your campaign page will look like, your pitch video and incentives, then it's time to figure out how your campaign will actually function. How it'll be scheduled, the communication you'll be doing, and how you'll update folks as it takes place.

This might sound like a second phase of pre-production, in addition to your actual film. That's because that's exactly what it is! This type of planning is vital for a campaign, and successful crowdfunders consider their campaign to be a second production, separate from but connected to their actual film. You'll find a lot of parallels between the production of a film and the running of a campaign. Many things are similar, like ...

Scheduling

You'll want to know when you'll be sharing things like updates, social media posts, emails (and follow-up emails), special events, and any other unique items your campaign will unleash into the world. The nice thing is that you don't need to be a producing whiz to lay all this information out. You can do it with something as simple as a Google calendar. Take a look (Figure 6.3):

This is the April 2020 campaign schedule for STAY WITH ME. In it, you can see a few different items:

- The lines on Sundays are the themes for each campaign week. We decided on a general theme that our outreach, social media, and updates would focus on, each of them being a special, unique element of our campaign. The first was crowdfunding education (since this was the first time I was running a campaign with a college class), week two was mental health during COVID (since the pandemic had literally started two weeks earlier), week three was mental health portrayals in film, and the final days in week four were about the state of film and television during the pandemic.
- The lines on Mondays, Wednesdays, and Fridays, are for backer updates. We decided we would put out three updates per week, each of them following that week's theme.
- There are lines specifically for special events. During our campaign, I had some press set up with local TV stations, a Twitter/X screenwriting group, and with Seed&Spark, watching some of their educational content.
- And if you look at each Monday, you'll see lines for four different groups, each doing different jobs. Those groups were groups of my students, and each group was responsible for overseeing one aspect of the

98 Crowdfundamentals

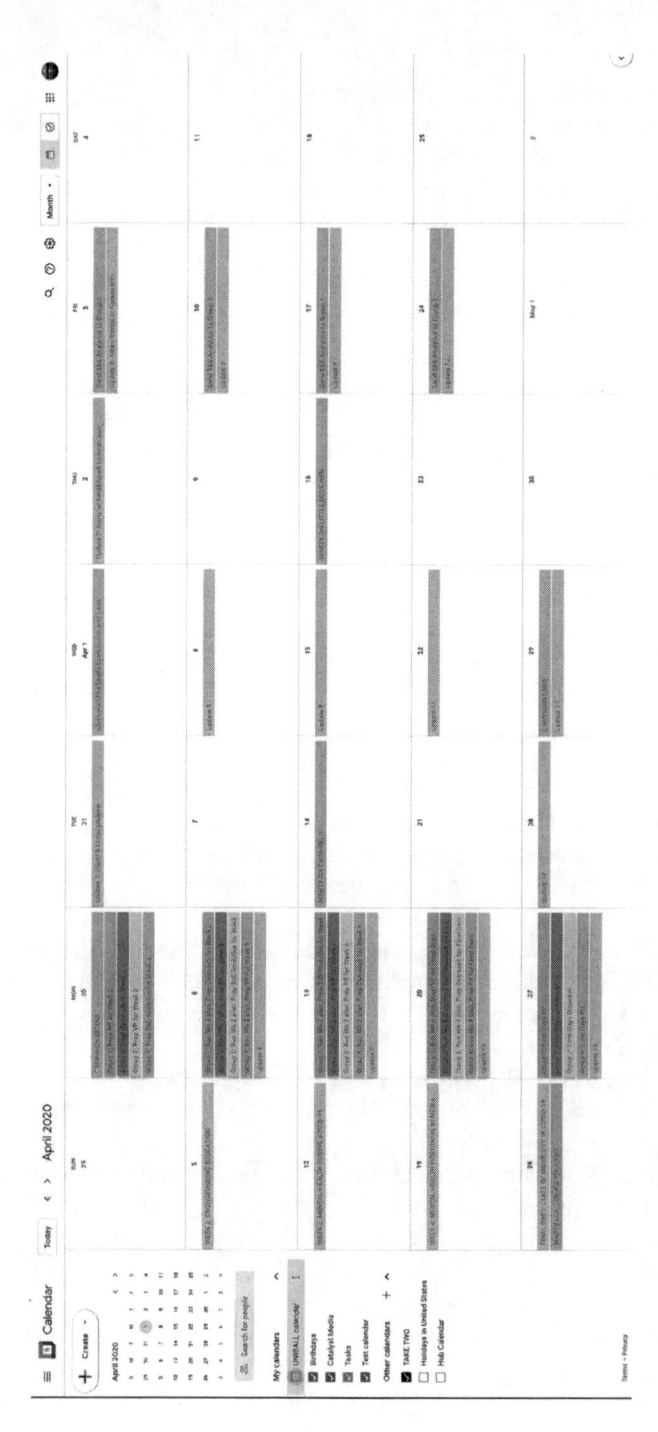

Figure 6.3 A Google calendar for the STAY WITH ME Seed&Spark crowdfunding campaign.

campaign each week: outreach, public relations, social media/analytics, and video production for backer updates.

This is a simple calendar – you'll see that I didn't include emails in this, or specific social media posts. But you can get as detailed as you want.

The key is to try and plan as much as possible. You can prewrite everything that you can schedule – social media posts, graphics – and that can save time. What days are emails going out? Who are they going out to? When the campaign is live, you can literally wake up, check your schedule, execute what must go out that day, and then just go about your regular day. You don't have to refresh the campaign page all day to see how much money you've raised. You can manage it better, and appear more confident, if you have a plan you can stick to, and then execute on.

Direct Outreach

Remember all that crowdsourcing work you did back in development and screenwriting? This is where it comes back to help you. You'll be able to leverage all those folks you've met along the way and invite them to become part of the campaign, before it even launches. This is the most important group to engage, because you've already connected with them (hopefully in person, but definitely through email/social), and they know about your film.

Another thing to remember is to ask those first contributors for data. You can find out how effective your pitch is by talking to the people you're pitching to. And if you find people don't care about what you're doing, stop doing it and try something else. What are people responding to? Lean into that; it may not be what you think. Restructure your outreach plan. It's like being flexible on set – you have to remember the ultimate goal of the day. You don't want to veer so far off the path because something new has happened, but you want to lean into things that are working, or away from things that aren't.

Pitching is another element of filmmaking that's sorely under-taught. When I talked with Leaf Maiman about our journey making STAY WITH ME, he had some surprising things to say about how much help a strong, concise pitch can be:

> "When I originally envisioned STAY WITH ME, I saw it as its own unique thing. It was about the characters and their situation. It didn't have a protagonist, and while it dealt with the issue of mental health, I never intended for it to have any particular mental health message. I wanted it to explore a messy, complicated situation while leaving the conclusions up to the audience. When having to advertise STAY WITH ME to a wide audience, much of those specifics became flattened into the

concept of 'mental health advocacy.' Being that STAY WITH ME explores what is intended to be a realistic portrayal of relationships when navigating mental health issues, saying it is a film about mental health advocacy is accurate. But as an artist, my film personally felt like more than that, like its own thing. What I learned in the crowdfunding process is that no one who donated to STAY WITH ME actually knew what the film was. How would they? The film didn't exist yet, and it couldn't exist without their support. The strangers who donated to the project largely donated to it because they support mental health advocacy and independent filmmaking. They want art that talks about and explores the realities of mental illness because it's a topic that needs good representation. It's easy as an artist to get caught up in your own work. It's understandable given that you've put hours upon hours of thought into your creation. But it's important to remember that the majority of the people who interface with your creation will not have the same level of understanding as you. This is especially true when the movie doesn't even exist. The people who supported STAY WITH ME did so because they supported the larger issue connected to STAY WITH ME, mental health advocacy. Mental health advocacy was the pitch. I used to shy away from boiling down my works to a pitch, fearing that embracing a simple pitch would somehow detract from the more complex film. If I learned anything from crowdfunding STAY WITH ME, it was to embrace the pitch. Lean into it. The pitch is what gets strangers to get passionate about your film before they've ever seen it. It's what gets people in the seats at movie theaters. It's what makes filmmaking possible. Knowing your pitch early on can help you prepare for crowdfunding before the first draft is written. When thinking about your film's pitch, think about the larger issues in the world that connect to your film. People care about mental health advocacy, diversity in media, trans rights, and so many other movements. Those people are the audience for your film, and often they will help you make it. Thanks to the work of all those involved in the campaign and our 154 contributors, we were able to reach our crowdfunding goal, and we had the money to go into post-production."

You can also take advantage of being in public at any time, wherever you have access to people, to continue your outreach as you prep the campaign. As we were preparing the RISING STAR campaign, my team and I often met at a Panera Bread restaurant near us, and we always had a sign up at our table that said ASK US ABOUT OUR INDEPENDENT FILM! Every time we did that, we always got multiple people stopping by to ask questions, at least one person to give us their email address, and some folks would actually give us money! Never underestimate how many opportunities you have to build that email list.

Backer Updates

Many crowdfunders consider backer updates to be nothing more than quick notes exclaiming, "We reached a thousand dollars funded! Please give us more!" If you're strategic about them, though, they can help you turn current campaign supporters or followers into more engaged teammates. Seed&Spark recommends that your backer updates are shareable, visual announcements that show the inevitability of success. They should share more than just what percent funded you are! If you include exclusive information or special offers in your backer emails, that can help train your people to open your emails. And you can pre-compose social media posts that have similar information.

One thing that can also be a big help when brainstorming backer updates is the opportunity to include your crowd in them. Did someone back your campaign because they thought your pitch video was incredibly cinematic and cool? Have them record a quick smartphone video and send it to you! The more you can show that people love what you're doing, the more they'll want to be a part of it. (And if someone doesn't have the money to make a contribution, this can be a fantastic way for them to help you in a way that doesn't involve cash ... and is just as valuable.)

Social Media

Putting a social media plan together can be a good way to engender goodwill from your online communities and keep building bridges with folks who could potentially become contributors. You should always plan to:

- Thank everyone publicly (whether or not they paid for it with an incentive)
- Promote your friends' work (they can do the same for you, and you could both benefit)
- Make announcements (especially if they involve anyone known in your community, or IRL events)
- Automate what you can (using social media programs like Tweetdeck, Hootsuite or Buffer can allow you to pre-compose social media posts, and the program will post them automatically for you, at whatever time you want, giving you more time to focus on direct outreach)

There's a great example of how promoting your friends' work can come back to help you, sometimes in much larger forms than just one contribution. Remember A YEAR WITHOUT RENT, the independent film transmedia campaign I talked about earlier? As creator Lucas McNelly was traveling around North America and Europe, he got to the eight-month mark of his year – and ran out of the money he got in his original campaign. So what happened? One of the coolest things I've ever been a part of an independent film. Once I learned about Lucas's challenge, I teamed up with Victoria Westcott, the producer of LOCKED IN A GARAGE BAND, one of the projects Lucas had worked with early on in his year, and we reached out to all the other filmmakers he had helped up to that point. We all put money in to help Lucas finish his year out, and we ended up getting some more help, too – our goal was $5,000 for his final four months, and we ended up raising about $5,400 from 142 backers.[1] All these filmmakers got a great amount of promotion for having Lucas join their teams (I can vouch for this personally). So it's only natural we would all return the favor and help out the person who helped us so much.

Bonus Elements

One other thing that every campaign should include is some sort of special event, something that Seed&Spark says, "puts the FUN in crowdFUNding." These can include live events or contests, matching contributions, short-term incentives (the one or two you've got in your back pocket, remember?) or anything else. The key is to be creative and give your audience a chance to have some fun.

I was a producer of a Web series called SELENE HOLLOW that crowdfunded on Kickstarter, and we had a live event I was pretty proud of. The co-creator of the web series was my best friend from high school, Damian Dydyn, and this was his first big project that he created on his own, so I wanted to help him fundraise however I could. I pitched Damian a crazy idea: what if we had a live social media "telethon," where for every $50 we raised, one of us would make a YouTube video, telling an embarrassing story about the other from when we were kids? He was game, so we tried it in the third week of the campaign, when we needed a little boost. We promoted on Facebook, Twitter/X, and backer updates, and we ended up raising $500 in one night. (Along with emails from people who were shocked at all the crazy things we did when we were younger.) It was personal, it was fun, and it showed Damian and I as human beings, not just mouths asking for money. The more events you can create that have that effect, the better.

Pushing the Button

Once you've done all your prep work, there's just one thing to do: hit launch! And once you do, you'll have a well thought out, multi-pronged plan to get your audience engaged, supporting, and reaching out to their own networks.

Hopefully.

As your campaign runs, you'll want to make sure that you stick to the schedule you created. You also want to review your messaging every day and make adjustments if it's not working. You want to let people know not only about the work you're doing in the crowdfunding campaign, but also the work you're doing to actually make the project. There were not many advantages to running the RISING STAR campaign right before principal photography started, but one of them was that we were quickly able to post backer updates from set, which our backers really loved. They were able to quickly see what we were doing and were able to follow us as we filmed at our different locations around Hartford, Connecticut.

The other important thing you should be doing is talking with your contributors, to find out why they ended up joining your team. In addition to the questions you asked your friends who liked your pitch, you can learn more about how you could find more people to join up by asking:

- How did you hear about us?
- What made you most excited to contribute?
- What would make you want to share this with your friends?
- How do you want to see this film?

Those answers can give you clues as to where to find more contributors, by honing in on the successful aspects of your pitch and campaign.

Engaging a Community: The Story of UNIBALL

When UNIBALL ran its Seed&Spark campaign, one of the things we knew we had going for us was that the topic of the film, testicular cancer, offered us the chance to engage a very specific audience: men with testicular cancer, their loved ones, and organizations that support them. So when the campaign began, one thing we did was reach out to nonprofit groups that advocated for those people. We were lucky to find the Testicular Cancer Awareness Foundation (TCAF), founded by Kim Jones, whose son Jordan passed away from the disease in 2016. The filmmaking team met with Kim via Zoom once the campaign was up and running, and she was kind enough to agree to help us promote the film on social media.

That was just the beginning. The same day we connected with TCAF, we were contacted by a second testicular cancer organization! This one, the Testicular Cancer Foundation (TCF), was actually having their annual conference in Las Vegas while the campaign was going on. They offered to fly Ben Eslick, the film's director and star, and Molly Phillips, the film's co-star (and now Ben's wife) to the conference, pay for their hotel, and let them give a 15-minute presentation about the film! Ben and Molly flew out to Vegas that same day they were contacted, and after their presentation, the campaign raised over $4,000 from conference attendees, including one who became an Executive Producer with a $2,500 contribution! Almost half the campaign's goal was secured because of contributors we didn't know when the campaign began, but who were intimately engaged with the subject matter of the film.

The campaign ended up raising $18,700 for production, over $8,500 more than its goal, so we were able to upgrade many technical and crew aspects of making the film. But even then, the story wasn't finished. A year after the campaign, in May 2022, Ben, Kim Jones and two urologists teamed up to make a presentation at the annual conference of the American Urological Association! It was called *"Stories Worth Telling: Documenting and Journaling Cancer Treatment as a Journey to Mitigate the Psychological Impact on Patient and Caregivers,"*[2] and it focused on the patient perspective, and giving his cancer a purpose. Ben said:

> I no longer viewed cancer as a pointless hindrance forcing me into a hopeless situation. I saw it as a challenge now, the kind of challenge it takes a hero to overcome, and I got to be the hero in my own story (Eslick et al., 2022).

All these things were due to connecting with an audience that was passionate about the subject matter of Ben's story. Yes, money was one thing that came from it, but Ben was also able to actually produce professional medical literature! You never know what opportunities a campaign might present; help can be found in so many ways other than financial.

A campaign can even provide inspiration for your filmmaking process. The UNIBALL campaign also helped the filmmaking team devise a unique strategy for the film's distribution: while working with the TCAF, we were inspired to begin the film's release not in theaters, but in testicular cancer hospitals. That way, the people who are most intimately involved with the subject matter, the literal people suffering from testicular cancer, will be able to experience the film first, and hopefully be inspired to become the hero of their own story. An example of holistic filmmaking, as we were thinking about distribution of the film before we even filmed it.

What Happens Afterwards?

Congratulations! You've gotten through the gauntlet of crowdfunding, and you've reached a successful result. Once the campaign is completed, you've got some responsibilities:

First, don't ghost your supporters! They've been there for you by contributing. You need to be there for them, by letting them know what's going on with the project. Filmmaker friends of mine who had made movies with traditional investment before crowdfunding often thought of backers the same way they did of investors: once they sign the check, you don't talk with them again until the film is done. They're not the same thing. Think of them as friends. So share production updates. Stay active on social media and create new calls to action, so that you can collect new emails from folks who might join your team in the future.

Second, make your thing! Obviously, you're thinking about that now that the campaign is done, but the reason all those folks joined up with you is because they want to see the project you were promoting. It's your responsibility to put it into the world.

Third, make sure you deliver all your incentives. Now some people send incentives in real time, while the campaign is going on, and if you're a higher level of organizer, I highly recommend you do it that way. If not, you can push off the incentives until after the campaign, so there's one less thing to worry about. That said, make sure you get on it right away once the campaign's done.

Finally, stay in regular communication. So many people forget that when you make one movie with a crowdfunding campaign, you can activate all those contributors later on in your career, to help you with a second campaign. (More on that later.) Keeping in contact with them is a way to show them respect, and gratitude for the help they gave you. The RISING STAR campaign was finished in October of 2010, and we kept giving backer updates all the way until August of 2014! Our backers knew every step of what was going on, and some of them have contacted me to let me know they appreciated it. One backer said he had been burned by ghosting crowdfunders before; he was very happy at the level of interaction we had with him. "It makes me feel like I'm getting something for my money," he said.

That's exactly what you want.

Crowdfunding DEADBRAINS

Putting a campaign together for DEADBRAINS offers some natural advantages. First off, since it's a zombie film, there's already a huge audience for that type of story. Second, since we've done so much crowdsourcing work already, we know where we can find them. So let's plot out what this campaign might look like.

As we prep the campaign, there's some easy decisions we can make. Since zombies are a big part of Halloween, October feels like the right month of the year to run it. We'd be able to capitalize on all the excitement around the holiday. We would also have some nice tie-ins for incentives. Maybe we could offer a Halloween outfit based on one of the zombie characters, to create a nice merchandising tie-in. (It would need to be at a high contribution amount, though – remember, we'd need to pay for shipping that item to backers.) We could also think about the world of the movie for incentives we could offer. What if the human characters saw that the zombies created their own compound, and that they had to attack it to defeat them? A map of that compound could be a cool incentive, too. And I always thought a cute perk could be a sticker or image file that says, "I LOVE YOU," but instead of the word "LOVE," we put a brain with a bite taken out of it. (Get it?)

For the pitch video, you want to show you can do a lot with a little. Remember how I mentioned that when writing the movie, you could concentrate on interior locations, with sound being the way we know zombies are closeby? You could use that for this, too.

Imagine this: let's say I'm directing the film. The pitch video takes place completely in a basement, with wood planks covering the windows. There's a few people huddled inside, and one light in the whole space.

POP! POP! POP!

We hear three gunshots from upstairs. The people downstairs recoil in terror. I come running down the basement stairs, holding a shotgun, talking to camera about how I just took down two zombies trying to get inside. Then, I start talking about the zombie army, how they've taken over the world, and how we're the last humans left – all while smoothly working in details about our crowdfunding campaign.

And here's the cool detail – as I'm talking, you can hear the sounds of zombies outside. Quietly at first, but then getting louder as I tell you about the cool incentives we're offering, what the crowdfunding will pay for, and the awesome partners we have in making it. And right when I get to the end, the zombies break into the house – but we don't see them on camera. We just hear them, and we see everyone in the room react to them coming downstairs! With one last scared look to camera, I make the ask. "Please help us bring DEADBRAINS to life!" And then I fire a single shotgun blast offscreen at the zombies rushing toward me.

Cut to black.

See how shootable that would be? It would all be in one room, with one light, and a few people dressed in tattered clothes. You wouldn't need any zombie makeup at all – the "zombies" would all come from the sound work you could do when you're editing it. With a good performance from the director, we could have a scary, thrilling sample of the filmmaking we could do.

The amount of our raise, frankly, would depend on who the filmmaker is, and how big their network is. I've got a bit of a network because I've been doing this for a while, but if a first-time feature filmmaker were crowdfunding this, I wouldn't suggest trying to raise more than $10,000. If all your backers were at the $25 level, you'd need 400 backers to get to that amount. For a first-time crowdfunder, that's a lot of work. If you can get above that amount in the campaign, that's great, but you don't want the stress of having to reach a goal that's too high. The work of the campaign is stress enough.

Leading up to the launch, of course, we'll want to schedule out our backer updates, our direct outreach, and social media posts. For backer updates, we could have each of the four weeks of the campaign focusing on a different topic related to zombies, where the filmmakers do 1–2 minute videos discussing:

- How Smart Are Zombies? (showing how zombies have never been smarter than the humans fighting them – and proving our hypothesis that this movie will be unique)
- Zombies in Pop Culture (their presence in film, TV, comic books, etc.)
- Independent zombie/horror films (maybe successfully crowdfunded ones, like SKINAMARINK)
- Building a Survival Kit (asking the filmmakers, and possibly early contributors, what they would put in their zombie survival kit)

Also, if you have access to a special effects makeup artist, like the one I identified earlier, one nice bonus element could be offering a special perk during the campaign, where that artist could do a how-to video on how to do your own zombie makeup. I've worked on horror films where you can do zombie makeup with balled up tissue paper and face paint. Something simple like that might be a thing backers would support.

Interview: Crowdfunding Consultant Bri Castellini

Figure 6.4 Headshot of crowdfunding consultant Bri Castellini.

Bri Castellini is an independent film and screenwriting consultant and a subject matter expert in arts crowdfunding, indie filmmaking, film festivals, podcasting, and the USA television show BURN NOTICE. As a filmmaker herself she's known for her short film Ace and Anxious (writer/director, 160k+ views on YouTube) and for her podcast BREAKING OUT OF BREAKING IN. She personally helped launch over $25 million dollars in crowdfunding campaigns with an 85% success rate while she was the Manager of Creator Success at the artist crowdfunding platform Seed&Spark, and she has spoken at over 200 events and festivals virtually and in person on the subjects previously listed. Full work history can be found on her website BriCastellini.com.

Marty Lang:	What is the hardest part of crowdfunding?
Bri Castellini:	Well for me, personally, it's finding enough people with money, because my communities are very generous, but are not very well off. So no matter how many best practices I can shove into my brain, I'm always going to be limited by the funds around me, and the funds that I have myself, and those are not significant. My cap for what is realistic for me to raise is much lower than I think a lot of people assume it is when they hire me, when I'm talking at festivals and that kind of stuff. For me, the challenge is just finding the crowd that will get me to the goals that I need, because it's a lot of work, and so much of it starts with your starting crowd. My starting crowd, bless their hearts, they can only get me so far.

Then I would say, even as an extrovert, that the hardest part about crowdfunding is often maintaining your energy and momentum throughout the entire campaign. Most people go into it with a decent amount of energy, but they expend it inefficiently. And by week two, they just give up. If they reserve energy, then there's still hope for them. When people don't immediately hit the goal that they want within the first couple of days, a lot of times I find people lose their energy, and they tend to never get it back. And it's a shame because they had a lot of great stuff. They had great material and they had a great idea. But they didn't have the momentum and the energy to carry them through the natural course of a campaign.

It's so rare for a campaign to get 100 percent funded in the first day. And I think that's what everyone secretly wants. And some people who depend on that secret, hope for it more than others, find the whole process a lot more challenging, and a lot more disheartening. |
| ML: | What would be the one thing that you hear most from people that hear you speak or that you consult with about the process? |
| BC: | As far as challenges, they say "Wow, this sounds like a lot of work." Genuinely, that's one of the first things that I get at the end of a workshop or during a consultation. Because nobody wants to think about this like a film production. They don't want to think about having to produce your crowdfunding campaign with the same energy and logistics as producing the ultimate film, but it is the nature of the beast. You have to buckle down and do it. Also, the thing that I hear most is "How much time do you think I need to prepare?" Usually preceding "Because I want to launch next week." So it's the |

twofer. "Wow, this sounds like a lot of work. So you're saying I shouldn't launch tomorrow?"

I'm going to be managing a project right now that gave me a week and a half's notice. They want to raise $20,000, and I was like, "I mean, we'll try it, I will get everything in place, but this is not ideal. We'll do our best, but guys, it's not ideal." It is what it is. But those are tough conversations to have. When I say that realistically, you should spend at least two months building your email list and learning all the processes. A week and a half is not a lot, especially when the two full-time people in that campaign have full-time jobs that are in offices, or on set. That means they can't be sending emails and setting things up in the middle of the day. So they have so little time, even with that week and a half.

Those are the two things. It's either, "Wow, that sounds like a lot of work. I expected you to just say email these two people, and they'll give you a million dollars," or "Oh, so I shouldn't launch immediately. How quickly can I launch this?"

ML: In your time working, as a consultant, with students, or on your own projects, what are the most innovative things that you've seen crowdfunders do? Things that sort of change the context around the act of crowdfunding.

BC: I remember one horror film's campaign that really stuck out to me. What was innovative about it is that it cost them no money. They just were in their house, you know, they turned off all the lights, they turned on a flashlight, and that's it. They had a flashlight, a camera, and a dark house, and they used that and their own ingenuity to create a little mini piece of art, that fully convinced me they could make the rest of their art.

When people have great incentives, that are just so unique to their particular project, that's so much fun. There was an audio drama project called ALPHA 8 that crowdfunded on Seed&Spark, that told a story of a society in space, kind of Star Trek-y. They made crew ID cards for their incentives. That was really fun.

Another campaign was about a dystopian society, where there was a wall around the city, and you were kicked out. You had to have an ID card to be in the city; the campaign made ID cards for people. And they would have to explain to people when they got that incentive, this will allow you into the city. Do not lose that ID! In a way, they initiated people into the world of their film. All through something they were selling. They also then got to use that design later in the process. And so, people got to say, "I have one of those!" when the movie eventually came out. And that's so fun because those sorts of things remind us that this isn't a soulless fundraising opportunity. We are building toward something together, and if you're clever you can include people as a part of that. You're not just an outside observer, you get to be in the world with them and that's so special. That's why people love movies, because they want to be immersed, and if you can give them some of that immersion early and then on the flipside, be able to use the conversion to make your movie and get people to it even before it exists, that's usually powerful.

And that's why we're all here. We're not here to make money. We're here to make movies. The money is just what we need to get started. The people who make crowdfunding about the money are almost always going to fail, but the people who make crowdfunding about the movie, are gaining a lot more than just their budget.

ML: Are there personality traits that you've identified as helpful when it comes to this process? Is there a certain kind of filmmaker that's more likely to be successful?

BC: Certainly, the extroverts have an easier time of it because just the first phase of starting a conversation with people is much easier. I would also say, I don't know exactly how to define this kind of personality, but, like, the kind of person who will lock themselves in a room for a weekend, and then come out the other side having learned how to do visual effects. Those are the kinds of people that do well, the people who are willing to get really nitty-gritty and learn new skills, so that they can use them immediately, even if they had no interest in that skill. The people who are the tinkerers, who are just good at sitting down and figuring things out. You know, those who have patience tend to do really well in crowdfunding, too, because so much of crowdfunding is psychology and momentum, and saving your energy and patience. The people who are more one-track mind, the instant gratification monkeys, they definitely struggle because there is no instant gratification and crowdfunding unless you're already rich. And if you are, why are you there, right?

ML: Have you gotten a benefit in your crowdfunding or in your consulting as a result of your podcast? You focus on every other aspect of filmmaking there. Have you seen benefits from that as a result of reaching out into the indie film community?

BC: Yeah, I got a client recently who listens to the podcast. They looked me up and saw I was offering crowdfunding support. There's been a couple of times where people who have discovered our podcast reached out to us to hire us for other work. So that's definitely a benefit.

It's also connected me to people who I now consider peers of mine who got to know me through the podcast and then they sent a nice email. We got to talking and now I know we're friends. Colleagues. So that's definitely been a huge benefit. The other is just, more broadly, getting to talk so regularly with other filmmakers that I respect.

The industry has just been a place of solidarity that is invaluable because we started this podcast at the very beginning of the pandemic, like the month before the 2020 election. There was a lot of chaos at the time, and still, so having a reason to continue being creative, valuing creativity, and talking to the many guests that we've had has been wonderful. It has saved my interest in being a part of this industry. Certainly, if I had just been in the pandemic working my job and just trying to get through the day, I don't think that I would still be as creatively fulfilled as I am now. That podcast gave me a lifeline and a community when I really, really needed it.

I think that's important too. People often don't think, "What's going on in the rest of my life, and how could that potentially be a benefit to my own creative work?"

ML: What's your best piece of advice for someone who's going to be crowdfunding a film for the first time?

BC: Emphasize direct personal outreach over social media. Nobody is paying attention to your social media. The social media platforms are not showing them your content, even if they wanted to pay attention to you. You cannot control those algorithms. They control you. And more often than not, they try to silence you because you are not as profitable as other people on their platform. So don't rely on them. Go directly to the source. It's going to be awkward, but it's worth it because when you make yourself vulnerable to people, and when you put yourself in the driver's seat of, "I want to talk to you about this movie that I'm making," you are going to get a lot more return. Higher risk, higher return. Higher work, but higher return.

Notes

1 https://filmmakermagazine.com/33587-a-thanksgiving-kickstarter-for-year-without-rent/
2 https://www.auanews.net/issues/articles/2022/may-2022/patient-perspectives-stories-worth-telling-documenting-and-journaling-cancer-treatment-as-a-journey-to-mitigate-the-psychological-impact-of-treatment-on-patient-and-caregivers

Reference List

Best, Emily. "Crowdfunding to Build Independence," Seed&Spark, 2023.

Eslick, Ben, Alkhatib, Khalid MD, Pierorazio, Phillip M. MD, Jones, Kim. "Stories Worth Telling: Documenting and Journaling Cancer Treatment as a Journey to Mitigate the Psychological Impact of Treatment on Patient and Caregivers," American Urological Association, 2022. https://www.auanews.net/issues/articles/2022/may-2022/patient-perspectives-stories-worth-telling-documenting-and-journaling-cancer-treatment-as-a-journey-to-mitigate-the-psychological-impact-of-treatment-on-patient-and-caregivers

Macauley, Scott. "A Thanksgiving Kickstarter for A Year Without Rent," *Filmmaker Magazine*, 2011. https://filmmakermagazine.com/33587-a-thanksgiving-kickstarter-for-year-without-rent/

7 Pre-Production

If you run a production crowdfunding campaign, and you're successful, the feeling where you know you can completely focus on pre-production is one of the best feelings ever. I speak from experience; when the RISING STAR campaign successfully finished, with two more weeks of prep before shooting, I celebrated with a bit too much champagne.

Believe me when I tell you: that moment felt GOOD.

Now that your plate has been cleared, you've got a daunting step in front of you: corral all the resources and people you need to physically produce your film. Now if you've successfully run a crowdfunding campaign, you'll have raised at least some money to help acquire these things.

But it's unlikely you'll have raised enough to pay for everything. So you'll need to look somewhere else for them.

And since you've spent all this time building an audience, and cultivating relationships, you already have the pool of people from which you can find them.

The crowdsourcing work you've done that helped you with your crowdfunding can instantly be transposed into pre-production. If you understand all the additional resources you have beyond that crowdsourcing, you'll find that there are many that want to help you.

Let's talk about how to find them.

The Power of the Open Call

Reading RB Botto's crowdsourcing book helped me to understand how widely it could be used to help filmmakers in pre-production. In it, he explained that crowdsourcing is a relatively new concept. It was first used by Wired Magazine editors Jeff Howe and Mark Robinson, and it was used in the context of businesses using the Internet to outsource work to individuals:

DOI: 10.4324/9781003295754-7

Simply defined, crowdsourcing represents the act of a company or institution taking a function once performed by employees, and outsourcing it to an undefined (and generally) large network of people in the form of an open call. This can take the form of peer production (when the job is performed collaboratively), but is also often undertaken by sole individuals. The crucial prerequisite is the use of the open call format, and the large network of potential laborers (Howe, 2006).

It's not hard to see how filmmakers could use an open call to incorporate peer production into the filmmaking process. The Google form we put together for RISING STAR, where we asked our audience if there's anything they could do to help us, is one broad way to do it, but you can extend it to specific items:

- Cast members (and maybe even a casting director)
- Crew members
- Equipment
- Locations
- Food/craft services
- Production design items

The pre-production of STAY WITH ME provided a lot of opportunities to take advantage of open calls. Leaf Maiman can tell you a little bit about how we put our cast together:

"First, we had to figure out the cast. Thankfully for us, one of our producers, Sarah de Leon, joined the team at the early stages. Sarah had a good working relationship with Marty, and had gotten us in touch with Lara Fox, who we would later cast as Katie. (Marty and Sarah worked together while she was a student at the Chapman University film school, and Lara was also an acting student there.) Lara joining the team was another key to the film's success. STAY WITH ME is a drama about mental illness, which, at times, can get very heavy. If the role of Katie had been poorly cast, the film could have easily come off as cringy and insensitive. Luckily, Lara was able to bring the subtlety and nuance to Katie that was needed to authentically bring the character to life.

Not only did Lara give a quality performance to one of the film's three leads, but she also acted as our casting director, eventually helping us cast our other lead roles, Gavin and Maya. This is where we truly lucked out. Talented actors are often friends with other talented actors. Because we had access to Lara's network, we were able to put an open call out, and get stellar acting for our indie drama that desperately needed it.

That said, the process was not necessarily easy. We were not able to finalize the cast until two weeks before production was set to begin. STAY WITH ME was very close to not existing because of it.

The good thing about being involved in a filmmaking community is that most of the people in that community have the same goal: they want to make movies and build filmmaking careers. Becoming connected to this community was a huge benefit of going to film school, though film school is not the only way to get connected. It also helped that we had a script ready to go. It can be much harder to find people willing to get a movie off the ground, but it is easier to get people onboard a train that is already moving."

What was great about this film, though, was that we put out open calls for other things that we needed during pre-production, too. One of the most creative things we did was to put out an open call for our meals. Leaf's parents were kind enough to offer to pay for our craft services on set (snacks, drinks, and small things for the cast and crew to eat), and they had lots of friends in their neighborhood. We ended up with a cast and crew of around 20 people, and they all needed to be fed. So we asked the neighborhood families to cook us one meal, for 20 people, to cover one shooting day. We had 13 shooting days, and we were able to find 13 different families that each made one meal (or bought us one meal from a local restaurant – hey, we weren't picky). They're all listed in our special thanks in the completed film, because they, quite literally, were the fuel for our shoot.

We were also able to get all our equipment for the shoot via an open call. I put the word out to the Cal State Northridge film community, on social media, in the hallways, and even by announcing it in some production classes, that we were making a film, and that it would be incredible if anyone had equipment they could let us use. We ended up hearing from the film school's equipment room that their gear wasn't used in the summer, and that we could borrow it for free! All we had to do was insure it and agree to pay for any damage that might occur. Needless to say, that saved us thousands of dollars, and it gave us professional equipment that our camera and lighting teams could use, which was a great professional experience for them.

Thinking in Symbiotic Relationships

When you learn that the only way to obtain products or services is through the exchange of money, you start to think of the world transactionally, and that's a hard mindset to break. When you're in pre-production, though, you must break it, because in most cases, money is the one thing you don't have. In order to make the deals you need for your film to happen you need something to GIVE to people. They'll be more likely to get involved with a project if they think there's something in it for them, as well as something for you. And there are all kinds of things that can be thought of as "currency" for these deals.

Rallying Your Community

When you're making a film in your community, the simple idea of local pride can be incredibly valuable to you. When we were making RISING STAR, we were filming in Hartford, Connecticut, and like I mentioned before, their professional hockey team, the Hartford Whalers, moved to North Carolina in 1997. The Whalers were the only professional sports franchise the state ever had, so their leaving was devastating. Any mention of the team in the state always brought about good memories. When we were preparing to film, I was able to get permission to use the Whalers logo in the movie – using it on a poster in a scene here and there, having a character wear an outfit with the logo, that kind of thing. When we approached some downtown Hartford locations about filming, the simple fact that we'd be using the logo was enough to break the ice with location owners, and helped us secure some of them.

Research Before You Ask

Anyone who's ever been involved in a negotiation can tell you that knowing your partner is one of the most important things. If you're negotiating with one person, you want to know the things they like, what kind of financial shape they're in, and if you know anyone in common. If it's with an organization, you want to know if they're looking for anything in particular, and how their finances are. That way, you can make a more targeted ask when you contact them and can increase the chances that you can make a deal that will work for both of you.

When RISING STAR was looking to film at the adulthood home of legendary writer Mark Twain, we were able to strike just such a deal. Before meeting with them, we researched and found out that the Mark Twain House and Museum had been struggling financially, and they needed events to happen in their museum (which had a 200-seat theater) in order to raise money.

We knew what they wanted, and we wanted something, too.

After meeting with their directors, they told us we could shoot in the house for $300 an hour. We did not have that much money to secure the house for the 6 hours we would need (a total fee of $1,800). In fact, at that point, we didn't have a budget for locations at all. So we offered them a deal. If they let us shoot in the house for $50 an hour (a total fee of $300), we would host a focus group screening of the film at the Museum, and they could keep all the ticket sales. That would help us both; we'd be able to get feedback on the movie while it was being edited, and the Museum could have an event that tied them into the local independent film community. The directors agreed, and we had permission to shoot at the Mark Twain House. We shot the scenes in the house in 6 hours, half a shooting day, and when the focus group screening came around, we were able to sell 275 tickets at $20 apiece. They had to create an overflow theater room, with a television that played the film.

They ended up making $5,500, more than three times what they would have made if we paid them the full amount to shoot there.

Everybody won.

They asked us if we wanted to screen the movie again with them, but we politely declined. We wanted to make some money, too!

Know Your Strengths

It's important to remember what your natural talents are, and the things you can offer to negotiation partners. Whatever skills you have, work you've done, anything that you can offer as assistance to people or groups that can help them, offer it.

My own background focuses on education (I've taught in high school and college), and workforce development. I was able to utilize those skills as part of arrangements I made with our partners on RISING STAR. When I met with the City of Hartford about the movie, I told them that our shoot would be a great opportunity for the city's department of tourism to get photos and video footage, to show how cool Hartford is now that an independent film was shooting there. I also reached out to Hartford schools as part of this meeting, letting them know that my team and I could do film workshops for students that might be interested. That led to us doing those filmmaking workshops with the Kinsella School for Performing Arts. In exchange for that offering, the City of Hartford gave us permission to shoot on any city-owned land for free, without having to secure permits! That was a huge help for us in pre-production, and it all came about because we knew what we could offer, and found the right partners who would want it.

What You Can Offer Other than Money

I'm pretty confident this will be the most controversial part of the book. Just by reading that headline, I can hear people scoffing, and saying "this guy wants to teach how to exploit people." And honestly, I can see your point of view if you think that way. Work deserves payment. We need payment to live. But since we're working with budgets that are so low on these types of projects, I believe you need to think of your film as a vehicle of opportunity, and not necessarily only as a means to a paycheck. As a result, odds are you won't be able to find the local professionals, who've been doing their job in film for years, willing to work on something this small. But there are lots of people who have goals of their own in film. Goals that might need training, or just a chance to prove they can do a job.

Those are the people you can recruit to your film.

Let's look at the things you can provide that they would want.

Educational Opportunities

This one is the most obvious, because so many films have been made using volunteers and interns. But you'd be surprised at the caliber of talent you can bring on to your film by providing the chance to learn.

Let's start with crew. Normally, these are the positions you'd be most likely to pay full freight for, in terms of a day rate, gas money, meal money, that kind of thing. But there are always ambitious people in our business. You might know someone who works consistently as a grip, but who has dreams of one day being a cinematographer. They might even have shot a few short films, to keep their dream alive.

That's the person you approach to be your cinematographer.

This can work for any of your major crew positions. When I was running the Connecticut Film Industry Training Program, I met a brilliant woman named Ginger LaBella. At the time, she had been working as a graphic artist on TV shows like **THE BLACKLIST**, but she always wanted to work as a production designer. Now she couldn't be on set full time, because she needed to work, and I couldn't afford to pay her what she was worth. But for the experience, she agreed that she would do the production design work for the movie off schedule (meaning before shooting, from home, on weekends), we would have other crew on set who could set everything up, and I ended up paying her less than $1,000. Based on the work she did, it was a steal, but it gave her a credit on a feature film as a production designer. This was something she always wanted, so even though the money wasn't good, everyone was still happy.

You can use the lure of education, like I mentioned earlier, to find interns for your film. Students have all sorts of opportunities built into their education, whether in high school, community college, or four-year universities, where they can find work experiences that would give them class credit. This works out great for the student because they can get a taste of the real world, and it's also great for the film because you're able to get people working for you that you don't need to pay. From an insurance perspective, it's also great to have interns, because if they're doing it for class credit, their educational institution usually covers the interns in case of accidents. (This isn't legal advice, though. Make sure you check with the institution.) You want to be sure, however, that any interns that work with you are provided with a meaningful work experience. You don't want interns getting coffee for you on set. Have them working in a department, where they're getting meaningful experience in an area they're interested in. Or multiple areas; I've produced multiple short films where we had interns, and I've moved them each shooting day, so they're working in a different department each day. That gives them a broader experience, and they can see how different parts of the film machine work.

Working with local public access television stations can be a great way to find folks who'd like to be a part of your film. The folks who work in public access don't get paid; they do it because they love the work, and because it's a way to give back to their community. Those people are in the same frame of mind we are, so it's possible they might want to help, especially if they could play the finished film on the station. Plus, public access stations usually have good equipment, so that could be another way to crowdsource the gear you'd need – bring public access workers onto the film as crew, and they could bring the camera, sound, and lighting you'll need.

Believe it or not, educational opportunities could help you get actors. High school and college theater programs are great places to find extras. So many young people want to work in film and television, so you'd be able to get excited people who want to learn how things work. (But make sure to schedule them on weekends. If they're not getting paid, it's hard to get them to come during the week, when they're either in school or working.)

Finally, the promise of education could help you find folks who could create marketing assets for your film. You can bring graphic design or Web design students to help you develop promo materials, and communication/film students could create behind the scenes video for you – they could even shoot stills and videos using their smartphones. I directed a short film called **PROTESTERS** with Catalyst Media, and we recruited college students to work as our assistant editor, and also to create our poster and social media graphics. And when I hired Ginger LaBella to be the production designer on **RISING STAR**, part of her job included making our poster and electronic press kit. Take a look at the great job she did (Figures 7.1 and 7.2):

Promotional Opportunities

Businesses, and governmental entities, love any chance to get exposure for what they do. Using their location as a location in the movie, or getting a

120 Pre-Production

Figure 7.1 Poster for the feature film RISING STAR.

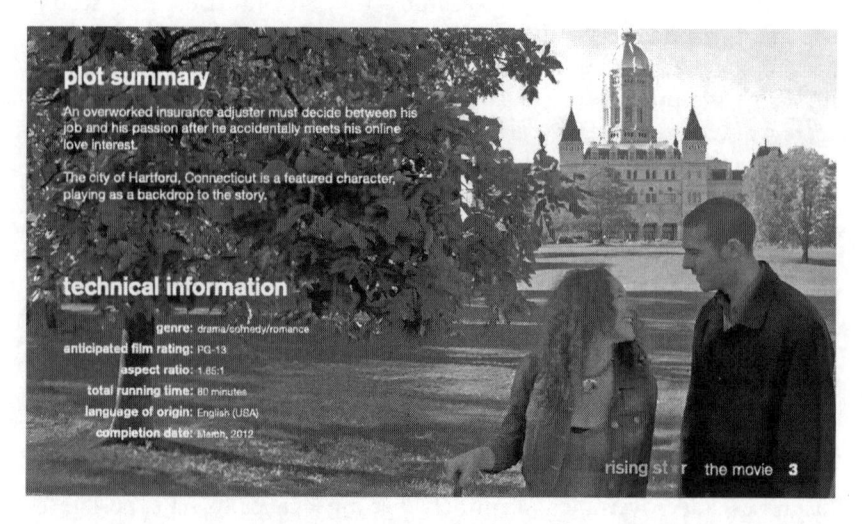

Figure 7.2 Plot summary page from the electronic press kit of RISING STAR.

service from them that could help your production, can be paid for by providing them promotional consideration. We were able to shoot part of RISING STAR in the Connecticut Science Center for free, in exchange for mentioning them on local news broadcasts and newspaper articles. We were fortunate to get a lot of press leading up to the finish of the film, so they were very happy with the number of times we were able to point them out for all their help. Our relationship continued with them after the film was done; since we worked together so well, we agreed to host our Connecticut premiere in their 200-seat theater. (More on that screening in a bit.)

You never know how much a business might want to help you, especially if they're a startup. Way back in 2000, I was working on my first-ever movie, a romantic comedy called A LITTLE BIT OF LIPSTICK. It starred Mia Tyler and Soupy Sales (remember him?), and it was about a Hollywood bad boy who gets sent to a small-town Connecticut theater to rehab his image, and falls in love with the plus-size girl who runs the theater. Since it was my first-ever film job, I was helping the producers try and find any kind of in-kind help to make our budget go farther. You may have heard of the beverage brand SoBe, or the South Beach Beverage Company; it's since been bought out by Pepsi, but at the time, it was a small Connecticut startup company, looking for ways to get the word out about their products. I knew three of their full-time employees because we all went to college together, and I had volunteered to help them after I graduated myself, while I was looking for my first full-time job. (They paid me in drinks and free T-shirts. It was a different world.) I approached one of my friends and asked if he thought SoBe would want to be a part of the movie. I offered them the chance for the main character to drink a SoBe drink during a scene, and have SoBe signage placed prominently in the background, in exchange for drinks and T-shirts, the same deal they gave me. Not only did they agree to it, but they also gave us 100 cases of drinks! It took three cars for us to get it all, and bring it back to the director's house. We were able to have our cast and crew hydrated for the entire shoot, and all it took was a small instance of product placement, which became a major promotional opportunity for the company.

Economic Development

A local area can always use help stimulating their economy, and making a movie in your area can help that happen. It can provide support to your area vendors that provide equipment, food, lodging, and gas. Making a movie in your area can help to grow your local economy. In addition to helping those vendors, there are governmental entities who would be excited about that. Specifically, departments of tourism.

One interesting aspect of RISING STAR was that it's a movie that takes place completely in Hartford, Connecticut. We used recognizable Hartford locations, like the Mark Twain House, Bushnell Park, the Connecticut Science Center, and the grave of Wallace Stevens. Shooting a movie in these locations helped those cultural attractions, as the attention and press from the film increased awareness, and in turn, increased patronage. Once the film was finished, we used the City of Hartford as a major part of its distribution, too. The Connecticut premiere took place at the Science Center, and the event was coordinated with the Connecticut Film Festival. We were also able to show the film in Bushnell Park, as part of their summer outdoor series program "Movies in the Park." Over 500 people came to see the film when it played there.

The goal through all of this was to create a tourism effect similar to that of Mystic, Connecticut, after the release of the film MYSTIC PIZZA. Mystic has received a longtime boost in tourism as a result of MYSTIC PIZZA shooting in town, as many vacationers make their way there to see the locations in the film, as well as to try out "the pizza that inspired the movie." Once the film was released, the Mark Twain House did get some visitors who came there because they saw it in RISING STAR. So mission accomplished!

Workforce Development

If you live in an area where film and television production is considered a high-priority industry, you can find lots of help by joining forces with any workforce development programs that might be going on in your area. If you live in Georgia, for example, that state has the Georgia Film Academy, a statewide film and television workforce development agency that partners with educational institutions around the state. Whenever a film arrives in Georgia to shoot, the GFA is activated, and they partner with institutions closest to where the film will shoot, so that local residents can be trained to work on it as crew.

When I created the Connecticut Film Industry Training Program, my job was to run a one-month program that taught state residents to work as below the line crew positions, like production manager, assistant director, location scout, prop master, jobs like that. We brought in union professionals from the Directors Guild of America (DGA) and International Alliance of Theater and Stage Employees (IATSE) to work as instructors, teaching classes about the jobs they were actually doing. And in the final week of the program, every student worked in their position on a short film that was eventually completed and released. (We made five of these films over the five years of the program, and they had known actors in them like CHEERS' John Ratzenberger and STRANGER THINGS' Amy Seimetz.)

As the program was going each year, I made sure to consult with the instructors and find out who the best students were. I knew that, when the time came that I would make my own feature film, I'd want the best crew members I could find who would want experience. And the graduates of a training program are the ideal group.

Cultural Enhancement

If you think about your local area, and all the cultural opportunities you might have, it could span a number of areas. Music, theater, film, art, photography – all those arts have a place in the life of a community. Film is unique in that when one is made, everyone in the community has an opportunity to actually see it be made in addition to seeing the finished, final product. There's an energy that builds around a film, a "cool factor," that's hard to describe, but very powerful. If you don't live in Los Angeles, New York, or Atlanta, seeing a movie filming gets people talking. I lived in New Haven, Connecticut, when INDIANA JONES AND THE KINGDOM OF THE CRYSTAL SKULL filmed there, and it was so exciting being able to walk downtown and see all the period cars lined up along the street. There was a magic seeing all the storefronts transformed to look like they were from the 1950s. Now your tiny film might not have the ability to send a whole street into a time warp, but when local folks see a camera, a director calling action, and actors performing, they'll want to know what's going on. They'll also tell their friends about it. That kind of excitement is something all cities and towns look for.

And it's something you can provide.

Getting the Community Involved

If you think about it, an independent film is a lot like a political campaign. They both consume the lives of the people that work on them, neither of them ever have any money, and working on one doesn't guarantee a successful result. But they're also two areas where that "cool factor" can be used to recruit local folks to help. Political campaigns recruit volunteers with the ability to be involved in the political life of your community, and films can do the same with its artistic life. And the farther away from the major film hubs you are, the more effective that recruiting can be. When INDIANA JONES was filming in New Haven, Connecticut had just instituted its own film tax incentive, along with the training program I created, so movies were still very new to the area. There hadn't been a film shot in Hartford since the tax credit was started. We were able to take advantage of the momentum that the tax credit created for the industry in the state. Everyone we talked to was excited to be a part of it. That also put a responsibility on us to make sure we worked well with everyone in the city, so films after us could work with them as well. And we were able to do that.

Meeting Them in Real Life

So much of this book has been about the importance of finding online communities, gathering personal emails, and building social media followings, but nothing beats hanging out with a person, showing them how excited you are about your film, and getting them to come on board. Running the Connecticut Film Industry Training Program had the huge benefit of spending lots of in person time with people who wanted a career in the industry. So when it came time to crowdfund RISING STAR, everyone knew me, and knew that I wanted to direct a feature. Many students, who were not hired as crew on the movie, backed the campaign because they believed in me, and in their classmates who would be working on it.

Finding the right individual can also open up worlds of support if you're in a community where you don't know anyone. I was an associate producer on a feature called OUT OF MY HAND, which was a 2016 Indie Spirit Award nominee, and was picked up by Ava Duvernay's distributor ARRAY. The film was shot partly in Liberia, and partly in Staten Island, New York – specifically, in Park Hill, Staten Island's Liberian community. The filmmakers were from Brooklyn (and I lived in Queens at the time), so we weren't members of this specific neighborhood. We needed to find someone who was part of this community, who believed in what we were doing. We were able to find an amazing woman named Jennifer, who lived in Park Hill, and was interested in the film. After we met with her, and she liked us, she was able to introduce us to just about every location owner we would need in the time we'd be shooting in Park Hill. And that goodwill carried into our actual shooting. There was more than one time when local people would see me walking down the street, a tall white man with a walkie-talkie, and ask me if I was a cop. When I told them I'm part of a crew making a movie, they would say "Oh! Jennifer told us about you," and then they'd be much nicer. That kind of community approval is so vital when you're trying to film in an area where you're not a local.

Getting Your Government Involved

So many indie filmmakers neglect one of the biggest resources they have: their government. True, in the United States, there isn't as much support for the arts as there is in Europe, Asia, or even Canada, but there are still ways that they can help, if you know how to speak their language.

A town or city government can give you access to use public land and streets and make the process more streamlined. That opened up the shoot for RISING STAR, and made the film seem so much bigger, since we were able to film in beautiful, open areas. A county government could have similar benefits as a town government, and both county and city governments often have chambers of commerce. Connecting with them could give you access to local businesses, who could provide location assistance, or become vendors for the project. State government can help, through their film or entertainment offices, tourism offices, and humanities councils (who are unusually adept, in my experience, at helping filmmakers find good locations). Some of these offices also offer grant programs, as a way to promote artistic activity within their borders.

Talking with government officials, however, requires a different kind of communication than businesses or vendors might. If someone is working in government, they're looking for ways to improve their areas; they're not looking for opportunities to give money or resources away. So you need to find a way to show them your film can provide something for the area. You can phrase that in terms of educational opportunities, cultural enhancement, tourism, or workforce development, but there's another term I've used that I've been successful with. If you talk with a mayor's office, they may not be excited to help your film if you pitch it as a chance for an artist to change the world. But there's a phrase you can use to describe your film that is much different and will get a government's attention:

Creative manufacturing.

Manufacturing provided 12% of the total US GDP, over $2.3 trillion dollars, in 2021, according to the National Institute of Standards and Technology.[1] And of that number, film and television production (which, technically, is manufacturing) provides $186 billion of wages to over 2.4 million people. And it pays out $21 billion per year to over 260,000 businesses in cities and small towns across the country.[2]

Calling your film an act of creative manufacturing presents an argument that your film will create jobs, contribute to a huge part of the American economy, and provide an economic boost to the community.

That's a much more compelling argument than your artistic drive to tell a great story.

If you know how to talk with government officials and show them how you can positively affect your community, the more likely you'll get them on board to help.

Know Your Tax Credits!

When I was early in my career, I was a producer on a small independent film that was shooting in a tax credit state. The tax credit had recently been passed, so not many folks knew about it. And what even fewer people knew was that the tax credit was applicable to films that had budgets as low as $50,000.

This film had a budget of around $250,000.

I told the producer about the tax credit the film would qualify for, excited that my research could lead to the project getting a boost in its budget. But the producer snapped back at me, "That's too much paperwork. We'll make our money back when the film plays in theaters."

Guess what? The film never played in theaters.

I share that story for two reasons. First, never let your ego get the best of you when thinking about the future of a project. No matter how much of a home run you might think it is, there are so many factors out of your control that can derail it. And second, always get your tax credits! The state you film in wants to promote film and television production, and they're willing to give you free money to do it. Even if you think your film is too small to qualify for one, always do the research. You'd be shocked how low the minimum spend is in some areas, and when you're making films this small, every dollar counts.

One of the most interesting tax credit states these days is the great state of Minnesota. They have film and television tax incentives available at multiple levels, and some areas of the state are incredibly indie-friendly.[3] Let's take a look at what they offer:

A State Credit

The Minnesota Film and TV Website explains the state's Film Production Tax Credit program. If a production company spends $1 million or more in the state on a project, they're eligible to receive a transferable tax credit equal to 25% of their spend. In addition, they have a Production Rebate program, where a production company spending at least $100,000 for qualified Minnesota production costs is eligible for a 20–25% cash reimbursement on their spend.

This is unusual for a state to offer more than one incentive program, at such disparate minimum spends, but it's great news for the indie filmmakers of that state. If you can put $100,000 together to spend, you're able to participate in a program that's usually reserved for much bigger projects. Now $100,000 is obviously a huge amount of money, but it shows that the state is cognizant of the smaller films that shoot within its borders.

It's not just at the state level where you can find incentives. They also have ...

A County Credit

If you shoot in St. Louis County, in Minnesota, you can qualify for additional money beyond the state credit. Their Production Incentive Program gives a production rebate of 25% on production and post-production costs spent in the county. Guess what the minimum spend is for this program? Ten thousand dollars! You can make a film for ten grand, and get $2,500 back, if you shoot it in St. Louis County! So now we're talking about films at our size.

But wait, it gets even better. Because within St. Louis County, there's also …

A City Credit

One of the most beautiful cities in St. Louis County is Duluth. It's home to the Catalyst Content Festival, one of the biggest independent television festivals in the country, it has beautiful waterfront views of Lake Superior – and it has a city-based film and television tax incentive program! The City of Duluth Production Incentive Program offers production rebates of up to 25% of production and post-production costs for film and television projects that are spent in the city. And this program also has a minimum spend of ten thousand dollars!

Now here's the best part. The incentives in Minnesota are what they call "stackable." So if you're filming and spending in an area that qualifies for more than one incentive, you can get them all! So if you have a $10,000 film you're making in Duluth, you qualify for both the City of Duluth Production Incentive AND the St. Louis County Production Incentive Program. This means that if you spend that ten thousand in Duluth, you could qualify to get up to $5,000 back.

Half price filmmaking!

(And entrepreneurial thinking.)

Making films at such a low budget level requires us to search for every possible advantage. And states like Minnesota are willing to help, because they realize the potential of the film and television industry to provide jobs and economic development for their residents. The filmmaker making a $10,000 film now might be making a $1 million film in a few years, so they want to support those Indigenous filmmakers as they try to grow the industry.

Make sure you find out if your community does, too.

Planning Far Ahead

As you prepare for physical production, it's vital that you consider every phase of filmmaking beyond the actual shooting of your film. The partners you choose can become part of every part of its life cycle and can provide benefits for both parties.

One of the best decisions I made when making RISING STAR was partnering with Patrick "Klokwize" O'Sullivan, a hip-hop musician from Hartford, Connecticut. I had learned about Klokwize from Gary Craig, one of our actors, and when I talked with him for the first time, he offered me something that blew me away: he said I could use any music of his that I wanted, for free! At the time, he had a few albums' worth of songs, and was working on a new album called HOOD HIPPIE: THE ALBUM, and he wanted to get the exposure that would come with a film's release. Because of his generosity, we were able to use seven of his songs on the soundtrack, making his raspy voice the soul of the film. (We also gave him a percentage of ownership in the film, but as I mentioned in the first chapter, that unfortunately didn't turn into any money. It's a mission of mine to work with him again, and pay him up front, as a thank you for everything he gave to us on RISING STAR.)

His willingness to work with us led me to start thinking about other ways we could include him. I learned he attended a performing arts high school (with one of our actors), and that he was a trained actor. So I decided I would write him into the film! The story's big finale has our two leads meeting up at a nightclub, and I wrote Klokwize performing one of his songs right before our lead female performs hip-hop for the first time. When we filmed, he was a total professional and was an energetic performer on screen every take we did. He was a pleasure to work with.

But once the film was finished, we still weren't done working together. Our lead actress, Emily Morse, is a musician herself, and he had the idea of doing a duet that could play over the film's ending credits. After we picture locked the film, they teamed up in the studio and recorded an incredible song, one that worked perfectly with picture. When we got our world premiere film festival, the Seattle True Independent Film Festival, he and his manager flew out with us for the premiere, and hosted a listening party for HOOD HIPPIE: THE ALBUM in town! That got the word out about the screening and helped us sell it out. And once our film festival run was done, he worked with us on its distribution, too; when we screened the film outdoors at Bushnell Park, the location included an open-air stage. Before the screening, we hosted a concert there, and he was our main act (with Emily as his opener!).

Because of his excitement for the project, Klokwize was a part of our production, post-production, and distribution. Those are the partnerships you want to make.

(Also, listen to Klokwize anywhere you find music online. He's a brilliant musician, and the epitome of an independent artist.)

Pre-Production for DEADBRAINS

The pre-production process for all films is usually the same list of jobs: scheduling, finding locations, getting cast and crew. But since we know we'll be putting a zombie war film together, there's a few things that could relate specifically to DEADBRAINS:

- A priority for this film would be to let the local police department know exactly where they'll be every day of the shoot. Having people in zombie makeup fighting all over the place is a recipe for a scared local resident to call you in. You want to make sure that when they do, the police can calmly tell them that it's just a movie shooting in town.
- Securing an army of zombies is a pretty heavy ask, especially for a microbudget film. Since we've already established relationships with the zombie groups around Memphis, we can approach them to be those extras, and potentially upgrade some of them to bigger roles, maybe featured extras, or even zombie military leaders. (I don't want to call them "speaking roles" per se, since, you know, zombies.)
- Because of the large amount of people that will be on set, they will need to be fed. I would reach out to restaurants that cater to young people, maybe ones that are close to colleges, and approach them for deals on meals. (Notice I didn't say pizza; I think I've eaten half the pizza in my life on film sets. Definitely do what you can to get good food for your people.)
- Looking for crew in Memphis wouldn't be a hard thing to do. There's a great organization called Cloud901 that provides filmmaking opportunities for high school students, so finding interns wouldn't be hard. The University of Memphis also has undergraduate and graduate film and video production programs, as well as a Film Club student organization, so there would be lots of young people interested in working on the project.
- Since we'd be shooting in Memphis, Tennessee, a look at the Tennessee Entertainment Commission's Website shows that their Grant Rebate program gives rebates up to 25% for production companies that spend at least $200,000 in Tennessee.[4] DEADBRAINS won't have that much money to spend, but the Memphis/Shelby County Film Commission offers discounted rates on Memphis police, discounted hotel production rates and after 30 days, you don't have to pay city/county hotel taxes.[5] So if there are out-of-town actors or crew as part of the production, you could get a little break on those expenses.

Interview: Hannah Black and Megan Peterson, Creators of DROUGHT

Actors and filmmakers Hannah Black and Megan Petersen met in a two-year Meisner acting program in 2014, where they quickly became business partners, collaborators, and best friends. With a desire to tell Southern stories and provide opportunities for Southeast actors, they decided to start their own production company, Same Page Pictures in Wilmington, North Carolina. In 2021, they released their first feature film, DROUGHT, which was executive produced by Mark & Jay Duplass. It went on to win multiple awards on the festival circuit and are currently in development on their second feature, a Southern gothic thriller.

Figure 7.3 Headshot of Hannah Black and Megan Peterson, creators of the film DROUGHT.

Marty Lang:	How did you guys decide to make DROUGHT in the first place? What was the origin of the film?
Hannah Black:	At the end of the two years of our acting class, we made a short film with our group. And we found out that we really loved working together and collaborating. So Megan and I made a short film directly after that, and it confirmed that we love working together. Then I came to her with the idea that would be DROUGHT. I said "I think there's a story about siblings. I think they're storm chasers." It's in the South, because we're Southern. We're really passionate about Southern stories. And I also used to work with students on the autism spectrum. So I said, I really want a character to be on the autism spectrum, because I feel like that's not represented in this industry, as much as I think it should be.

I thought this wasn't a short film; this was a feature. So how do we write a feature? We didn't know, so we got Save the Cat, we would meet every Tuesday night, map it out. And then I would go home, I would write five pages a day and send to Megan, she would look over it and give notes. And then after a month, we had our first script. And then over three years, we continued to rewrite more and more drafts until we landed on our final draft. |
| ML: | While you guys were writing, were you letting people in your community know that this was on the horizon? Were |

	you working to get people excited about it as you were writing?
Megan Peterson:	Yeah, sure. That first draft happened so quickly, we didn't really tell a lot of people about the first draft as we were writing it, because it just happened in a month. And then we thought it was awesome. So we said to some friends, we're gonna make this movie. We have friends within the industry that we really respect, and they read it and gave us notes. And that's when we took it back and started to rework it. We wanted to play the main characters in the film, and we were getting older. So we said, we've got to do this thing. Now let's really start telling people about it. I think that was when we were like, "Okay, we've got to figure out a way to make it." That means people have to know about it to get behind it. That was when we really started spreading the word.
ML:	Your crowdfunding campaign was a big part of that. You ended up running a Seed&Spark campaign, and it won the Hometown Heroes crowdfunding rally there in 2017, where you won a grant and support from the Duplass Brothers. How did that come together?
MP:	I had not heard of Seed&Spark. At that point we had a GoFundMe campaign for a different film we made. Then Hannah saw this article on No Film School that said the Duplass Brothers want to fund your feature film. And then we read about the parameters, about wanting to make a film in your hometown with your local cast and crew. And I was like, "Hold on Hannah, I think this would actually work." So putting the whole thing together was a lot of work. The pre-production to crowdfunding was one of the harder parts of it, basically, because at that point, we were new to filmmaking. So we didn't have the amount of email contacts that are helpful or necessary to have. And Seed&Spark gently told us that when they saw our goal was $24,000. We only had, like, 200 email contacts. They said you really need around 1,000. And you've got two weeks before you launch. They said, either lower your goal or get more emails. We said, "Okay, we'll get more emails." And I think we hit 850 people.

To find them, we used Facebook Messenger, we did everything. We were in a coffee shop and we would see someone and be like, "Oh, hey, you look like you like movies. Are you interested in helping us make ours?" We would be buying random stuff at a store for a launch party, and the cashier would be like, "Oh, you're throwing a party?" We said |

	"Yeah, we're making a movie. Would you like to give us your email address?" We were shameless.
ML:	Your crowdfunding campaign was successful, and then you won the Hometown Heroes rally. What happens after that? To the point when you're in active prep? How long did that take and what was going on during that time?
MP:	Hometown Heroes happened in November. And then we were in active prep and started production in August. So when we won in November, it took a few months. And I think in January, we did a full rewrite. And then we were back and forth for a couple of months with notes on the rewrite, and then it was locked in April.
HB:	Yeah, April or May. I think we originally wanted to shoot earlier in the summer, but the script just wasn't ready, which we were super grateful for. Mark Duplass really helped us pare down the script, so we can make it with the budget that we had. That meant paring down locations, and also cutting some characters that just weren't necessary. And even just shortening the script a little bit. We started crewing in June.
MP:	While all this was going on, we were looking for locations. And we were both working full time jobs. So we were doing it on the weekends or at night.
ML:	I read in one of the articles about the film that you worked a lot with a local man named Lee Carberry. Who is Lee? How did you meet Lee and how did he help you guys?
HB:	Oh my gosh, if Lee ever reads this book! He's such a character. We actually found Lee through one of our other locations. Our motel that we found, which is in White Lake, North Carolina, the owner's daughter was married to Lee. So he said, "My son in law Lee, you know, he's a city commissioner." And we met up with him and he took us around,
	He was so great. These small towns, if you're ever making a movie, and maybe you're in a city, like we are in Wilmington, but you have smaller towns outside of your area, the folks there were so kind, so excited, and so willing to help. We had a great time in these little towns. And Lee was really, really helpful. And in fact, we were going to shoot in a different field for our last scene of the movie. And for some reason, it didn't work. But Lee was like, "Let's go to this other field," and we're like, cool. Let's do it. And we shot it there. It was the most beautiful, perfect spot. So yeah, we're very lucky to have Lee.
ML:	What was it like looking for crew for the film? Did you guys have folks that you had already worked with?

MP: Yeah, sure. When we decided on our DP, Brad Walker, he helped us so much with connecting us with people who would be a good fit for our team. And what was cool is a lot of those folks were stepping up into a new role. So it helps us all learn, or gain new experience. But they're all awesome.

HB: I mean, when we were running the crowdfunding campaign. Brad texted me because I actually did like a commercial shoot with him. My boyfriend at the time, now husband, he was in a band and Brad was shooting him for this band. He messaged me and said "Hey, I want to shoot your movie." Now Brad Walker is a very established, very kind, very talented DP. And I was like, "Megan, Brad Walker wants to shoot our movie!" Like, what? This is crazy. And he really just connected us with pretty much everyone.

Then Michelle Roca, who was our unofficial pre-production supervisor, she worked at Lighthouse, a local production company at the time.

And our gaffer was John Knudson, so talented. He had just moved to Wilmington, like maybe two months prior. And he was on Craigslist. He saw this ad that was saying "Wanted: 1990s ice cream truck for feature film." And he was like, "What is this? I gotta figure this out." And so he looked into us. He was just like, "Hey, can I just meet with you guys? I'm in the film industry and don't have an ice cream truck. But I just want to meet you guys." And we met him. And we're like, we love this guy. He's amazing. And so he came on as our gaffer.

ML: Were there any other people who helped you as you were going through pre-production?

MP: The person who actually did get us an ice cream truck! His name is Garrett, and he owns it. We were looking for this ice cream truck, and Hannah pulled into a gas station. She told him about our story. He was filling up his truck with gas. And he's like, look, I got a truck that matches what you're looking for. Let's talk. So bless him. We had come to this agreement that during pre-production on Fridays and Saturdays, we would take the ice cream truck out and help sell ice cream. And then he would give it to us for free. So we're gonna run the truck on the weekends. And when we showed up to get the keys, he was like, "Look, I just want to give it to you guys." So we did not actually have to run it. But we would have! We were fully prepared. We were there to get the keys and learn the route.

ML: What's the best advice you guys can give to people who will be making their first feature film?

HB: I don't think I necessarily have advice. But I think something that really was important to us at the beginning of shooting DROUGHT, but also something that I will always, always, always bring in to anything else that I make, would be when you're creating, that when you're casting, finding people, that those people have the same vibe, and that you mesh well together. But I think more than that, having the same heart for what you're making. I know, it's cheesy, but if you find the people that are the kindest, and most fun to work with, it helps so much. Because at the end of the day, if you have someone who is the best at their job, but they're total jerks. It ruins the making of the film. And I think the product of the film is incredibly important. But I also think making it and the experience of that is just as important, because it's such a special experience that only a handful of people get to do. You want that experience to be memorable and wonderful and magical. I think finding the people that have the same heart as you do for making this movie, and kindness is the biggest thing.

MP: I love it. And I think mine might be just as cheesy, but it's just don't give up. It's friggin' hard. Like, it's really, really hard. Hard work. And there will be times that you question if it matters. It does, your voice matters. There's a reason you want to tell the story, no matter the genre, and somebody is going to need to watch it to know that they can tell their story, too. So I think from the person who was voted most shy in high school, that you can do it. And you will find your way. You don't have to do it like anyone else. You will have to be flexible, and change directions, and find a way that works for you to be able to do it. Yeah, that's my advice. Don't quit.

Notes

1 https://www.nist.gov/el/applied-economics-office/manufacturing/total-us-manufacturing/manufacturing-economy/total-us
2 https://www.motionpictures.org/what-we-do/driving-economic-growth/
3 https://mnfilmtv.org/incentives
4 https://www.tnentertainment.com/film/incentives/
5 https://www.filmmemphis.org/incentives

Reference List

Howe, Jeff. "The Rise of Crowdsourcing," *Wired Magazine*, 2006. https://www.wired.com/2006/06/crowds/

Pre-Production 135

Memphis/Shelby County, Tennessee Film Commission tax credit information. https://www.filmmemphis.org/incentives

Minnesota Office of Film and Television tax credit information. https://mnfilmtv.org/incentives

Motion Picture Association economic data. https://www.motionpictures.org/what-we-do/driving-economic-growth/

National Institute of Standards and Technology manufacturing data. https://www.nist.gov/el/applied-economics-office/manufacturing/total-us-manufacturing/manufacturing-economy/total-us

Tennessee Entertainment Commission tax credit information. https://www.tnentertainment.com/film/incentives/

8 Production and Post-Production

Once you've done all the work to build your audience, crowdsource and crowdfund your resources, and prep your film, there's just one thing left to do.

Actually make the thing.

Now in terms of effective production, a lot of the work should be done by this point. The script has been written so that there are no extraneous characters or storylines. The film has been scheduled in the most efficient way possible. You should have your transportation, food, and shot lists all figured out. So when you show up on set, the only thing you should worry about is getting the best performance from your actors, and the coverage you need for every scene.

This book isn't about directing, though, so the way you decide to direct, if you're in that position, is totally up to you. You can make sure your script is performed word for word, or you can allow improvisation through every scene. You can keep the camera still the whole time, or have it moving to follow your actors as they perform. You can use production design to create whole worlds, or you can show up to a location and film it the way you find it. That's all up to you.

In keeping with an entrepreneurial mindset, though, you want to make sure every part of your shoot is as efficient as possible. And there is one method you can use to make sure your shoot proceeds as smoothly as possible, moment to moment. It was taught to me when I started working in film.

And it's five letters long.

The BLRTS Process

B, L, R, T, S. It sounds like "blurts," and it's an acronym for the five steps you need to get through shooting a scene, while providing the most opportunities for all your crew to spot problems and fix them. Getting through each step will involve the director, the cinematographer, the

DOI: 10.4324/9781003295754-8

assistant director, and your actors, along with your crew. This is what each of the letters mean:

B is for Blocking. In addition to being the traffic officer on the set, the assistant director, or AD, is responsible for managing the time it takes to complete shots and scenes, as well as announcing the calls through the BLRTS process. When the director and actors begin their work, creating the blocking for a scene, the AD will oversee it, and keep the crew quiet. When they're ready, the AD will call a blocking rehearsal, where the actors will go through the scene, showing all the movement they'll do. Once it's done, the AD will cue the cinematographer to go through the shots the scene needs (wide shots, closeups, etc.) This is vitally important for all the departments on the film, because this is the first time they're seeing the scene as it will be filmed. This will allow them to plan, knowing exactly how the scene will happen, and to discover issues and problems they can address before the cameras are rolling. Once that's done, the AD will release the actors, and the crew will begin to light the scene.

L is for Lighting. Once the actors are released, the AD will meet with the director and cinematographer, and determine how long it will take for the crew to prep the lighting, production design, and other elements the scene needs. (This time will be determined by the shot list and schedule.) Once the time is determined, the AD will be pleasantly persistent with the crew, to make sure they stick to that time, and keep on schedule. When the scene is lit, the AD will bring the actors back to set, and they'll begin to rehearse.

R is for Rehearsal. When the director and actors are ready to rehearse, the AD will tell the crew, "quiet, please," so they can work without noise. The AD will call "rehearsal is up," to let everyone know it is about to begin, and then the director will call "action" to begin the rehearsal. The director will call "cut" when the rehearsal is finished, and the AD will repeat that, saying "cut on rehearsal." This continues until the director is ready to shoot. But crew members may find things they want to change, so they'll have an opportunity to tweak things.

T is for Tweaking. If the cinematographer wants to tweak things after a rehearsal, or another department finds a problem they need to fix (like if the sound mixer needs to plant another microphone), the AD must find out how long the tweaks will take to complete. Once a time is established, the AD will be pleasantly persistent in finding out how they're coming along, to stay on schedule. Once the tweaks are done, the director can then move to shooting.

S is for Shooting. When the director is ready to do a take, the AD will call "quiet please," to make sure the actors can perform without noise. When everyone is ready, the AD will call "picture is up," so the crew knows they are about to record a take. After this, the AD will check with the two departments responsible for recording, the sound and camera departments. The AD will call out "sound ready?" to the sound team. They will respond "sound speeding" once they are recording sound. Once sound is recording, the AD will call out "camera ready?" to the camera team. They will respond "camera speeding," once the camera is recording. Once camera and sound are both recording, the AD does not call action. The director will call "action" after the camera is recording. When the director feels the shot is complete, they will call "cut," and the AD will follow up with "that's a cut on action." Once the shot is complete, the AD will confer with the director to see if another take is needed, or if they can move on. If the director is happy, the crew moves on to the next shot in the scene, or the next scene in the film.

And this process continues, one shot at a time, one scene at a time, until the entire movie is filmed.

The Story of Your Shoot

When principal photography begins, obviously, shooting the film will be your biggest priority. You have the responsibility to your audience to complete the film, because that's what got them involved with you in the first place. Even though your most important job will be shooting the film, you also need to realize there's a group of people that are excited about it – and want to know how things are going. Keeping in touch with your audience during production and post-production is an incredibly important part of the process.

Providing crowdfunding backer updates during production should be something your team plans for. And any person involved with the production can be the one who creates them. When we shot RISING STAR, we were able to post 15 public backer updates (and four more private backer updates, only for our backers) over the 18 days of the shoot. Those updates included all kinds of activities beyond just shooting the film, and we used them as opportunities to teach our audience more about the filmmaking process, along with introducing them to the people helping us create it. We had backer videos that included:

- A commemoration of the first completed shot of the movie
- Me taking a shot of wheatgrass at Alchemy, a juice bar that we used as a location, along with a quick interview with Imani, the owner (and cameo actor!)
- Our assistant director playing dance critic, explaining the level of dance skill our two lead actors have (we filmed a dance scene at a local park that day)

Production and Post-Production 139

- Our lead actor highlighting our on-set lunches (we decided to have Meatless Mondays on set, to help with the environment)
- Our lead actor documenting local folks playing drums, and our attempts to get them to stop so that we could record good sound
- Our lead actor giving a tour of ArtSpace, another location we filmed at, and interviewing the loft owner who let us film in his home – and who painted a painting of our lead actress to use in the movie! (We had no idea he had done it. We saw it for the first time the day we showed up to film.)
- Our sound mixer and boom operator teaching about room tone, the quiet, ambient sound that must be recorded at the end of every scene
- A commemoration of the final shot of the movie

Your videos could include literally anything; these are just examples of what we did. As long as your backers and audience have an opportunity to follow what you're doing, you're on the right track. And don't forget to post those videos on social media – posting on YouTube first is usually the easiest way to repost on other platforms – because people can catch an on-set video and become interested in the film, even if they had nothing to do with your crowdfunding. You'll want those people on board as you build excitement later, when the film is released.

Transparency in Post

Once your film is finished (and especially if you've run a crowdfunding campaign for post-production), your audience will want to see the process of the film coming together. This phase is something a lot of people don't know as much about; production is something that's more recognizable to them. You have an opportunity to educate your audience by walking them through the process. While we were in post-production on STAY WITH ME, we were able to come up with some interesting update videos. While editor Jessie Green and I were editing, I did an update right before we picture locked, showing the entire 80-minute timeline of the movie, before showing a completed scene from the movie. Once we picture locked, I recorded the spotting session between me and our sound designer (I was in Tennessee and he was in California, so it was all on Zoom). We were able to show backers the discussions a director has with their post-sound team, pointing out lines of dialogue that need to be re-recorded, new lines that must be recorded for the first time, and sound effects ideas. When we were doing ADR with the actors, we recorded a Zoom ADR session with our actress Addison Turner, so backers could see how she was literally putting her own words back into her mouth as she performed. The video also showed me directing Addison, changing her performance over multiple takes, to get different versions of her lines. I got a few emails from backers, thanking me for that video, because they had never seen that process before. We didn't get a chance to make any backer updates focusing on the color correction of the film, but that's another great chance to teach your audience. Showing stills before they're corrected and after they're corrected could be a great chance to show your audience how your film is evolving.

There were also other opportunities to contact backers in post, as we created marketing materials for the film. Backers got exclusive access to the first trailer we made, and our poster, before the rest of the world got to see it. We also made two different trailers for the film, so as we're getting ready for distribution, one thing we could do is show our backers both trailers, try to find out which one they like better, and what type of movie each trailer suggests the film will be. Getting this type of information from your audience is a fantastic way to identify problems in your marketing ... or in your film.

The Incredible Opportunities of Focus Groups

When RISING STAR made the deal to shoot in the Mark Twain House, we agreed to host a focus group screening in their museum, where they could sell tickets and keep the revenue, as a tradeoff for a break on the fee to shoot in the house. That screening would be of a version of the film, but not the final, locked edit of it. This would not only be an opportunity for the Mark Twain House to raise money, but an opportunity for our filmmaking team to see how we'd been addressing major story points in the edit, as well as how much an audience likes certain characters. We were so lucky to have about 275 people show up for the screening, and they were all ages, genders, and ethnicities. So we were able to get a real cross section of people, and data that we could trust.

We distributed a feedback form to the audience that attended. We handed it out on physical paper and pencils, and also had a Google form that audience members could fill out online. (This was in 2011, though; nowadays, the Google form would definitely be the only method we'd use, since everyone has smartphones.) Here are the questions we asked:

1 What is your age?

   a 13–17
   b 18–24
   c 25–29
   d 30–39

e 40–49
 f 50–59
 g 60+

2 What city and state do you live in?
3 Gender:

 a Male
 b Female
 c Other

4 Ethnicity:

 a Caucasian
 b African-American
 c Hispanic
 d Asian
 e Other

5 Did you enjoy the film?

 a Yes
 b No

6 Were there any parts of the film you particularly liked?

 a Yes (prompt for writing)
 b No

7 Were there any parts of the film you particularly disliked?

 a Yes (prompt for writing)
 b No

8 Did the story make sense to you?

 a Yes
 b No (prompt for writing)

9 Did the ending of the film make sense to you?

 a Yes
 b No (prompt for writing)

10 Were there any unanswered questions after watching the film?

 a Yes (prompt for writing)
 b No

11 Please place an X in the box that best describes the likability of each character (1 X per character) Table 8.1

Table 8.1 RISING STAR characters and degrees of likability in the film

	Very likable	Likable	Neither likable nor unlikable	Unlikable	Very unlikable
Chris					
Alyza					
Brent					
The Boss					
Jaime					
Isabel					

12 How do you think Chris and Alyza met?

   a Local bar
   b Online dating site
   c At a party

13 Who do you think is 3XL?

   a Chris
   b Brent
   c The Boss
   d Jaime

14 Do you think Chris and Alyza had sex at Brent's party?

   a Yes
   b No

15 Do you think Chris and Alyza are going to stay together?

   a Yes
   b No

16 Where do you think Chris lost his keys? (prompt for writing)

17 What do you think Chris learns over the course of the movie? (prompt for writing)

18 What do you think Alyza learns over the course of the movie? (prompt for writing)

19 What do you think Chris fears the most? (prompt for writing)

20 Who do you think was calling Alyza over the course of the movie? (prompt for writing)

21 What would you suggest to make the movie better? (prompt for writing)

22 We love our fans, aka Stars!, and we'd like you to be a part of our teaser trailer. It will be made up of responses to the following question: "What don't you like about your job?" (prompt for writing)

As you can see, there's a number of questions about how much the audience member liked the film, a scale on how much the person liked all the major characters, and questions about certain story points. There were specific reasons for why we asked these questions, and they all had to do with clarity, and the ability for an audience to understand the entire story. If there was an element that an audience didn't get, or was confused on, that could pull them out of the film. That's something we didn't want.

Thankfully, a majority of the audience members who filled this out liked the film, either very much, or a normal amount. So generally, we thought we were on the right track. We received some interesting data from the scale about character likability, though. It turned out a lot of people didn't like Alyza, our lead female character. Multiple people pointed out how much she laughed, and that she seemed especially annoying. That was something we missed, so after the screening, we were able to go back and edit out a lot of her laughing, so that she didn't seem as much of a "manic pixie dream girl," as one audience member called her. And the story questions clarified that we edited the film in a way that audience members could follow most of the important relationships, like how Chris and Alyza met, and who 3XL was (spoiler alert: it was Brent, played by THE AMAZING SPIDER-MAN actor Michael Barra). There was one question that no one knew the answer to, though: how Chris lost his keys. This is a vital piece of the plot as it leads to everything else Chris does throughout the weekend of the film. There's a point where Chris is at a bar, and he drops them on the ground, but no one noticed that in the focus group screening. We then went into the sound design of the film afterwards, and raised the volume of the keys falling to the ground in the bar. That helped more people realize that was the point where the keys were lost.

Thankfully, the audience was able to pick up on the things that both lead characters learned over the course of the story; Chris learned that he can have a work/life balance that isn't completely tilted toward work, and Alyza learned that she can find one thing that she loves and focus on that, instead of spreading herself so thin in doing all sorts of different things that she loves. This was an important thing for me, and I felt good seeing the responses to those questions. I got that across very early in the edit.

One other thing we did was to give an opportunity for audience members to be a part of our teaser trailer, by asking them to tell us what they didn't like about their job. We were able to take some of those quotes, and put them into that teaser, which came out later that spring. We got answers like "The 9 to 5 part," "The vacuum, the emptiness," and "I would like a job ... stinkin' economy." The responses we got to that question confirmed that we had struck a nerve with a film about work/life balance.

The beauty of these focus group screenings is that you don't only need just one. You can show as many cuts of the film as you want as you progress through post-production. It's preferable that you show each new version to new audiences, though, for two reasons. First, you can get more objective feedback when you're always showing the film to people who've never seen it before. But just as importantly, every time you show it to a new audience, that's a new group of people who could potentially come back to see it when it's completely finished! When I lived in Los Angeles, I loved going to focus group screenings, and then seeing the finished films later. It's so interesting seeing how the films evolve, and seeing an earlier cut of the film can give you some insight into how the filmmakers put their vision together.

Creating Film-Adjacent Content

In terms of publicity, production and post-production are the phases where there's the least video-worthy things going on. I mean, sound design is fascinating, but you can only watch so much footage of people sitting down at their computers, talking on Zoom calls. While your film is being shot and put together, you need to figure out more ways to keep your audience engaged with the film. Creating content that's related to the film is the best way to do it.

When we were in post on RISING STAR, we accidentally fell into a cool way to keep people excited about the film. One of the perks we had in our Kickstarter campaign was an "Awesome Video," where producer Matt Giovannucci and actor Michael Barra created original videos based on questionnaires filled out by backers – and the videos were all about how awesome the backer was. When the campaign was going on, we were able to make five or six of them, but with the tight schedule for shooting, we stopped making them once we got into production. When we got into post-production, that opened up a little bit of time, so we got back to making the other 13 videos we needed to make. Each time we made a video, we promoted it on both our film's social media channels and our own personal ones. These videos were very popular; the people we made them for spread them all over the place on social media, and whenever someone watched them, we made sure to have a link back to the film's Web site, which created fresh traffic for us throughout post-production. The Awesome Videos started off as simple ones – Matt and Michael wrote a song about how awesome one backer was in one of them, and Michael impersonated a celebrity in another – but as we went along, more people started watching them, so they got more complex. We even made an animated video for one backer, and we made another video that turned into a five minute, mini-true crime "documentary." People who didn't even know the subjects of the videos wanted to see the new ones – those were people we brought on to the project who had nothing to do with the crowdfunding campaign. We were building our audience, even while the film was being edited and sound designed.

But the content you create could be almost anything, so long as it has some tangential tie to your film. You could create a podcast talking about independent film, where you can mention your project during each episode, as you make your way through production and post. You could create a Web series that follows a supporting character in your film (or maybe repurpose scenes that don't make your final cut and create short films from that footage). Anything that keeps the name of your film in the ether is enough for the possibility of attracting new fans to your team.

Production and Post for DEADBRAINS

When a zombie film is in production, the type of content you can create is pretty self-explanatory. Following a zombie extra as they're put into makeup, a group of zombie extras learn how to "accurately" walk and hunt, or the sound team as they record sounds of zombies screaming are all cool ideas for video updates while the film is shooting. Interviewing the owners of the locations where the film is shot is a good idea, especially if they own a location that the zombie community spends time at, outside of the film. As the main zombie actors work, talking with them about how they get into the mind of a zombie military leader could be a fun look at how an actor works.

Once the film is finished shooting and in post, updates can include all the things we talked about in the chapter. But focus group screenings can be a big help in making sure the audience feels like the zombie characters are smarter than the human ones. Since this intelligence is what makes DEADBRAINS unique, you want to be sure it's communicated very clearly. If the audience feels like the movie doesn't get that across, that's a problem. The filmmakers would want to be sure they've clearly shown how smart the zombies are.

This type of movie could also give a cool opportunity to create film-adjacent narrative content. Television shows like THE WALKING DEAD and FEAR THE WALKING DEAD created a number of successful webisode seasons that told stories of minor characters. Something like that could work here as well – especially if we took the opposite point of view and made a zombie character the lead character of the webisodes. Perhaps a military character who's not at the head of the zombie army, but also has ambitions of leading the army of the undead. Might make an interesting drama.

Interview: Director/Cinematographer Noam Kroll

Figure 8.1 Headshot of director/cinematographer Noam Kroll.

Noam Kroll is a Los Angeles-based narrative filmmaker, known for his incredibly DIY approach to the craft. Over the past decade, Noam has written, directed, shot, and edited numerous acclaimed short and feature projects that have screened at international film festivals, including his microbudget features SHADOWS ON THE ROAD and PSYCHOSYNTHESIS. Committed to sharing his expertise, Noam reaches millions of filmmakers each year through his popular podcast, "Show, Don't Tell," newsletter, "Micro-Budget Weekly," and his personal filmmaking blog, NoamKroll.com.

Marty Lang:	You come from a technical background, working as a cinematographer and colorist. How important is it for independent filmmakers to understand the technology that they're using to make their films?
Noam Kroll:	I think it's very important. I think there are a lot of filmmakers that fall into one of two categories. Some believe it's all about story, and we shouldn't focus on gear, that doesn't really matter. And then there's the gear people. And they're kind of dismissive of how important the story is. Of course, the story is important, what you want to tell, but the equipment that you're using is critical in order to tell that story, and to tell it the way that you want to. To have the most well-rounded, holistic approach to filmmaking, I think you want to embrace storytelling, but also technical. Now that doesn't mean you need to become a full time DP or understand every single feature that's included in DaVinci Resolve, or anything like that. But I do think at a bare minimum, what it means is that you understand what technology you need in order to achieve your vision, which may be as simple as an iPhone. Because if you don't understand what technology you need, you'll assume that you need the best thing. And that may prevent you from making your movie, because you think you can only make a good movie with an Alexa or with a RED or whatever. But you don't know that you can download the new Blackmagic app on your iPhone, or Filmic Pro, and you can shoot in you know, RAW log. You can use your phone, or you can use a mirrorless camera, or whatever tool is the best way for you. So I think that understanding the technical component of filmmaking is important. It can very much liberate your ability to make films, because you'll know what you need, but more importantly, what you don't need.
ML:	Let's talk a little bit specifically about cinematography. What are some of the things to keep in mind when trying to create a visual plan that can fit a microbudget?
NK:	When you're choosing a camera, it's all about the utility. It's not about the resolution, or the dynamic range, or any of those other things that do matter. We've been sold by marketing from camera manufacturers whose job is to sell you more cameras, not necessarily to make you a better filmmaker. There's no shortage of cameras; you can go into Best Buy and buy any camera off the shelf, use your phone, you can make something beautiful with anything. But is it the right format and use case for your particular movie? For example, when I started my last

feature film DISAPPEARING BOY, I had my Alexa Classic, which is a big, bulky camera, sitting here, and I chose not to use that because if I chose that camera, I wouldn't be able to shoot anywhere I wanted. I couldn't just knock off a shot with one actor at the beach one day, or I couldn't sit in the backseat of the car without an AC. It came down to why am I choosing the camera? Is it because I want to tell people the movie was shot on Alexa? Or is it because I want to have the best camera for not just the story, but my production? So I ended up shooting on my little Fuji X T4 because I knew that camera so well. I had one lens – I shot the entire movie on a 50 millimeter vintage Leica lens. And it just made it so much more fun, so much easier.

I think your job as the filmmaker, first and foremost, is to determine what your story is, what production scope you have, and then what camera will best serve both of those things. And if you're operating yourself, like I have on some of my films, then what's the easiest for you? I could operate my Fuji and not even look at it. I just know where the dials are. But if I switch to a Sony that might have superior stabilization, I'm going to spend an hour each day figuring out what I'm doing with the menus. All those things are very important to consider.

ML: How about lighting? What insight can you give about lighting on microbudget productions?

NK: I always suggest that filmmakers take a less is more approach, especially if you do not come from a lighting background or cinematography background. I think a huge mistake that filmmakers make on microbudget productions is trying to emulate big feature film lighting without having the right lights, or without having the right crew, trying to either do it themselves or with somebody who's understaffed.

If I can shoot entirely with natural light, that's what I'm going to do. Because, in my opinion, when it's done well, natural light is the most organically, aesthetically pleasing, beautiful light. That's why Terrence Malick and many other filmmakers prefer to shoot with it. That doesn't mean it's always the easiest – there's other workarounds you need to know, how to shape natural light, what time of day to shoot at, how to use windows to your advantage, that kind of thing. But it's generally easier to work with natural light and get good results than it is with traditional film lighting, especially if you're not experienced in the lighting department.

If I can shoot natural light, I will, but if I can't, how do I augment the natural light to be as simple as possible? That's usually just a single light source. So if I had to choose one light to shoot everything on, I would probably just take a soft LED panel or, if I had the room to walk around with it, a China ball with some black wrap on the back, to control the spill. That can make your movie look like a million bucks. No exaggeration, it's just the lightest, so soft, it's so natural. And it's very warm and inviting.

You don't want to overcomplicate things, because the second that you start doing traditional three-point lighting, on these microbudget productions, we usually don't have the resources to do that well. So what ends up happening is you turn on one light, a key light, and it looks good. And then you put on a hair light, and it looks good. But now there's spill, and you're trying to control the spill. Now a seasoned DP and a grip and a gaffer, they know exactly what to do in these scenarios to keep moving. But when you're shooting without the resources, that's usually not the best use of your time.

ML: You make your films with small crews, sometimes as small as just you. What are the benefits and drawbacks of crews that small, and how do you arrive at that decision about how big your crew should be?

NK: That's a great question. To me, crew size largely comes down to how many days do I have to shoot the movie? And those two things very much go hand in hand. I shot a feature film a couple of years back called PSYCHOSYNTHESIS, which was in two locations, and the movie was written for two locations. And I knew that in order to have good locations, I'd need to pay a decent amount to rent them. I would basically have to shoot the whole movie in nine days, so it was going to be fast, because it had to be shot that quickly. And because there were only two locations, that essentially meant that I needed a slightly more traditional crew configuration. Because we were going to operate like most other nine day feature film projects.

But my film DISAPPEARING BOY, I knew that it was written in a way where there were so many different locations, it was basically written in tandem with the editing. We wrote, shot, edited, back and forth, over the course of a year. I knew there was no way for that film to have a traditional crew. The only real way to do it was if I shot everything myself, and treated it more like a documentary project, in a weird way.

So the first step is identifying your story, and realistically, how many days, based on your budget, you'll be shooting. If you're shooting for more than 10 or 12, maybe 15 days at most, you probably want to scale things back significantly, so that you have the bandwidth and the time to be looser with your production. Generally, I prefer the smaller, the better. And it's not an anti-collaborative thing, I think it's pro-collaboration, because my biggest fear when I worked with no crew, I didn't think I'd have people pushing back and sharing new ideas. I leaned into the actors, and they became such an integral part of the process. They're just as much the filmmakers on this movie as I am. We met every day, they read every script and gave me notes, we rehearsed, we did so many things together. Even down to when we're shooting, they would help me come up with camera angles and ideas. There's this sort of misconception that if you do something with a smaller crew, or with no crew, then that means you're lacking collaboration. That's what I thought. I actually think one of the benefits, if you choose to lean into it, is that you can have a deeper collaboration with the actors. Unlike on most sets, where the director is usually huddled over at the monitor with the DP and the actors are in many ways an afterthought. That doesn't make any sense to me, because the actors are the movie. That should be the number one thing. So this allows you to be as connected to the actors as possible.

    I think the drawback of doing something on a very small scale, is you have to have a lot of self-motivation. You don't have a partner in crime, or a team looking at the footage with you saying, "No, it's great," you know, getting you riled up. You must dig deep for that self-motivation, especially if you shoot it the way that I did, over the course of a year. We shot the first day, and then there was three weeks until we shot the second day. And in those three weeks, I'm like, "Is this gonna be a movie? Or did I just shoot a few shots?" It wasn't until eight months into it that I was like, "Okay, this is going pretty well." On the flip side, having a slightly larger crew, like a 15-person crew, the benefit of that is you have more control over visual aesthetics. So if you want to do a dolly move, or you want to do a zoom, or just light in a more specific way, you do have the extra crew to do that without it looking bad or taking too long.

ML: Let's talk about post. What tips do you have for streamlining the post process?

NK: If there's one thing, it's sound. It always comes down to sound. Get good sound on set, get wild lines, record actual sound effects, like doors opening, on set, record room tone. And use that to drive your edit in post, because for most people, sound is an afterthought. It's not just about getting good audio, it's about leading your edit with the audio because otherwise, we pick the prettiest shots, and we pick the angles that we spent time on camera, or whatever the effect is that we want to showcase. And then we try to get the audio to match with that. We sacrifice audio in that process, because we're choosing takes where the performances might not be as good. If you can really prioritize your sound bed, that paves the way for everything. And that doesn't mean you have to do a ton of ADR. It's almost more of a mental shift, of thinking about your job as editing a soundtrack that has visuals attached. It's not really the other way around.

So much of production comes down to the organization, whether it's in camera and on set or in post, making sure that bins are set up with your folder structure, the way that your files are tagged, syncing everything up first. So many of us are just so eager to dive right in and start editing, and then we get halfway through the movie, and then our system won't run because we didn't generate proxy files on day one, because we were so eager to start! If we just did the proxies up front, we'd be fine. Now we must go back and do those and relink everything.

If you're shooting in any 4k or 6k format, and you don't have the computer system to play that back, then generate proxy files. Give yourself and your system some bandwidth to work with. I have a pretty good system, and I shot on a Fuji XD4, and it still takes a while to open up the project file and edit. You're gonna run into bottlenecks and technical issues. So try to mitigate that up front.

ML: What's the most important advice you can give for someone going into production on their first large scale indie project?

NK: No matter if you have a small or a large crew, the most important thing is that you surround yourself with the right people, the people that understand what you're doing. People that you like to be around, and they like to be around you. And then it can feel like a genuine collaboration, that's fun and enjoyable for everybody. Because if it's not, then there's no point. If we wanted to work on things we didn't enjoy, we wouldn't be making art. The longer I do this, the more I just want to work with people that are fun, where I value them, and they value me. If you can find the right people, you can solve almost any problem, and you can come up with the best ideas. We're not working on movies with 200 person crews, where you don't even know the names of the PAs. That's not how I want to work. That's not where I think good work is born out of.

Also, don't take it too seriously. I've made the mistake of taking things very seriously, and stressing myself out to the point where it was not sustainable. I would finish a movie and not be able to work on anything for months, because I was getting sick, stressed out, and my body was worn down. That's just not sustainable. And it doesn't make the final product better. You don't have to feel like you're suffering in order for the movie to be good. You can just have fun, be around good people. Sometimes it's going to come out the way you want. Sometimes it's not, but you can at least control your own energy and feeling on set, and the other people that you surround yourself with. I think that generally in creativity, good things are born out of casual and fun environments. So if you can embody that, I think that's always a good choice.

9 Marketing

You've finished your film! Congratulations!

Your work is now half done.

With apologies to the old saying about the tree in the woods, if a movie is released and no one knows about it, does it really exist?

I'd argue no.

Letting people know about your film is the most effective way for them to see it, and that marketing work has to be done by someone. Movie studios have entire departments dedicated to marketing their films, and they have every possible advantage:

- They can spend hundreds of millions of dollars, and years upon years, building their brand (Hello, Marvel Studios!)
- They can partner with major brands for their releases (whenever a James Bond movie comes out, you'll see Heineken ads, starring Bond, plastered all over your TV)
- They can bring major movie stars into their campaigns (the first two Deadpool movies had the benefit of including Hugh Jackman in their marketing, even before he was cast in DEADPOOL & WOLVERINE)

So they can do pretty much whatever they want.

We can't.

For microbudget film marketing, we need to focus our efforts on using elements we can create and utilize. I can think of five of them:

- Crowdsourcing work
- Digital marketing
- Digital advertising
- Press elements
- Trailers and posters

Let's find out more about how we can use these tools.

DOI: 10.4324/9781003295754-9

Re-engaging the Engaged

In the studio world, a longtime marketing practice is to determine who the audience is for a film while it's being made. Marketing executives can sometimes be in the room with the creatives actually making the movie (especially if toys and merchandise are involved). Their goal is to maximize the reach of the film to the people they think will be most likely to watch it.

Indie filmmakers don't have the luxury of waiting even that long. Right from the first glimmer of an idea, you need to be thinking about who your audience will be.

But since you're reading this book, you already know that information! Thanks to the crowdsourcing work you've already done, you know who your audience is, where they gather, in person and online, and you've gotten them to take part in some part of the film's creation, whether it's by having them contribute to a crowdfunding campaign, watch social media about the film, or take part in an event related to it.

If those folks have been kept aware throughout the filmmaking process, they should be excited to find out that the film is finished, and that it will be coming out soon. (You might have offered a perk in your crowdfunding campaign, where those who backed at a certain amount could see the finished film first. That's a great way to seed excitement about a release. Think of it as the film equivalent of advance copies of new books.) If they haven't brought their friends and family to the film through the crowdfunding campaign, this is the perfect time for them to let those people know about the film, and its upcoming release.

Since our audience for RISING STAR was in touch with us all the way through the completion of the film, once we got our eventual distribution deal, it was easy for us to re-engage our people to get excited about its release on Amazon Prime. I made a video at the Mark Twain House, breaking the great news to everyone, and within a day of the video being posted on Kickstarter and emailed to our backers, I received dozens of emails from backers and friends, excited about seeing it. A big reason we were able to get that kind of response was because we had stayed in touch with them all through the filmmaking process. Since we kept them in the loop, they felt the excitement we did, after all the hard work and challenges we went through.

In addition to your backers, you can re-use the public relations information you did during your crowdfunding campaign to help expand your audience, too. If there are print magazines that focus on the subject of your film, their subscribers can be part of your target audience. You can reach out to those magazines and ask them for their subscriber demographics. Are they mostly men or women? Do they have jobs? What's their income? Where do they live? You can use that information to help create audience profiles, along with the information you gathered while preparing for your crowdfunding campaign.

Expanding Your Digital Footprint

You'll have social media infrastructure built at this point because of your crowdfunding work, but you'll need to increase your online presence when you get to the marketing phase. And the biggest piece of that is creating a website for your film. Since everything online is so accessible, you need to bring all your Internet traffic to one specific point of sale and turn those visitors into paying customers. Your film's Website will be that point of sale. It will give information about your film, provide related media (trailer, poster, behind the scenes photo and video), links to the film's social media accounts, and anything else you feel would be relevant.

But the most important aspect of your film's website is that it must offer some way for visitors to actually purchase the film. Even if the film is available on multiple platforms, it's vital that all those platforms be available through the site. That way, the choice of where to watch the film belongs to the customer.

You also need to have a strong call to action about the movie – and make sure it's at the top of the front page of the site. Whether they access the film by desktop or by mobile, you want to give your visitors a simple way to see the film is for sale, and a simple way for them to buy it.

If you go to the official Website for SKINAMARINK, you'll see a really simple layout, and a very clear call to action (http://www.skinamarink.com/).[1] The front page is a rotating loop of ten short video clips from the movie, which gives off a really creepy vibe. But the text over those videos does all the work here: it says SKINAMARINK, NOW STREAMING ON SHUDDER, along with a link to a page where you can buy tickets to see it in a theater. That's simple, evocative of the film's tone, and gives you two different ways to see the film, without even having to scroll down on the front page.

You might be wondering why a website would be created this late in the process, and it's a fair question. My personal opinion is that you don't want to confuse potential audience members as you go through the process of making your film. If you're running a crowdfunding campaign, the only site you want people coming to is the campaign page. Having a website at that stage, for example, could confuse potential backers as to where they're supposed to go – they could ask "I'm interested in contributing. Do I go from a social media platform to the campaign page, or the website?" Keep it simple and put the website out only when you need it.

Always Be Tracking

Remember how when we were crowdfunding, a big part of outreach was testing your message, to make sure it was resonating with your backers? You can do the same thing with your digital marketing ideas. The only way for you to know if an idea works is to test it. Ever notice how big movies are sometimes advertised as one type of film, but then changed to be advertised as something completely different? Maybe you see a trailer for an action film, but then see another trailer, where the film is now a love story? That's because marketers are always testing movie messaging in front of test audiences. It's so important to remember: the audience, and not the filmmaker, will determine what aspects of the film are the most interesting and engaging.

You can also add tracking tools to your Website, and based on the data you get from them, you can modify your site to influence the activity of your visitors. They can provide information to you in a few major areas:

- Visitor behavior: how long visitors spend on certain pages, where people click, and how that behavior differs by user type, demographic, or the referring source for the visitor (how they found their way to your site)
- Visitor identity: Most tracking tools can't identify individual users, but they can identify the region they come from, company IP addresses, and other information about site visitors
- Website analytics: Page views, session duration (how long they're on your page), and bounce rate (how many visitors leave your site after viewing only one page)

Using those tools can help you communicate your story in the most engaging way possible.

Creating Relevant Content

One big way you can generate marketing without paying much is to create your own content that will drive traffic to your Website. And once they're there, your simple call to action on the front page will turn those visitors into customers. You can do that by utilizing SEO, or search engine optimization, to ensure your Website appears high up on lists of search engine results. You can research and select certain keywords that are popular in content, and make sure you use them in yours. You'll want to use those keywords across your Website, in your blog posts, and meta descriptions of assets you might upload, like trailers and posters. Once you know the SEO keywords that fit best with your film, story, or genre, you can create targeted content on your site, to drive traffic there. That content can be text-based, audio or video – and the key to it is making sure that it offers something educational to your audience, related to your film. Think of all the backer updates you generated during your crowdfunding campaign. You could repurpose those, and include those SEO keywords, and it can help drive more traffic.

You can also look beyond your Website to find places for your SEO-infused content to live. Articles on external blogs or magazines is one excellent way to build SEO buzz. Low-cost advertisements, on sites like Facebook, Instagram, Google, or TikTok, can incorporate those keywords. Even if you put a trailer, poster, press release, or EPK (electronic press kit) out, naming your files with SEO keywords can help drive traffic, too.

You've also got the same big tool you had during crowdfunding: email. You can send targeted emails out to different portions of your audience. Depending on what messages different audience segments respond to, if you're making a romantic comedy set in high school, you could send different messages to:

- Fans of romantic comedies
- Your friends from high school
- People who live in the town in which you filmed

And each of those messages can include SEO keywords as well.

Here's a few examples of materials we created for RISING STAR. We wrote up a press release for the Connecticut premiere of the film, I wrote a blog post for Film Courage, the website run by the filmmakers of GOODBYE PROMISE, and our production designer created an EPK that gave a lot of information about the film, and the people involved. You'll see many of the items I've talked about in previous chapters, in terms of how we put the film together, and different ways we engaged our audience.

Press Release

"Rising Star" Red Carpet Movie Premiere Illuminates Hartford
   7:00 pm – August 3rd – Connecticut Science Center
   On August 3rd, The Connecticut Film Festival presents "Rising Star." The revolutionary and very independent film is making its Red Carpet Premiere when it graces the screen of the Connecticut Science Center in downtown Hartford. Writer/Director Marty Lang's film "Rising Star" was filmed entirely on location in Hartford, utilizing many of the city's major architectural landmarks and scenic parks. The Red Carpet begins at 6:00 pm, with the film and after party starting at 7:00 pm.
   Rising Star is not your typical romantic comedy. It's about living carefree, finding your bliss, and feeding your passions. It's also about drowning in

fear and anxiety, but most importantly, it's about letting nature take its course, and letting opposites attract, to create balance.

The film is about Chris, an overworked 20-something insurance adjuster who must decide between his job and his passion. Alyza is a carefree opposite who writes poems, counts beats, and lets the bills pile. The two couldn't be further apart on what is and isn't important in life. But after 24 hours together, they both learn a thing or two about each other, themselves, and their passions.

Making a Rising Star

The making of Rising Star began in 2009, when writer/director Marty Lang saw the independent film "Medicine for Melancholy" at the IFC Center in New York City. After that, Lang wrote the script over the next year while visiting Hartford cultural landmarks and neighborhoods.

Lang quickly found out that while writing a script is one thing, raising funds for even a microbudget film is another. Fundraising began with a Kickstarter campaign in mid-August 2010, and lasted for 45 days. When it was completed, the production had raised $15,211 from 176 backers. These backers were family members of the filmmakers and actors, graduates of the Connecticut Film Industry Training Program, and independent film fans worldwide who found out about the project on Twitter. One backer even gave $2,000 to the project. The Independent Feature Project (IFP) also fiscally sponsored Rising Star, where they were able to raise $2,300 through tax-deductible donations from family, friends, and supporters. There were also three private investors for the film.

Due to the tiny budget of the film, the production had to come up with some innovative ways to secure the locations it wanted for shooting. The Mark Twain House plays a major role in the film, but securing it wouldn't have been possible had it not been for Lang's offer to screen a rough cut of the film at the Mark Twain Museum, with the Twain House keeping all the ticket sales. The rough cut screened in February 2011 – to a sold out house.

There were no major setbacks once the funding was all in and the shooting schedule began. Post-production, however, caused a few delays as members of the post team needed to focus on their higher-paying priority projects. The film was in post-production from November 2010 until March 2012.

Tickets for Rising Star are available in advance online. A second show has just been added at 9:15 pm. Tickets to the Red Carpet Premiere and After Party are $20.00 in advance online and $25.00 at the door. Tickets to the second show are $10.00 in advance and $12.00 at the door.

Tickets will be available at the door for both screenings beginning at 6:00 pm on August 3rd. The Connecticut Science Center is located at: 250 Columbus Boulevard, Hartford, CT 06103.

YouTube Trailer: http://youtu.be/CD_TN8uXrD8
YouTube Trailer Embed Code: <iframe width="640" height="360" src="http://www.youtube.com/embed/CD_TN8uXrD8" frameborder="0" allowfullscreen></iframe>
Facebook: http://www.facebook.com/risingstarmovie
Twitter: http://Twitter.com/risingstarmovie

"The Rise of the Political Filmmaker," on Film Courage

The title of indie filmmaker infers many roles. Worker. Leader. Psychiatrist. Conflict mediator. (And many times, financier.) When my friends and I decided to make my feature directorial debut, Rising Star, last summer, I knew we'd fill all those jobs, plus plenty others. But an interesting thing happened as we went through fundraising, prep and production: we also became politicians. We didn't know it as it was happening, but looking back, we didn't treat Rising Star like an indie film.

We treated our film like a political campaign.

Strange, huh? It seems weird when you think about it, but indie films and political campaigns have a lot in common. We can learn a lot from the way political campaigns reach out to people, and how that outreach translates into dollars and production support. Things like ...

1 **Keeping it local.** Ever heard the phrase "All politics is local?" It's definitely true. During campaign season, you see people waving signs on street corners and knocking on doors, and you get phone calls supporting this or that candidate. When you go to the polls, you remember those personal interactions. As filmmakers, we can't forget how important those personal interactions are. Utilizing social media will be an integral part of any crowdfunding campaign, but eye contact and shaking hands are just as important. During our Kickstarter campaign, we sent out more emails than I can remember, but we also spent time every day calling people, and going out to talk with people. I invited people over to my house to explain what our project was, and how they could get involved. Our producer, Matt Giovannucci, met with his local Unico chapter, and was able to raise money by meeting with their officers. The numbers back this up: our social media director/ producer/lead actor determined that of our 176 Kickstarter backers, we knew 146 of them. That's 84%. That's huge.

2 **Helping your community.** Politicians make their name in part by volunteerism, by serving on boards of non-profit organizations, or preparing meals at their local homeless shelter. This engenders community goodwill and gives a positive connotation to their name. Filmmakers can do the same thing, helping their local communities, while increasing the public profile for their projects. I'm a film professor, so I wanted to offer something education-related to Hartford, Connecticut, the city where we shot Rising Star. We found the R.J. Kinsella Magnet School for Performing Arts, a K-8 school that was looking to increase its classroom offerings. I taught filmmaking classes at Kinsella for their 7th and 8th grade multimedia students before and after production. We also had Matt, and other crew members, come in to teach, and we helped the students write and shoot their own short movie. We had a blast, the kids loved it, and the school diversified their class offerings. Did we get paid? Nope. Did it help us? Absolutely. We wanted to shoot at the Mark Twain House in Hartford but couldn't get anyone to talk with us. I mentioned that to Kinsella's artistic director after our second class, and he told me he had worked with the marketing director of the Twain House at his last job. A few phone calls later, we had permission to shoot there. The good karma came around back to us.

3 **Working with your local/state government.** When politicians want to garner support among voters, they'll look for endorsements from others working in government. Think a gubernatorial candidate getting a thumbs-up from a sitting senator. This is a strong way to demonstrate a candidate can get the job done. And so it can be for indie filmmakers, too. Getting support from local and state government can be a big aid to your production. We were able to utilize our state film commission to help find and secure locations, and the Mayor's Office of the City of Hartford got us free permits to shoot on any city street. Hartford's Economic Development Department also referred us to grants we were eligible for after meeting with them. These people have serious titles, yes, but don't be scared of them – your taxes pay their salaries. Working with government can also lead to dollars for your movie. Our state offers the Connecticut Film Industry Training Program, a workforce development program that trains state residents to work as crew members on film and television projects. I was able to get the list of program graduates and emailed them to tell them about Rising Star. A number of them became Kickstarter backers, some became volunteer P.A.s on the film, and others actually became crew members. And to top it all off, the director of the FITP thought enough of our film to pledge $500 on Kickstarter.

4 **Going green.** Government is embracing all things environmentally friendly, whether by offering tax credits for buying electric cars, or encouraging recycling. Helping save the earth is a priority for many politicians. Filmmakers can do this, too. We collaborated with a Sustainability Planner on Rising Star, and she came up with eco-friendly plans like using biodegradable plates and silverware on set. She also incorporated the environment into the film's story. She wanted a sustainable character in the movie (and our producer wanted to engage online with a new community), so they asked me if I would change our lead female character, Alyza, into a vegetarian or vegan. This would make the film's story eco-friendly, since eating those types of diets puts less strain on the environment, and it would allow our producer to engage the online veg community. I said if our fans decided she should change, I would do it.

And so began "The Alyza Challenge," a Twitter/X campaign our producer ran. He asked our fans to tweet #VeganVegRS or #OmnivoreRS to the movie's Twitter/X feed, depending on what they wanted Alyza to eat. The challenge caught fire online, being featured on ELEVEN vegan/vegetarian and eco-friendly blogs and news sites. We also had so many fans wanting Alyza to be vegan, I called the challenge off a week before it was supposed to end. And I rewrote the script to make her a vegan character. So in addition to helping the Earth, being green turned into great press for us, too, and revved up our fan base.

5 **Utilizing volunteers.** I know this sounds obvious; many of us have made films entirely with volunteers. But political campaigns utilize volunteers as well as anyone, given how little money they often must work with. They can recruit people by offering them involvement in the political process. Guess what? Filmmakers can recruit people just as easily by offering them the chance to be in show business. You'd be surprised what types of help you'll be offered if you ask for it. Once we began fundraising, our producer suggested we create a Google Doc, populated by a form on our Facebook page, that fans could fill out if they wanted to help us. In any way. We had 159 people respond. We found a still photographer in that group, as well as a family that let us shoot in their house. We also got some amazing offers: one woman offered us a flock of sheep we could photograph, a classical violinist offered to play for us in the movie, and a tradesman offered us welding and excavation services. You never know what you'll get.

So try thinking like a politico when you start your next movie. It could help you in every phase of your project. As for us, we're in post-production on Rising Star now, so we're looking for champions to get behind us as we prepare for our distribution.

I hear Connecticut's new governor is a big movie fan ... Figure 9.1

Figure 9.1 Electronic press kit for the film RISING STAR.

Marketing 163

contents	
plot summary and technical information	3
one-sheet posters	4
cast	5-7
about the director	8
press	9
soundtrack	10
credits	11
social media	12
contact information	13

Figure 9.1 (*continued*)

164 *Marketing*

plot summary

An overworked insurance adjuster must decide between his job and his passion after he accidentally meets his online love interest.

The city of Hartford, Connecticut is a featured character, playing as a backdrop to the story.

technical information

genre: drama/comedy/romance
anticipated film rating: PG-13
aspect ratio: 1.85:1
total running time: 80 minutes
language of origin: English (USA)
completion date: March, 2012

rising st r the movie 3

Figure 9.1 (*continued*)

Marketing 165

one-sheet poster

Click to link to the full-size (27"x40") downloadable file online.

Figure 9.1 (*continued*)

166 *Marketing*

cast

Gary Ploski (Chris)
Gary is a Prospect, Connecticut native with over 10 years of stage experience and an MFA in acting from Sarah Lawrence College.

He has performed in each of the Connecticut Film Industry Training Programs from 2008 to 2011. Gary was an Assistant Director of Education and presenter for the 2010 Connecticut Film Festival.

Gary recently won "Best Acting" in OBJECTS OF TIME (Best Film) during the 2011 New Haven, CT 48 Hour Film Project. Follow him in his behind the scenes web series CAST TO CURTAIN.

Gary is also available at: http://garyploski.com

Emily Morse (Alyza)
Emily is a Bristol, Connecticut native, and works as an actress, writer, producer, editor and singer.

Her latest short film, SWING VOTE: WHOSE SIDE ARE YOU ON?, won Best Short Film at the 2009 Connecticut Film Festival. On this film she worked as an actress, co-writer, producer and editor.

She also records music under the name Emilyis, and is a Music Education Director for the Connecticut Film Festival.

Emily is also available at: http://emilyis.com

rising st r the movie 5

Figure 9.1 (*continued*)

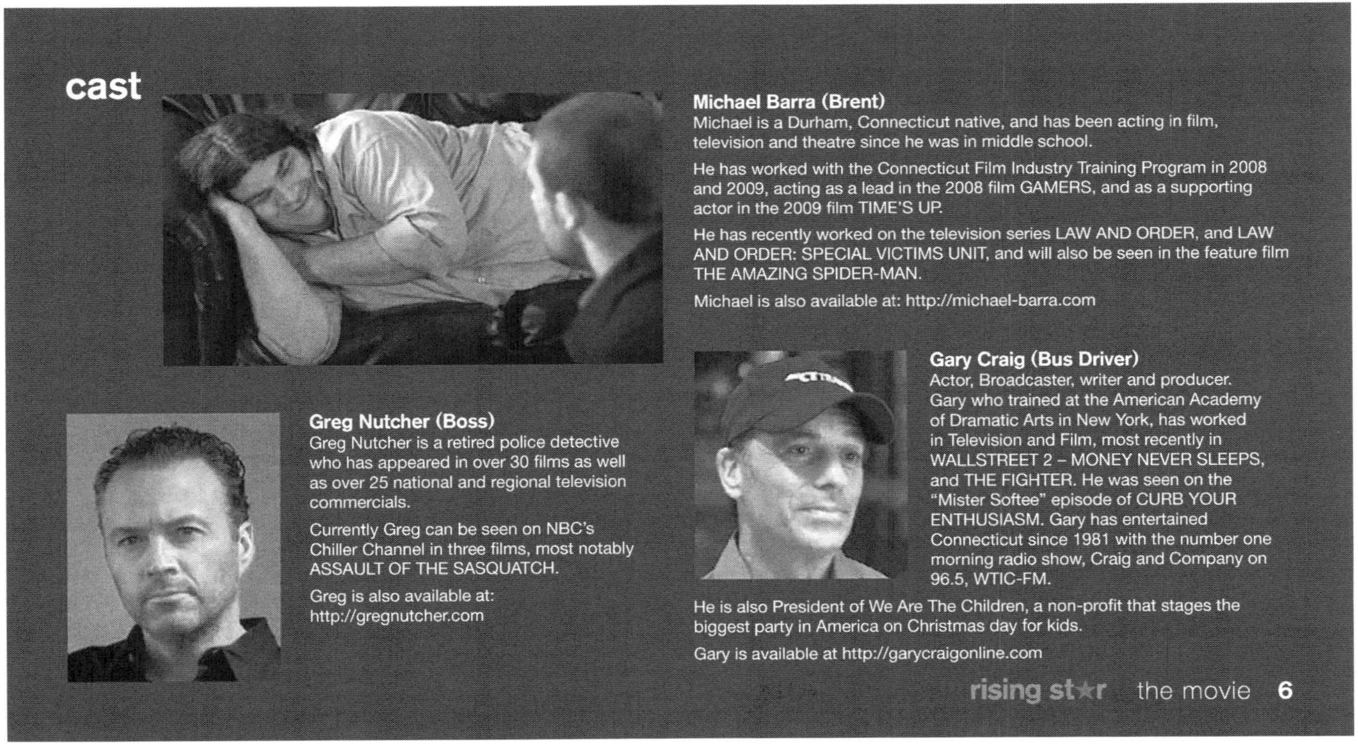

Marketing 167

cast

Greg Nutcher (Boss)

Greg Nutcher is a retired police detective who has appeared in over 30 films as well as over 25 national and regional television commercials.

Currently Greg can be seen on NBC's Chiller Channel in three films, most notably ASSAULT OF THE SASQUATCH.

Greg is also available at: http://gregnutcher.com

Michael Barra (Brent)

Michael is a Durham, Connecticut native, and has been acting in film, television and theatre since he was in middle school.

He has worked with the Connecticut Film Industry Training Program in 2008 and 2009, acting as a lead in the 2008 film GAMERS, and as a supporting actor in the 2009 film TIME'S UP.

He has recently worked on the television series LAW AND ORDER, and LAW AND ORDER: SPECIAL VICTIMS UNIT, and will also be seen in the feature film THE AMAZING SPIDER-MAN.

Michael is also available at: http://michael-barra.com

Gary Craig (Bus Driver)

Actor, Broadcaster, writer and producer. Gary who trained at the American Academy of Dramatic Arts in New York, has worked in Television and Film, most recently in WALLSTREET 2 – MONEY NEVER SLEEPS, and THE FIGHTER. He was seen on the "Mister Softee" episode of CURB YOUR ENTHUSIASM. Gary has entertained Connecticut since 1981 with the number one morning radio show, Craig and Company on 96.5, WTIC-FM.

He is also President of We Are The Children, a non-profit that stages the biggest party in America on Christmas day for kids.

Gary is available at http://garycraigonline.com

rising st★r the movie 6

Figure 9.1 (*continued*)

168 Marketing

cast

Sari Gagnon (Jamie)
Sari Gagnon was born, raised, and still lives in Hartford County. After completing intensive training at Circle in the Square Conservatory Theatre on Broadway, Sari has performed in dozens of independent Films Her latest appearance was in a film called OPPONENT co-staring with Jeremy London and "Rowdy" Roddy Piper. Aside from filming Sari also teaches performing arts classes to elementary school kids all over the state.

Julia Frisoli (Mary)
A native of Columbus, Ohio, Julia moved to Connecticut in 1989. She discovered her passion for acting at Curtain Call Theatre in Stamford. She can be seen in Disney's COLLEGE ROAD TRIP with Martin Lawrence and Donny Osmond. She has also worked with Robert DeNiro in THE GOOD SHEPHERD and Meryl Streep in THE DEVIL WEARS PRADA. Her television credits include LAW & ORDER, THE SOPRANOS and UGLY BETTY. Julia is a Board Member of Curtain Call Theatre.

Darrell Sullivan (M.C.)
Darrell a Wethersfield, CT native working as a musician, actor, writer, producer & entrepreneur. He is most widely known in Connecticut for his many years of service in the food & beverage industry as owner of Lena's Pizzaria and Sully's Pub in Hartford CT. Sully's Pub has been the pulse for original music and artistry in Hartford CT since 2000. Darrell is also available at: http://sullyspub.com

Matt Heron-Duranti (Antonio)
Matt Heron Duranti is an accomplished actor and writer. He has recently trained at the Stella Adler Studio in NYC, along with the Meisner Method under the tutelage of Lyralen Kaye in Boston, and let's not forget his background in Irish Liturature. Matt has appeared in tons of films and commercials all over the New England area. He is most recognized for his role in SOMETHING REMOTE by Broken Wall Films, which won Best Feature and Funniest Flick at the 2009 Silk City Flick Festival in Manchester CT. Matt is also available at: http://www.mattheronduranti.com

Luz Ramos (Isabel)
Luz is an actress for film and television, and can most recently be seen in the film AFTER LIFE, with Liam Neeson and Christina Ricci. Her work has been seen in GOSSIP GIRL, BROTHERHOOD, and the film THE INVENTION OF LYING. She also runs the New England Actors Group, a Hartford-based educational company. She is a Connecticut resident. Luz is also available at: http://luzramos.com

rising st★r the movie 7

Figure 9.1 (continued)

about the director

Marty Lang, writer/director/producer

Marty Lang is an award-winning filmmaker, professor and journalist. He attended the University of Connecticut, graduating with a B.A. in Journalism and covering entertainment for the New York Times after graduation. His first producing credit was on the independent feature "A LITTLE BIT OF LIPSTICK," starring Mia Tyler and Soupy Sales.

Armed with this experience, Lang was accepted into the Florida State University Graduate Film Conservatory in 2002. He worked on over 50 short films at FSU, associate producing the Student Academy Award-winning comedy "THE PLUNGE" in 2003, and co-producing the drama "FIELDS OF MUDAN," which qualified for the 2006 Oscar for Best Short Film. He also wrote and directed the comedy "CHEAP AS HELL: A CHRISTMAS STORY," which won "The Precious" at the 2005 New Haven (Conn.) Underground Film Festival. After working for Zide/Perry Films and Magnet Management in Los Angeles, he moved back home to Connecticut.

Since then, Lang has co-produced the satire "Being Michael Madsen," starring Michael Madsen, Virginia Madsen, David Carradine, Daryl Hannah and Lacey Chabert, associate produced the supernatural drama "The Other Side of the Tracks," starring Brendan Fehr, Tania Raymonde and Shirley Knight, and produced the vampire thriller "Fog Warning." He was the Educational Director for the 2010 Connecticut Film Festival, in Danbury, Connecticut. Lang developed the curriculum for the nationally-recognized Connecticut Film Industry Training Program, and has been its Assistant Director since 2008. He has also taught film at Quinnipiac University in Hamden, Connecticut.

Marty can be reached at http://martylang.com, and on Twitter @marty_lang.

Figure 9.1 (*continued*)

170 *Marketing*

press

Click on an article to link to the full-size downloadable file online.

Figure 9.1 (*continued*)

soundtrack

Michael Barra – In addition to acting, Michael is a standup comedian and musician. He makes his hip-hop debut on RISING STAR.

Emilyis – A veteran of the New York City and Connecticut music scene, Emilyis has released two CDs, Emilyis and Quietly Dying, and her work was featured in the short film SWING VOTE: WHAT SIDE ARE YOU ON?

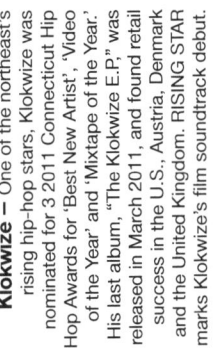

Klokwize – One of the northeast's rising hip-hop stars, Klokwize was nominated for 3 2011 Connecticut Hip Hop Awards for 'Best New Artist', 'Video of the Year' and 'Mixtape of the Year.' His last album, "The Klokwize E.P." was released in March 2011, and found retail success in the U.S., Austria, Denmark and the United Kingdom. RISING STAR marks Klokwize's film soundtrack debut.

Tom Varga – A veteran musician and production sound mixer (including the Oscar-nominated film PRECIOUS), Tom makes his feature composing debut on RISING STAR.

Figure 9.1 (*continued*)

172 *Marketing*

credits

written and directed by   marty lang

starring   gary ploski
emily morse
michael barra

supporting cast   sari gagnon
greg nutcher
luz ramos

producers   marty lang
matt giovannucci
gary ploski

co-producers   jennifer arzt
magda grover
gary fierro

assiciate producers   ty edge
darrell sullivan

production design   ginger labella

director of photography   rachael levine

1st assistant camera   chris daddio
2nd assistant camera/dit   jessica barbosa
1st assistant director   zach polhemus
editor   alec asten
post-production sound   tom varga
location manager   ben barker
eco/sustainability planner   ali berman
composer   tom varga
prop master   linda ginter
leadman   vicki wasylishyn
set dresser   michael dunne
wardrobe supervisor   sarah trobaugh
makeup artist   jackie zbuska
sound mixer   aaron miller
boom operator   david mcrorie
key grip   mike merli
gaffer   bob paré
script supervisor   rebecca schwab
accountant   michael finick

photo: Christine Paluf

rising st★r the movie 11

Figure 9.1 (*continued*)

Marketing 173

social media

http://www.youtube.com/risingstarmovie

http://www.risingstarmovie.com

http://www.facebook.com/risingstarmovie

http://twitter.com/risingstarmovie

Figure 9.1 (*continued*)

174 *Marketing*

contacts

Marty Lang
marty@risingstarmovie.com

risingstarmovie.com

Figure 9.1 (*continued*)

Marketing for DEADBRAINS

Because of all the crowdsourcing work we did for DEADBRAINS during development, screenwriting, and crowdfunding, we'll have a solid core of supporters who would want to see the film. Reaching out to them to let them know the film is done, and about to be released, will undoubtedly get them excited.

Once they are, we have an opportunity to build the audience beyond them – by asking them to bring more people in. We can put out a call to action, where we can ask every supporter to bring a friend or two into the fold and get them interested. Asking your audience to serve as marketers can be highly effective, especially when you're talking about films that have a specific, dedicated audience. Zombie movies certainly fall into that category.

And because they have a specific audience, there are in-person events that we can attend, to find more folks who would be interested. As mentioned earlier, zombie walks are common events all over the United States, where zombie fans can dress up like the undead, and wander around a downtown area, or predetermined path. We could set up a booth at the beginning of the walk, or at the end, so people can stop and find out about the film's release (and hopefully give us their email addresses).

Zombie conventions, and horror conventions more broadly, are other big in-person events that we could become a part of, in order to get the word out. Looking around Memphis, Tennessee, there's a horror/Halloween convention in Knoxville each year called CreepyCon, which could be a great place to find more Tennessee-based fans. Nashville has a Horror Con each July, and Jackson, Tennessee actually has a zombie trail paintball competition. These three are all great opportunities to build our audience.

The social media platforms we created for the DEADBRAINS crowdfunding campaign will still be active, and we can use them as funnels to get potential customers to visit the film's website. Let's hypothetically call it www.deadbrains.com. The site's front page can have a simple image of our zombie characters leading a military operation against the humans, clearly communicating the story of the film. It can also provide links to the film's trailer, poster, EPK and behind the scenes photo and video. The most important element of the site will be the call to action, at the top of the front page, which will provide a one-click link to where you can pay to watch the movie. (We'll talk about where, exactly, the film will play in the next chapter.) And we'll also have tracking tools on the site, to see what the reactions are to the image we have on the front page. Over time, we can change the front page image, maybe to one of the human characters fighting the zombies, or possibly a human parent with their child in the midst of the war. That way, we can compare and contrast the reaction to those different images, and find out which one gives us the best chance to convert those visitors into customers.

Finally, we'll spend a good amount of time creating content about the film that can be posted on media outlets relating to our audience. The mere act of engaging a local zombie-loving audience in the making of a zombie movie could be interesting enough to write about for zombie-related media. A quick Google search will reveal blogs, magazines, and even audio dramas focusing on zombies, all great places to contact and see if you could publish there. You could even broaden your media target out to horror, thriller, or Halloween-related media.

Interview: Filmsnobbery CEO Nicholas Larue

Nicholas LaRue has been a vocal supporter for independent film and filmmakers throughout his career and is the Founder and Editor-in-Chief of FilmSnobbery, which has been around since 2008. Nicholas also runs the full-service marketing agency LaRue Entertainment Group, LLC which helps clients find and connect with their audiences and drive revenue for their businesses. He is the author of BEHIND THE SCENES OF INDEPENDENT FILM MARKETING, published by Routledge.

Figure 9.2 Headshot of Filmsnobbery CEO Nicholas LaRue.

Marty Lang: You've been in independent film marketing since 2008. How has film marketing changed from then until today?

Nicholas LaRue: At a microbudget level, the basics of it really haven't changed. If you go to a film festival, or even to a film market, you still need to have these certain things that will get your film sold, whether it's a poster, whether it's a trailer. Back then was when you first started seeing more custom websites being set up, too. It's also when social media really started to take off, because Twitter/X was really starting to gather a lot of traction from various communities, the film community being one of them. People were seeing the value of conversation on sites like Twitter/X.

As far as how else it has evolved, we've gone through a lot of technology shifts in a very short amount of time. So now there's not just VR, but there's AR, there's social media. Now Facebook and Instagram are dominating the ad space portion. So if you're looking to do marketing on a microbudget, any type of paid marketing, that's probably where you're going to put the majority of your money. That will help you to hit the widest audience net.

Marketing

Twitter/X would probably be the second. If you could, you could also put some money into TikTok. But with TikTok, you really want to see more organic views. And it's very easy to do that with how their algorithm is set up. There is also email marketing to consider. As much as some things have changed, some things have stayed the same. More traditional methods are still really important and really viable. Email marketing is one of those things. 99% of the people in the world have an email address, if not more than one. Unlike phone numbers, which can frequently change, most people just keep the same email address. And those are still viable ways to getting in touch with people. Email marketing is one of those things that has remained really consistent, because it also allows you to target specific audiences, you can segment audiences off per campaign. It can help people through that sales funnel if that is your goal with your microbudget film. If you've made it, now your goal is to sell it and you want to kind of walk people through that process, that absolutely works.

ML: What, in your mind, makes for a successful independent film marketer?

NR: I think someone being charismatic. A successful filmmaker, one that's able to connect with their audience, is going to be somebody who has charisma. And they have an ability to be vulnerable with their audience. Both with their art and with themselves. And I don't mean like, everything's got to be a sob story, or everything's got to be drama. I mean vulnerable as in approachable, vulnerable as in sharing the things that were difficult for you, as well as the things that went well. They can make people feel like they can come to you.

But also, like a lot of things, 99% of anything is showing up. And whether it's show up to the film festival, show up to the interview with folks like myself, put yourself out there, I think that's why when you see a lot of crowdfunding videos, the people who are the creators of the idea, they often want to be front and center on those videos, because you want to see it in their eyes. You want to see the passion that they have, and they want to see that connection that you have with them, and you want to see how you can help them.

So I think success is a little bit about being vulnerable. It's about being charismatic. I think at times, it also is about being bolder than you think you should be. I think a lot of people get embarrassed. I think that they feel that if I promote myself too much, it's going to turn people off. They feel that if I am saying that something I'm doing is great, then someone a level above them is going to slap their hand and tell them no. And that's what stops people from being a success, to some degree.

Let's use the phrase "Dance like no one's watching." I think there's a level of embarrassment that comes with that. And I get it. I mean, there's a reason why someone sits behind the camera and isn't acting in front of it. I think actors get the embarrassment beaten out of them a little bit. So they're a little bit more comfortable doing certain things, to promote their work, to promote themselves. I think filmmakers have a little bit more of a difficult time with that, It's a different part of your brain. That is just as vulnerable as when an actor is doing something dramatically.

I think that you need to be unabashed in this industry. You see someone like Dan Mirvish; he is out there every day, finding any angle he can to promote his movie. He'll be out there wearing a sandwich board, he'll be out there with a bullhorn, he'll be out there doing whatever he can to make himself look like whatever amount of ass he needs to, to draw in an audience. And he doesn't just do that because it's this movie, he does that on **every** movie. Because it's not just about this movie, it's about every movie. And when you have that kind of passion, and the audience sees it, they will be attracted to that. The person who is doing something gets attention. And that's just how that works. What you want to do as a filmmaker is create some kind of heat. You want to have some story, or several stories, related to you, related to your film, the making of your film, your background, whatever. And you want to keep that heat moving for as long as you can, preferably until you hit the next movie.

ML: What would you say are the biggest misconceptions that new filmmakers have about marketing their work?

NR: That their job is done once the movie is out. They don't realize the job doesn't end. I also think that they feel like this is someone else's job. They don't understand that yes, they paid money to submit to a film festival. And they got accepted. And that's great. But it's not 100% of the festival's job to put butts in seats for your particular screening. They're busy thinking about the festival, and bringing in an audience, but not necessarily your audience. I think that there's a distinction that needs to be held there for filmmakers, where you have to know who your audience is, and you need to make sure that they're there, regardless of where you are in the country or in the world.

I think another big misconception is that if they put something out for free, that people will buy it. I think that is a gross misconception. I also think it's completely devaluing of something that cost money to make, and also took the time and effort of people, and all those things deserve to be valued. It really comes down to valuing your work.

It's great when you could put something out there and it hits on YouTube, you get a few 100,000 hits here or half a million there, but when it comes to monetization, the key is consistency. Because YouTube's monetization guidelines require a level of consistency. It's not that you hit this threshold, and you're done. Now, you must hit this threshold every month, consistently, and they move the goalposts all the time.

I think the misconception really is that at some point, you can put the camera down, or that you can put the pen down, or you can put the microphone down. No, you must keep going. I don't care if the movie cost $1,000 or $100,000, you should be striving to not only make that money back, but also to make a profit and to have a career. I think that's another thing, too – this is not a job. For some people, this is a job, you know, for actors on your shoot, this is a job for them. But this is part of a larger career plan that they hopefully have for themselves. You as the director of your work, the head of your own production company, or the head of your own business, should always be looking to profit. I mean, that's how businesses stay in business.

ML: The majority of the filmmakers you work with have budgets around $50,000. Are there pieces of advice and strategy you give to films of that size? As opposed to films of bigger sizes?

NR: Yeah, a lot of it is setting expectations, and moving around marketing budgets. So if I'm working with a filmmaker, I'll say, you made this movie for $50,000. Ideally, you'd like to have, you know, at least $20,000 for a marketing budget. Now you're gonna hear this from the filmmaker, "We want to put every penny on the screen." And I get that notion. You feel like if you just make the movie better, more people will see it.

My response to that is, "Well, explain Troma." And I say that, as someone who's known Lloyd Kaufman for many, many years, and I've been a fan of Troma movies going all the way back to my childhood. They're a 50-year-old production company. And whether you're a fan or not, they make movies that some people call schlock. But Lloyd understands the value of, "I have to put on the bowtie, and I have to go to this convention, set up the table, and I gotta sell the merch, I have to move the action figures, I have to move the DVDs, I have to move the Blu-Rays," all those things. And he will consistently take chances on smaller budget things, but he will package them well. And he will sell every single one of them. He will sell Trey Parker and Matt Stone's movie, Jenna Fisher's movie, James Gunn's movies with the same level of fervor that he will sell POULTRYGEIST.

So if I'm going to talk to a filmmaker about if the marketing budget really matters, just understand if you have a higher budget, and you can put more money toward marketing, you may not need to work as hard as someone like Lloyd Kaufman, well into your 80s to reach a similar level of success. If you're a $50,000 filmmaker or lower, and you're not putting any money into your marketing budget, don't be surprised if you must work harder to earn those eyeballs. You'll have to convince people every single minute of every single day, why they should be watching your movie and not someone else's.

And you're earning eyeballs by being a charming, charismatic person. You're earning eyeballs by hopefully having a good movie. With that, you're earning trust, you're earning eyeballs, you're earning all of this stuff that hopefully amounts to dollars at the end, or at the very least, some level of fans that you can carry over to another project, where dollars may factor in.

In terms of advice, you know, at any budget level, it really doesn't come down to budget economy, it comes down to how hard do you want to work?

ML: What's the most important single piece of advice you can give to a filmmaker who's going to be marketing their film for the first time?

NR: I would say don't be afraid to try anything, but understand that trying anything can often have just as poor results as being calculated. I think that you can get lucky with a shotgun approach. Just like with a shotgun, you might hit something, you might get that bear. But the more time you spend really delving into yourself, your work and your audience, and having as much information as possible at your disposal at any time, the easier and the more time and money you will save later.

It also gives you a lot of responses to arguments from people when they say, "You can't do that." If you're going to talk to someone who may be interested in buying your movie, and they say "Well, I don't see this playing to more than x amount of people." You can say "Well, I have data here that suggests otherwise." The more information you come in with, the stronger your position is. Don't be afraid to ask for the sale either. Whether that sale is an actual selling of your movie, or a waiver for a film festival, or a discount on your posters. Or just getting some damn help. Ask for what you feel that you're worth. Never be afraid to ask for help.

Note

1 www.skinamarink.com

Reference List

Lang, Marty. "The Rise of the Political Filmmaker," Film Courage, 2011. https://filmcourage.com/2011/01/18/the-rise-of-the-political-filmmaker/

Official Website for horror film SKINAMARINK. www.skinamarink.com

10 Distribution

It's taken a long time for us to get to the part of the book where filmmakers can actually become self-sustaining, hasn't it? Now we're here. We've developed our story, written, produced, and finished a film, and gotten the word out about it to an engaged audience. Now it's time for us to reap the rewards!

At least, that's the idea.

Here's the truth: like I mentioned in the first chapter, indie film distribution is broken. If you look at the long-time practice of indie filmmakers, the all-important step of distribution is often outsourced to distribution companies, instead of handled completely by the filmmaker. A completely anti-entrepreneurial practice, and one that rips away so much of a film's potential revenue from the person (or team) that did all the work to make that film exist in the first place.

Since our films are being made for such little money, it doesn't make sense to give away all that revenue-generating potential to another company, no matter how effective they might be at marketing and distribution. Besides, after reading the last chapter, we've already done the marketing work ourselves!

We need to think of our film as a product, offered by a startup business. We need to distribute our films ourselves, without giving our rights up to distributors.

Before we get into how to do that, though, I want to explain two things. The first is a concept called the "waterfall," which is the path of profits from a traditional theatrical release of a film. That path can differ a bit, depending on how a film is released, but I want to explain it so that it's clear how low on the totem pole filmmakers are when it comes to making money on theatrical releases. Then, I want to show you some hard data, collected by two incredible indie filmmakers, who confirm how bleak the landscape really is.

This might have you thinking all is hopeless, but fear not! That's definitely not the case. The world of film distribution is being transformed

DOI: 10.4324/9781003295754-10

right now, by someone you probably wouldn't expect. Their exploits in our field give me so much hope for the future and give us a blueprint for how we can self-distribute our own work.

But first?

The Dried-up Waterfall

When a film is released, and it makes money, the revenue that's generated is paid out in a certain order. That order is called a waterfall. And if you want to make money as an indie filmmaker, it's least likely that you will – because you're last.

Here's a fictional example. Let's say we make a drama feature about police officers in Memphis, Tennessee, called BLUFF CITY NIGHTS. The film is produced for $50 million, and it's released theatrically in the United States. Over the course of its opening weekend, it makes $50 million.

Great opening, right? We made our budget back in one weekend!

Not so fast.

The beginning of the waterfall is the exhibitors. So all the theater chains get the first piece of the pie. And it's a big piece. Exhibitor grosses are usually around half of what the film makes. So of that $50 million, we're already down to $25 million.

After exhibitors, the P&A costs, or prints and advertising, are paid back to the distributor. These days, the prints are usually hard drives instead of the film prints of the past, but it's still a cost if you have a major release with hundreds or thousands of screens. The big money is in the advertising. For a film of this budget, it's not unusual for P&A costs to total about $20 million. So just after exhibitors and P&A, we've already paid out 90% of our opening weekend.

But wait, there's more! After P&A costs, the distributor gets a distribution fee for their work marketing the movie. They don't just get their money back, they get paid for their work spending it! On a $50 million budget, that fee could be as much as $3 million. So we're now down to $2 million.

After the distribution fee, the unions whose workers acted and crewed on the film must be paid residuals, which are negotiated payments in addition to their salaries. If you work with all professional unions, for actors, writers, directors, and below the line crew, those residual payments can be as much as $1 million.

So now we just have one million dollars left!

And we haven't even paid back the budget of the film yet!

If you objectively look at a model like this, it's kind of strange to think so many filmmakers willingly distribute their films this way, since you have to give away the first 98% of what you make. If you're making a microbudget film, it just doesn't make sense.

And the hard data bears that out.

Golden Elevators and Free-range Films

In March 2023, filmmakers Naomi McDougall Jones and Liz Manashil wrote an article for Filmmaker Magazine that was, in my opinion, the biggest wake-up call for independent film distribution I had ever seen. It was called "Producer Data: The Numbers Don't Lie (The Truth about Independent Film Revenue," and I recommend you read it top to bottom.[1] They put an open call out to filmmakers (crowdsourcing!), asking for revenue data on their independent films, including budgets, best and worst-performing revenue streams, their casts and how much the films made. They focused on films that were released from 2018 to 2022, as those films were released in a distribution climate most similar to today. (Streaming services really didn't become dominant until that time.) And when they analyzed that data, they came to some sobering conclusions. They classified the films they analyzed in two distinct categories, what they called "golden elevator" films and "free-range" films. Here's how they explained them:

> At this moment, there are only two possible paths for an independent film. The first is what Naomi refers to as the 'golden elevator.' A project that manages to get on the golden elevator is very likely to bear out a filmmaker's wildest dreams: premiere at a top film festival, big dollar sale to a streamer, maybe an Independent Spirit Award, distribution by NEON or A24. These high-profile stories keep the rest of us dreaming as the filmmakers breezily explain in interviews a charmed path up into the stars. But there are only a tiny number of highly elite and tightly gate-kept tickets onto that golden elevator. A place in a highly prestigious lab might get you on board (though certainly isn't guaranteed to do so). So may the attachment of a hugely famous actor (not a sort-of-famous one) or the full-throated backing of WME or CAA (but only if they're really pushing the project, not just casually attached).

> We call the non-golden elevator films - the *actually* independent films - 'free-range films' (a term coined by director Maria Nieto) because they are made fully outside the institutional industry apparatus. In the current landscape, these films find themselves scrambling down a well-worn set of uninspiring distribution paths. Out here, in the land of mid-level film festivals or no-one's-ever-heard-of-them film festivals, filmmakers encounter unrealistic projections from predatory distributors or the candid and depressing truth from honest ones that recoupment is near

impossible after platforms, agents and distributors take their pieces of the pie. This is because content has been and continues to be devalued on a daily basis as audiences are sold more and more SVOD and AVOD platforms that allow them unlimited viewing for small monthly fees—fees effectively subsidized by low license fees to creators—that pale in comparison to the true cultural value of all the films in those libraries.

Of the films they were able to analyze:

- 94.4% of films with budgets between $200,001 and $900,000 did not break even
- 81.8% of films with budgets between $50,001 and $200,000 did not break even
- 60% of films with budgets under $50,000 did not break even

Of the budget ranges under $900,000, the best chance you have to make your money back would be with a film under $50,000.

And they also found eye-opening data regarding the distribution methods of these films. They learned that 83.3% of films released solely by a distribution company (that is, films where the filmmakers did not take distribution into their own hands) did not break even. And 100% of the films that employed a hybrid release (working with a distributor for part of a release, but also doing some distribution work on your own) did not break even. But 53.5% of films that were completely self-distributed actually did break even, or make money! So this data bears out that if you distribute a low-budget film yourself, you have a better chance to pay your budget back, and potentially more, than if you outsource that task to a distributor.

So what should we do? Now that we see how important it is that we distribute our films ourselves, what should our best practices be? For a glimpse of how things are changing, we need to look to the music world.

Tay Leads the Way

In summer 2023, singer/songwriter Taylor Swift was in the middle of her Eras Tour, an international phenomenon that resulted in close to $5 billion in economic activity in the United States alone.[2] What no one knew, however, was that she was also shooting a concert film at the same time. Once the film was completed, Swift and her father, Scott, approached movie studios to release the film, but they were disappointed with the offers they received.[3] So they tried something very different – they approached the film exhibition company AMC, and asked if they'd be interested in releasing the film directly, without the involvement of the studios.

AMC said of course, and CEO Adam Aron negotiated the deal directly with the Swifts, with no talent agency involved, and no lawyers involved until the contracts needed to be written up. The Swifts will end up receiving over 50% of the gross revenues, with 57% going to the Swifts and AMC, and the remaining 43% going to theaters, a far better arrangement than any film studio offered.

Now if you think about it, Taylor Swift really doesn't need a movie studio. As Puck reporter Matthew Belloni explained:

> What do modern movie studios do, anyway? They *produce* the product (often with partners), but since the Swifts had hired director Sam Wrench and paid for this movie themselves (it actually cost between $10 million and $20 million, I'm told, and was shot during her recent L.A. stop), they didn't need production help. The studios *market* - increasingly their core competency - but Swift, with a couple social media posts to her 365 million followers, is her own best marketing machine. And the studios *distribute*; meaning they actually secure and deliver the movie to theaters. On that front, AMC could coordinate its own theaters and then hire a small, independent sub-distributor, Variance Films, to book Regal, Cinemark, and eventually the other chains, as is planned.

The studios ended up missing out on a financial juggernaut. In just its opening weekend in mid-October 2023, TAYLOR SWIFT: THE ERAS TOUR posted a domestic opening weekend of $93.2 million. And throughout its theatrical run, the film made over $261.6 million worldwide, and $180.7 million in the United States and Canada.[4]

Now I know what you're thinking. It's easy for someone with over a quarter billion social media followers to leverage their huge audience into sweetheart distribution deals. What about filmmakers that raise their budgets with crowdfunding? Can indie filmmakers self-distribute theatrically?

I can report that it's possible.

When I finished producing CHOMPY & THE GIRLS, we were on the hunt for a distributor to put the film on streaming and digital – but we kept the theatrical rights for ourselves. That's because, as a pretty bizarre horror/comedy, we had dreams of the film one day becoming the ROCKY HORROR PICTURE SHOW of a new generation, with midnight theatrical screenings all over the country, and revenue generation for years. We were able to secure a distribution deal with Freestyle Digital Media for streaming, cable and on demand, and once we did, we thought we had enough momentum to approach a theater chain for a direct release. We decided on Malco Theatres, a Memphis-based chain with theaters in six states.

How did I make a deal with Malco?

I emailed them and asked them.

After contacting their booker, they asked to see the film, and our marketing materials (trailer and poster), and once they did, they offered us a one-week run at one of their theaters, with a 50/50 split on ticket sales! We needed to create a digital cinema package (DCP) for the film to play in the theater, and we needed to print two posters to put outside the theater. The posters were $45 each, and we already had a DCP made, so the release cost us $90. And that was it! We played the film there for seven days, and it made $500 in ticket sales. So we ended up making $250, and after paying for the posters, the total revenue from the week was $160. This was in September 2021, so pandemic fears were still keeping many folks from theaters, but we were thrilled that people came out to see it. And while we couldn't retire on what we made, it got us lots of local press coverage, and it helped get the word out about the digital release. So it was a positive experience for us all around.

Now think about the economy of scale here. We only ended up showing CHOMPY in that one theater, for one week. But what if we found ten theaters, and played at each of them for a week? And we were able to get about the same amount of tickets sold? We'd only pay for the posters once, and the DCP was free; the nine theaters we would play at after that would be all revenue after the 50/50 theater split. So they would give us $250 each, or $2,250, on top of the $160. That's $2,410, assuming you'd get COVID-era audiences. Post-BARBENHEIMER, that's a very conservative estimate.

You can also find some interesting partners you might not normally think of when it comes to theatrical distribution – film festivals. If you're thinking of doing one-off screenings in an area with a film festival, you can approach them and ask if they'd like to partner with you 50/50 for the screening. That way, you share in the cost of the event, if you need to rent a venue, for example, but you also share in the potential revenue the event could create. You may find some festival personnel who are progressive enough to think of filmmakers as their financial partners, and who might be open to the idea.

I was lucky enough to find one such festival director. When RISING STAR had its Connecticut premiere at the Connecticut Science Center, we partnered with the Connecticut Film Festival for the screening. We had to pay to rent their theater and hire bartenders for a four-hour block, and that cost about $1,500. But we were able to keep all the ticket sales. That's where we did the revenue split with the film festival – the first $1,500 paid for the theater rental, and then the rest of the ticket sales were split between the film and the film festival. We ended up selling out one screening of 200 seats at $20 per ticket, and sold about 40 more tickets for a second screening we set up within our four-hour block. So we ended up making $4,800 on ticket sales. The first $1,500 paid for the theater, bringing us to

$3,300, and that was split, giving $1,650 to the film, and $1,650 to the film festival. Everybody won. (We ended up spending that money immediately on distribution deliverables, though. Those were costs we didn't anticipate when we budgeted the film. An expensive lesson!)

Community filmmakers can take advantage of every theatrical screening opportunity in their community. If you have three theaters in your hometown, play a week at each of them! If you want to reach farther out to your county, or wider, do it. There are scores of independent theaters, who are always looking to support independent filmmakers – especially if they can quantify an audience of their own, that they can bring to their theater. And if there are places in your community that could potentially be transformed into theatrical screening venues, go back to Chapter 2 and utilize the work we did with Reel Life Entertainment. Create experiences to show your film theatrically. Engage your audience to attend these "events," which can be more than just a film. Partner with locations and groups who can engage their own followers to come and see your film. Welcome them to your film and introduce them to you and your team. And invite them to join you.

Digital Distribution

Of course, there are lots of ways to show a movie other than in theaters, and this is where things can get tricky with self-distribution. There are a number of ways you can have customers access the digital version of your film. They boil down to two strategies:

1 Put the film up on commonly used video on demand (VOD) sites, or
2 Sell the film yourself, through a video hosting site (YouTube, Vimeo, Dacast, etc.)

Now here's the really cool thing about distributing your film yourself: since you're not giving up your film's rights to a distributor, you can do either – or both – without any restrictions. And that will offer you the broadest possible reach for the film, and possible viewers.

If you're interested in selling the film on VOD, one way to go about it is to use what's called an aggregator. These are services that place your film onto networks where it can be purchased. It's different from a distributor in that they don't do any marketing for the film – but that's okay, because we've already done that work. Some charge a fee up front, letting you keep all the revenue, and others charge a percentage of what the film makes on the platforms it's placed on. But most importantly, they do not take any rights – they're providing a service to the filmmaker. So you retain all control of the film, and the revenue it ultimately makes. Some popular aggregators are

BitMax, Filmhub, and Premiere Digital – check them all out, and see what would make the most sense for your project.

Working with a video hosting site isn't putting your film out onto large platforms, but it's providing viewers a chance to purchase and view your film in a simple, clean way. Those sites also allow you to embed your film into other sites, providing filmmakers a chance to place their film in locations where they know their audience will be. This could be on message boards, on media sites related to the topic of the film ...

And on your film's Website.

Working with a video hosting site will provide you with the most direct way to get interested folks to buy your film, because it will allow you to place your film on the front page of your site when it's finished. If the film is on the front page, above the fold, anyone who visits the site will see the film, and be able to buy it, as the first thing they see. Once your film is finished, this should be the first place it goes. That way, all the effort you spend increasing traffic to the site will pay off, giving visitors a one-click process to become a paid audience member.

Hire Your Crowd!

You also have one enormous advantage at this point in the process, when it comes to distribution: after you've crowdsourced, crowdfunded, and built community around your film, you now not only have a group of people who want to pay to see your movie, you have a group of people that are motivated enough to play the film for THEIR friends and families. And since we're thinking in terms of radical collaboration, guess what that means?

You can pay them to do it!

Once you play your film, theatrically or at a film festival, you have an opportunity to recruit people who can become part of your team as screening organizers. Again, since you have control of all rights to your film, you can actually bring audience members on to your team to host screenings of their own. With ticket sales and everything. And you can pay them a percentage of whatever they make, as an incentive for them to bring out as big an audience as possible. Maybe you can pop in for a Q&A, in person or virtual, after the screening to help spur turnout. If you work with a ticket processor, like EventBrite or Brown Paper Tickets, you can make an arrangement where the event organizer will get a percentage of the sales. You can also negotiate a flat fee, where for that amount, the organizer will get 100% of the ticket sales. Either way, you're including your audience as a part of your business, which will guarantee a higher level of engagement than if they were doing it for free. And it will also help you build a network of people you can return to when you make subsequent films.

Distribution for DEADBRAINS

Getting DEADBRAINS out into the world would definitely be a ton of fun. Starting with a theatrical release, in the month of October, to coincide with Halloween. If you began in Memphis, and worked with Malco Theaters as the largest (and most indie-friendly) theater chain in the area, it's possible you could secure screens in Memphis and beyond. In addition to the Memphis area, Malco has theaters in Oxford, Mississippi (right near the University of Mississippi) and Fayetteville, Arkansas (where the University of Arkansas is). Securing a theatrical release in those three cities, even if they're just one night screenings, could be a great way to get full theaters for the film's opening, along with the (hopefully) good reviews from local critics. This could also involve partnerships with local film festivals, like Indie Memphis, the Hub City Film Festival in Jackson, TN, the Oxford Film Festival in Mississippi, and Filmland, run by the Arkansas Cinema Society in Little Rock. If they were interested in revenue sharing, the film could get exposure to the audiences those film festivals have built, as well as the audience we've built for it over the time we've made it.

We would also have an opportunity to do some really cool things with additional theatrical screenings outside of theaters. When I was in middle school, one of the most frightening things I ever did was a Halloween train ride through the woods, at a local train museum. Once we got into the ride, the train suddenly "malfunctioned," and stopped in the dark.

Then the zombies came out.

They came on the train, all made up in makeup and groaning. One of them even had a chainsaw, without the chain on it, that was really running. That zombie put the (harmless) chainsaw against my arm, and I started screaming like I put my hand in boiling water.

It was the best Halloween experience I've ever had.

What if we found a local train museum, had an event similar to that ... but once you got to the end of the train ride, there was an outdoor screening of DEADBRAINS ready for you? Zombie lovers would fall over themselves to attend an event like that. And it would get plenty of press attention, because of the additional elements beyond the film screening.

Once theatrical is finished, and digital distribution begins, this is where the marketing work we've done will bear fruit. If we post the completed film on a hosting site so that viewers can purchase it, we'll be able to post it on the film's Website, front page, above the fold. So all the traffic we generate will bring visitors to a point where they can purchase and watch it. Then, we can approach every single zombie-related blog, online magazine, and Internet community that we found and have them post it on there. Maybe we could offer additional items to media outlets, like Q&A sessions with their reporters to go along with the film being posted. However it works out, we'll have our film right in the middle of engaged groups of zombie lovers.

Once the film has been on those sites for a while, we could decide to work with aggregators to get the film placed on bigger sites. And since it's a zombie film, there's already an audience that loves those films, so we'd be able to reach those people through the wider reach of platforms like Tubi, Google Play, or Roku.

And since Halloween happens every year, we'd have the possibility of continuing theatrical experiences for the film year after year, whether in traditional theaters or through experience-based screenings like that zombie train ride.

The film could make money for us every fall.

Interview: Director and Slamdance Co-founder Dan Mirvish

Figure 10.1 Headshot of director and Slamdance co-founder Dan Mirvish.

Award-winning filmmaker/author Dan Mirvish directed and produced such features as 18½, BERNARD AND HUEY, BETWEEN US, OPEN HOUSE and OMAHA (THE MOVIE). Dan's films screened in over 100 festivals on 7 continents, sold to 150 countries, all had theatrical releases and played on everything from Netflix and Showtime to Virgin Atlantic and JetBlue. He co-wrote the critically acclaimed novel I AM MARTIN EISENSTADT (Farrar, Straus, Giroux) and wrote two editions of THE CHEERFUL SUBVERSIVE'S GUIDE TO INDEPENDENT FILMMAKING (Focal Press/Routledge). Dan's lectured in over 50 film schools around the world and he co-founded the Slamdance Film Festival.

Marty Lang:	In the time that you've been making films, from the mid-90s to today, how has traditional film distribution changed?
Dan Mirvish:	My answer is that things haven't changed a bit. In the grand scheme of things, things haven't changed. And the reason I say that is because 25 years ago, or almost 30 years ago, when I was starting out, there were a limited number of gatekeepers. And a limited number of distributors that could get you what I call "culturally relevant" distribution, which is to say that people have heard of the show. I don't think that that has changed in the sense that the percentage of culturally relevant films is still about one or two percent. The gatekeepers for those films, it's

still almost 90% Sundance, which was as true now as it was then. There's maybe a couple other ways to get a film out there and get it distributed. But not many, like the kind of number of breakout festivals where you can get a big distribution deal or get the film initially noticed.

On the distribution side, the technology has changed in terms of both making the film and exhibiting films, and how consumers see films. That obviously, has gone digital, for the most part, in all kinds of ways. But I think the gatekeepers once you get distribution haven't changed much. The number of distributors that are picking up films and wind up getting culturally relevant distribution are about the same as it was 30 years ago. Back then, it was Miramax and Fine Line. Now it's A24 and NEON. The number of players are about the same.

The thing that I think is often overlooked is that the way to get cultural relevance once you have distribution, whether you're doing it yourself, you have a big distributor, or you have a small distributor is the significant film critics. And the way to get them hasn't changed, which is that you have to have a theatrical release in New York City to start with and nationwide to finish. That's the only way you're going to get a New York Times review, one that gets awards consideration. And the gatekeeper for indie films is all the New York critics because they're the ones who vote on the Gotham Awards. You know, if you can get noticed by the New York Critics Circle, that means you're a noticeable indie film, it's had cultural salience. If you get ignored by them, you don't. And that's 98% of films.

So that's why I say it hasn't really changed.

ML: You were able to self-distribute your first feature, OMAHA (THE MOVIE), and over six months, it played all over the country. What was that process like?

DM: First of all, huge shout out to the late, great Bruce Sinofsky. I met Bruce when he was a juror at the Florida Film Festival, when I had the movie there. And he had self-distributed the documentary BROTHER'S KEEPER. It was kind of hot in Filmmaker Magazine. It was one of the rare self-distribution success stories. I mean, people have been doing self-distribution for 100 years, but this was sort of a recent, really great example. And the one reason people weren't doing it, or didn't know how to do it, is because you didn't know how to contact the bookers at the theaters. And Bruce said he would give me his secret list! So that was a huge help. So we embraced his information, his list, but then we also kind of knew Mike Corrente, who self-distributed FEDERAL HILL. We'd met him on the festival circuit, and kind of knew about his stories. He had done a similar thing to what Richard Linklater did with SLACKER, and that is we called the FEDERAL HILL/SLACKER strategy, which is you open your film in your hometown. You hope that it does really well. You then contact distributors and say, "Hey, my film is doing really well." And then someone swoops in and gives you national distribution.

So that was kind of our plan. We opened the film in Omaha at a big multiplex, and it did well. We're beating some of the big Hollywood films, we're getting all the local press and everything. And then we'd open in Lincoln, and then we kind of slowly worked our way out, just kind of expanded geographically from there. So we played in South Dakota, and Iowa, Kansas and Kansas City and St. Louis. And we worked our way down to Texas, and then Atlanta, and then made our way westward. We played five weeks in Tempe, Arizona.

The key thing was at the time, we shot our film in 35 mm, you had to project in 35, and we made trailers, 35 mm trailers, but you could only get about seven or eight prints off your negative before the negative can start to disintegrate. That was a really expensive process. But if you were doing a handful of prints, it was a lot cheaper. So we would take the money that we made in Omaha, to pay for an extra printing that we needed in Kansas City, or some things like that. In the end, we wound up with four prints. But each of those additional prints was like $4,000. They weren't cheap. And then we also had to pay for ads, right? Newspaper ads, print ads. But the idea was that it was kind of self-generated. We never raised additional money to do our distribution. It was always, you know, the money we made in one place paid for the advertising in the next place. It was kind of a zero sum endeavor. We didn't make money, we didn't lose money, which basically meant you're doing as well as the studios do. It was fun.

ML: What were the highest points in that process?
DM: I think for me, personally, a lot of it came at the end of the run. We're in LA, and we got a great review. We got a half page profile on the Sunday LA Times. And it was a fun story, too. I always tell people, you never know what's going to happen when only one person comes to your screening. We did a press screening in a 400 seat theater at Laemmle, and only one person showed. I was like, oh my god, this is horrible. But he liked it. And he was the editor of the LA Times calendar section! So he assigned a half

ML: page profile. So I'd rather have one person in the audience who likes it. So that was great. And then just working with Bob and Greg Laemmle, you know, just on a personal basis, because they booked the film for a weekend, at the theater they had in downtown LA. Another highlight was at that screening, I threw raw steak and corn at the audience. And that got us on Channel Five, on KTLA, in LA. Because no one else was throwing raw meat at the audience.

ML: That sounds unique.

DM: It was wrapped in plastic. But that kept us in circulation, because we had a good review, and a great review of the LA Times and the LA Weekly. So we had a one solid week run. But then they kept us in the rotation as a midnight movie, like at the Sunset Five. And as a morning movie at the Laemmle Monica. for 11 weeks total. So that meant that I could strap on my sandwich board. And we met everyone. Tarantino, Drew Barrymore, Seth Green, you know, like all kinds of crazy people. Everyone cool went to the Sunset Five at the midnight shifts.

ML: What would you say are the biggest things you learned throughout that process?

DM: That you've got to do it all yourself. Like I mentioned, we started with the FEDERAL HILL/SLACKER strategy. But the reality was that then we'd call these distributors and say, "Hey, we just did great in Omaha," and they'd be like, "Oh, that's a shame. You just blew your biggest audience." So yeah, now we're not interested. So that strategy either works, or they use it as an excuse to say to keep saying no. Right? No matter how we did or what kind of crazy stunts we pulled, it was never going to get someone on board to distribute. It was like Mark Duplass's phrase, "The cavalry is not coming."

         The other thing I learned is that all this stuff is worth doing, if you're having fun doing it. So the minute it becomes a chore, don't do it. I think something that I've come to appreciate even more since then is realizing exactly what these films are. If you just look at these films as three weeks of set, directing for three weeks, it's not just that. The project takes five years to get done, and then another 20 years of distribution afterwards. Looking back at it makes perfect sense, which is that these things are not just 90 minutes of entertainment. They are five year long, community-based performing arts projects, that encompass everything from the crowdfunding, to the filming, to the festivals, to the interaction with the crowd, and the audience attitudes and screenings to whatever kind of performance art you do at the screenings, like throwing steak at the audience, or Nixon protesters? Whatever it is, if you look at them as these multi-year, multimedia, multi-geographical art projects, then it makes a lot more sense. It's easier to justify.

When you get to a certain age, you look back, you're like, Oh, wait, I did all that just for a 90-minute film? No, I did all that because we got a lot of people involved at various stages. We also had fun along the way, at all the different phases. And I think once you take that holistic look at it, this is really what it is we're doing. It's not just getting your little 90-minute film to audiences, because there's easier ways to do that. But it's the long-term engagement with those audiences that is emotionally fulfilling, and creatively and artistically fulfilling.

ML: For theatrical releases, you talk in your book about the idea of "eventizing" your film, a term coined by filmmaker Jon Reiss. Can you talk about what that means?

DM: Jon's the one that really started talking about that a few years ago. So I'm just copying off him. On the one hand, the distinction between film festivals and theatrical is getting a lot fuzzier because more festivals are doing year round programming, either because they own the theater, or they're working with a theater. Some have been doing this for years, but some, it's more recent. Also, more festivals are revenue sharing, at least during COVID, with filmmakers. And that was kind of a new thing for non-gay, non-Jewish festivals. The gay and the Jewish festival circuits have, for years.

I think that theaters need to be more like festivals, in that they need to "eventize" their theatrical screenings. And if you're in LA or New York, this has been commonplace for years. People do Q&A's after their theatrical screening. If you're in New York, you know, you're at the IFC Center, you do a Q&A after screening, so it's pretty commonplace. But in other parts of the country, I don't think as much because realistically, you know, if your film comes out in 10, or 20, or 60, theaters, you physically can't get to all these different places. And that's where the technology can help. I mean, look, Tom Cruise did introductions for TOP GUN: MAVERICK. It came out and people's reaction was, "Oh, my gosh, that's crazy." But it works. It's a way to engage with the audience, even if it's Tom Cruise on 6,000 screens. But, you know, but if you're screaming in Wichita, you can do a Zoom Q&A, even if you're not there. Theaters have figured out the technical side of that in a way that pre-COVID they really hadn't. Before COVID, it was Skype, and it was complicated. But I think, for actors, and for directors, you know, Zoom has just gotten more normalized like, "Oh, do a Q&A on Zoom. Yeah." Every actor has a little ring light and a microphone. They know how to do this stuff. It's not strange. So there's no reason you can't do that kind of thing now.

I think, fundamentally, theaters figured out that they've got to get people off the couches, they're gotta get them to stop watching Netflix at home. So what are they going to do to bring people back into the theaters? Back into that theatrical experience?

There's another interesting lesson, though, in addition to the Zoom Q&A. And it kind of goes back to my paradigm about it being a community-based project. If you've got 300 backers around the country, you don't have to be the one doing the Q&A. You can have one of your backers doing Q&A, or one of your investors during the Q&A. Forget about the idea of doing the Zoom Q&A, get a live body. That's great because all those people know all the same stories about the film. So why not get other people to do it? And I think that's something that decentralizes it. The director is not the only filmmaker. You can have the DP or the writer. I once had a key grip go to a festival, because it was the only one I couldn't attend. He was thrilled, you know, and he knew as many stories about the film as I did, about the making of it, probably better than I did. On 18½, largely because of COVID, but also financially, I couldn't make it to Detroit. That said, our executive producer in Detroit could be there. So great! You're hosting the event, right? He ended up doing the whole thing. And that worked out great. You got a lot of a lot more people involved.

ML: What's the biggest piece of advice you can give to new filmmakers who will be self-distributing their film for the first time?

DM: I would tell them no matter what, marry well! Which sounds goofy, but it's kind of true in the sense that self-distribution either takes time, or takes money. But it does not necessarily take both. So I think that's a crucial thing. Because I've heard a lot of people go out and self-distribute, and they find they need to pay money for a booking, or pay money for a poster Or you take the time for putting your own screenings together. You do your own publicity, you do your own booking, and make it work that way, but that takes time. So if you've got a job or career, or family that can support you during that process, then it makes sense to put the time in to do it. Or if you're not already working on your next film. If you don't, if you've got a really solid day job. Yeah, you may not have the time to do it. In which case, okay, how much money does it take? It can be one or the other.

Notes

1 https://filmmakermagazine.com/120384-truth-about-independent-film-revenue/
2 https://time.com/6307420/taylor-swift-eras-tour-money-economy/
3 https://puck.news/how-the-swiftie-cinematic-universe-came-to-theaters/
4 https://www.boxofficemojo.com/title/tt28814949/

Reference List

Belloni, Matthew. "How the Swiftie Cinematic Universe Came to Theaters," *Puck News*, 2023. https://puck.news/how-the-swiftie-cinematic-universe-came-to-theaters/

Box Office Mojo box office data on TAYLOR SWIFT: THE ERAS TOUR. https://www.boxofficemojo.com/title/tt28814949/

Jones, Naomi McDougall and Manashil, Liz. "Producer Data: The Numbers Don't Lie (The Truth about Independent Film Revenue," *Filmmaker Magazine*, 2023. https://filmmakermagazine.com/120384-truth-about-independent-film-revenue/

Kopstein, Jeannie and Espada, Mariah. "The Staggering Economic Impact of Taylor Swift's Eras Tour," *Time Magazine*, 2023. https://time.com/6307420/taylor-swift-eras-tour-money-economy/

11 You're Done. Now What?

My God.

You're finished.

Your film has been made, marketed, and put out in the world. And you've been wildly successful in doing so. You've got film festival laurels, pictures from the film playing in theaters, and glowing press coverage about the obviously genius filmmaker who made it. Maybe you've gotten social media messages from people who enjoyed it – I got the sweetest Facebook DM from a RISING STAR viewer in Klerksdorp, South Africa, saying how much she loved it when it came out on cable in the country. You're feeling a well-deserved sense of accomplishment.

So what do you do now?

You bring your work with you, over to a new project!

The brilliance of this style of filmmaking is that when you're done, you've built the foundation for a second film. Then a third. And as many films as you'd like to make. I call this foundation the Loop of Kindness.

The Loop of Kindness

The great thing about building community for your film is that after you do it once, you can pick up right where you left off for a subsequent one. Your audience isn't going anywhere, so if you make a project that's similar in some way (the same genre, same actors, or just a new film from you), they'll be interested in learning more about it. Your resources are still in place, so you can return to them, and ask to utilize them again. If you remember one thing, remember this: If you're good to your community, they'll be good to you!

DOI: 10.4324/9781003295754-11

For STAY WITH ME, even though I made the film in California, I had the community I had built by crowdfunding RISING STAR in Connecticut to help get us off the ground. When we began our Seed&Spark campaign for STAY WITH ME, I reached out to all the backers of RISING STAR. Happily, there were dozens of backers who wanted to support the new film, including a Connecticut Film Industry Training Program alumnus who donated $1,000! There were ten years between crowdfunding campaigns for these two films; it doesn't take much to get people excited again about something new.

You could also find folks who join your team on a first project, and then grow into a bigger role on subsequent projects. Our Facebook promotion of RISING STAR landed us a location – as well as a producer. When I wrote the script, I wrote a pivotal scene to take place at Sully's Pub, a bar and music venue in Hartford, that I had never been to. I wrote it there because my lead actress, Emily Morse, performed spoken-word poetry there for the first time, and her character, Alyza, raps for the first time in a music venue. I thought it would be perfect for Emily to draw on that experience, in the same place, while giving that performance in the movie. I had no connection to Sully's other than Emily, but I was thinking once we got into pre-production, I would contact them and see if we could film there.

Once our Kickstarter campaign started, though, I got a Facebook message from Darrell Sullivan, the owner of Sully's! He said he read an article about the film, loved the project, and wanted to help in whatever way he could. We had never met before! I went to Sully's soon after to meet him, he showed me the venue, and said we could shoot there for free. Darrell also ended up with a cameo acting role in the movie, and an Associate Producer credit, for all his help. He told me that the next time I make a movie in Connecticut, he wants to collaborate with me on it as a producer.

All from a connection I didn't even initiate.

Building Your Ecosystem

An amazing byproduct of community filmmaking is that you can contribute to the film scene of your local area by literally building it. If you happen to be the first filmmaker who makes a big project, the people you work with will no doubt follow behind you with projects of their own. And this is where radical collaboration comes in. Your filmmaking team gave you time, resources, and sometimes money to make your film, and they have dreams to tell their own stories. If you can help them as they make their own films, the goodwill that you build from it will pay you back multiple times over – and it will continue to familiarize your community with filmmaking. You don't need to be the only filmmaker working in a community – if you help others make their films, you're building momentum that you can take advantage of later down the line.

After RISING STAR was finished, there was an explosion of independent filmmaking in Connecticut, and I was thrilled to help on a bunch of them:

- Our co-producer Gary Fierro directed a comedy feature called THE MEAN OF GREEN, which I executive produced and acted in (four other RISING STAR actors were in it, too)
- Our editor, Alec Asten, directed an action feature called DIAMOND RUFF, and I acted in it as a prison inmate (this one had three RISING STAR actors in it)
- Our actors Sari Gagnon and Matt Heron-Duranti eventually founded their own production company, Counterfeit Cow Productions, and I produced a feature documentary with them called HOMELESS IN A COLLEGE TOWN, about the struggles of Amherst, Massachusetts with the homeless
- Second unit cinematographer Michael Shove directed a short called VANILLA PLOT, which I worked on as second assistant director (two RISING STAR actors acted in it, too)
- Graphic artist Jim Hawk directed a short film called UNFORGIVEN, which I produced (two RISING STAR actors are in this one)

These guys aren't world-renowned filmmakers (yet), but it's important to see how small a film community is, and how often people work with each other. If you can help those in your community, they'll be there for you when you need it.

Bridging the Indie Gap

The other great thing about this type of filmmaking is that it can provide a seamless transition into professional filmmaking, at any point in your career. If your first film doesn't get you an offer to get paid to make something, the Loop of Kindness will allow you to continue building support until you do, over as many films as you'd like to make. Each time you make something new, you have a new chance to build your audience and supporters.

If you make a film that's a huge hit, though, you'll be able to get out of the Indie Gap! And if your film gets you enough heat that someone wants to pay you to make another one, you'll have assets you can monetize. You'll have an audience you've proven you can engage, and direct contact to them. That could help you get a bigger paycheck, more equity in the film, more of a say in the marketing and distribution – maybe even final cut.

What if you get that chance, and the film you get paid to make isn't successful? Perhaps it doesn't make the money the investors thought it would. It doesn't get the cultural discussion the producers wanted. That might mean you won't get hired a second time.

Here's the good news, though: all the work you did on your community-supported films didn't go anywhere. You can move from a bigger budget to a smaller budget for your next film and go back to your community to help you. You could even make a smaller film while you're trying to get a bigger film off the ground. Some might think it's a step backwards going from a bigger film to a smaller film, but to me, the only step backwards is not making a film at all.

This is a personal thing for me, because even though I've worked as a writer, director, producer and actor in films and television for over 20 years, I'm still in the Indie Gap. And I don't consider it a bad thing. Because I think in terms of radical collaboration, entrepreneurial thinking and holistic filmmaking, I've been able to create my own work over all that time. And I've never had to get anyone's permission to do it. Do I hope that one day, a film of mine will create enough excitement for someone to pay me to make it? Absolutely! But if it never happens, I'll still have a body of work that people can watch. I'll still have made films.

No matter what stage of your career you're in, that's the most important thing.

You Can Build Anywhere

You might live somewhere where films aren't produced very much (if at all), but this style of filmmaking can make it happen for you, no matter where home is. I know because my film career started in one of those places.

Growing up in northern Connecticut, the idea of working as a filmmaker was the most foreign thing in the world to me. My mother was a secretary and my father was a mechanic, so films were just things we watched. I never seriously considered the idea of making films at home.

In fact, I never seriously considered the idea of making films at all until I was out of college. I was a journalism major in school, and after I graduated, I worked as a reporter for the New York Times. And it was through that work that I met HEAT actress Amy Brenneman. She was also a Connecticut native, and at the time, the star of a TV show called JUDGING AMY. I interviewed her for the Connecticut section of the Times because she was getting an honorary degree at a state college. And at that interview, she asked me the question that started my journey in this crazy world:

"You ever think about working in the movies?"

Up until that moment, I hadn't. But she gave me the motivation to see what was being made in Connecticut, and I found one film – A LITTLE BIT OF LIPSTICK. I spent two years on that film, eventually becoming a producer, and that led to my working on a few more as a producer. Those early jobs got me into film school.

Even in film school, though, I assumed I would spend my career living and working in Los Angeles, because that's just where you went to work in film and television. But I couldn't afford to live there, partly because my parents couldn't help me financially, and partly because of my student loan debt. So I was forced to start my professional career in Connecticut.

I didn't know it at the time, but that was the best thing that could have ever happened to me. It allowed me to start teaching, it plugged me into a passionate indie film community, and it gave me the chance to find my tribe. That was the only reason I could put RISING STAR together – and that film began my education in crowdsourcing, crowdfunding and community filmmaking – which led to this book.

I know how hard it is for people who want to be filmmakers, but who don't have the means to live in the traditional industry hubs. That's why I'm so excited about this style of filmmaking – there are so many of us outside of those places! We want to make films! And we want to be part of creative communities! We just need to find each other, help each other, and build our local film scenes up.

I know it can be done. I've done it. And I know you can do it, too.

So get out there. Make your dreams come true, and do it on your terms.

Become a self-sustaining filmmaker.

Index

Note: *Italicized* and **bold** page numbers refer to figures and tables.

28 DAYS LATER 26, 68

A24 2
AI *see* artificial intelligence (AI)
ALOHA 54, 59
ALPHA 8 109
"The Alyza Challenge" campaign 161
THE AMAZING SPIDER-MAN 144
Amazon 5, 14
AMERICAN HUSTLE 43
American Motion Picture & Television Producers (AMPTP) 5, 6
AMPTP *see* American Motion Picture & Television Producers (AMPTP)
Anderson, Chris 65–66
Aron, Adam 186
ARRAY 124
artificial intelligence (AI) 5–6
THE ART OF ASKING 85–86
Asten, Alec 200
A TIME TO KILL 72
audience 46–50
A YEAR WITHOUT RENT (AYWR) 101; crowdfunding 80
AYWR *see* A YEAR WITHOUT RENT (AYWR)

Barra, Michael 144–145
Belloni, Matthew 186
BERNARD AND HUEY 191
Best, Emily 32–37, *32*; on career 36; on entrepreneurs 32–37; on revenues 34–36
BETWEEN US 191

THE BIG LEBOWSKI 63
BitMax 189
Black, Hannah 130–134, *130*; on origin of *DROUGHT* 130; on writing for *DROUGHT* 132
Black, Skinny 77
THE BLACKLIST 118
BLACK LOVE 35
BLACK SNAKE MOAN 73
BLAIR WITCH PROJECT, THE 21
BLRTS process 136–138
BLUFF CITY NIGHTS 182
Botto, Richard "R.B." 39
Braff, Zach 65
Branin, David 84
BREAKING OUT OF BREAKING IN 107
Brenneman, Amy 201
Brewer, Craig 71–77, *71*; on coffee shops writing 73–77; on locations 71–73
BROTHER'S KEEPER 192
Brown Paper Tickets 189
BURN NOTICE 107
Bushnell Park 122
business, in real world 31–32
business model 22–24, *22*; mindset into filmmaking, translating 29–30
business questions, answering 13–24; benefits 18; business model 22–24; competition 18–19; market 19–21; problem solving 14–18

capitalism: definition of 12
Carberry, Lee 132

carding 61–63
Castellini, Bri 107–111, **107**; on consultation 108–109; on crowdfunding 108, 110–111; on personality traits 110
Catalyst Media 88
THE CHEERFUL SUBVERSIVE'S GUIDE TO INDEPENDENT FILMMAKING 191
CHOMPY & THE GIRLS 16, *17*, 18, 186, 187
Collins, Gregor 84
COMING 2 AMERICA 61, 71
COMMITMENTS, THE 62
community-based story building 41–42
Connecticut: audience 47; film scene 47–48
Connecticut Film Festival 187
Connecticut Film Industry Training Program (FITP) 48, 49, 118, 122, 160, 199
Connecticut Science Center 121, 122
CONNECT TO 80
Counterfeit Cow Productions 200
Craig, Gary 43
Creative Works Conference, Memphis 53
crowdfunding 6–7, 78–86; conflicting emotions 84–86; holistic 82–84; as networking 79–81
"Crowdfunding to Build Independence" (Seed&Spark) 88–107; after effect of 104–105; backer updates 101; bonus elements 102; community engagement 103–104; direct outreach 99–101; filmmakers, role of 96; incentives 93–95; leadup to launch 97–102; pitch video, creation of 96; prepping 89–97; schduling 97–99; size of audience 92–93; social media 101–102; team building 91–92; time to lauch 90–91
crowdsourcing: *DEADBRAINS* 52; definition of 39–40; screenwriting 63–66; story of 40–46
Cuban, Mark 12
cultural enhancement, pre-production and 123
CURB YOUR ENTHUSIASM 43

DAWN OF THE DEAD 28
DCP *see* digital cinema package (DCP)

DEADBRAINS 26–30, **27**; audience identification 53; crowdfunding 84, 105–107; crowdsourcing 52; development for 52–53; distribution 190–191; marketing 175–176; post-production 145–146; pre-production 129; production 145–146; publicity 53; screenwriting for 68–71; team building 53
de Leon, Sarah 114
development 38–59
DGA *see* Directors Guild of America (DGA)
DIAMOND RUFF 200
digital cinema package (DCP) 187
digital distribution 188–189
digital footprint 155
Dinucci, Nancy 64
Directors Guild of America (DGA) 122
DISAPPEARING BOY 148, 149
distribution 182–196; digital 188–189
DOLEMITE IS MY NAME 61, 71, 74
DROUGHT 130, 130, 134
Duplass, Mark 132
Duvernay, Ava 124
Dydyn, Damian 102

economic development, pre-production and 121–122
ecosystem, building 199–200
Edson, Eric 61
educational opportunities, in pre-production 118–119
ELIOT: THE LITTLEST REINDEER: crowdfunding 80
ELVIS 16
emotions, conflicting 84–86
EMPIRE 71
entrepreneurial mindset 8–9, 38; creation of 12–13
entrepreneurs: creative 36–37; definition of 32, 33; disruption of industry by 33–34
Eslick, Ben 103
EventBrite 189

Falco, Edie 2
FEAR THE WALKING DEAD 146
FEDERAL HILL 193, 194
Fierro, Gary 200
film-adjacent content, creation of 144–145

film education 3–5
Filmhub 189
FINDING NEMO 22
FITP *see* Connecticut Film Industry Training Program (FITP)
Florida State University (FSU): film school community 48; Graduate Film Conservatory 48
FOOTLOOSE 71
Fox, Lara 114
"free-range" films 184–185
FSU *see* Florida State University (FSU)
FULL HOUSE 68

Gagnon, Sari 200
Galuppo, Mia 4
GAME OF THRONES 44
GARDEN STATE 65
Gay, Andrew Kenneth 65, 66; "Screenwriting 2.0 in the Classroom? Teaching the Digital Screenplay" 64
Georgia Film Academy (GFA) 122
Gerwig, Greta 36
GFA *see* Georgia Film Academy (GFA)
Giovannucci, Matt 49–50, 145, 146
Glass, Ira 37
GOATS 79
GoFundMe 78
"golden elevator" films 184–185
GOODBYE PROMISE: crowdfunding 84; marketing 157
Grant, Adam: Re:Thinking 12
Green, Jessie 139
Griffin, Clay 74
Gunn, James 180

Harriet Beecher Stowe House 42
Hawk, Jim 200
HBO 54
hedging 10
Henson, Taraji P. 71
Heron-Duranti, Matt 200
holistic filmmaking 9–10, 60
HOMELESS IN A COLLEGE TOWN 200
HOOD HIPPIE: THE ALBUM 128
Howard, Terrance 62
HowardArtSPFX 52
Howe, Jeff 113

Hulu 5
HUSTLE AND FLOW 61, 62, 71–73, 76, 77

I AM LEGEND 25, **27**, 68; screenwriting 69
I AM MARTIN EISENSTADT 191
IATSE *see* International Alliance of Theater and Stage Employees (IATSE)
IFP *see* Independent Feature Project (IFP)
IFP Made, New York Center, Brooklyn 88
IMAX theater 16
Independent Feature Project (IFP) 158
independent film 6–7
INDIANA JONES 123
Indie Gap 2, 3, 10; bridging 200–201
IndieGoGo 6, 78, 79
International Alliance of Theater and Stage Employees (IATSE) 122

JAWS 16
Jenkins, Barry 2
Jones, Kim 103, 104
Jones, Naomi McDougall 34
JUDGING AMY 201

Kickstarter 6, 55, 78–80, 145, 160
Kid 'n Play 37
Kinsella School for Performing Arts 48, 117
Knudson, John 134
KRISHA 41
Kroll, Noam 146–152, *146*; on large scale indie project 151–152; on lighting 148–149; on post-production 150–151; on small crews 149–150; on technology 147, 148

LANDLINE 2
LAND OF THE DEAD 25, **27**, 68
Lang, Marty, interviews of: with Brandi Nicole 54–59; with Bri Castellini 107–111; with Craig Brewer 71–77; with Dan Mirvish 191–196; with Emily Best 32–37; with Hannah Black 130–134; with Megan Peterson 130–134; with Nicholas LaRue 176–180; with Noam Kroll 146–152

LaRue, Nicholas 176–180, *176*
Lawrence, Martin 37
Lee, Spike 71
LIGHTS OUT 2
A LITTLE BIT OF LIPSTICK 202; pre-production 121
local celebrities 42–43
LOCKED IN A GARAGE BAND 102; crowdfunding 62
Ludacris 77

Maiman, Leaf 43
Malco Theatres 186
marketing 153–180; digital footprint 155; press release 157–161; re-engagement 154–155; relevant content, creation of 156–161, *162–174*; tracking 156
Mark Twain House 42, 116, 117, 122, 154, 158
Mark Twain Museum 116, 158
McNelly, Lucas 80
THE MEAN OF GREEN 200
MEAN STREETS 72
MEDICINE FOR MELANCHOLY 2
MEMENTO 41
Memphis Museum of Science & History 16
Memphis Zombie Hunt 53
Memphis Zombie Walk 53
mental health advocacy 100
"Micro-Budget Weekly" 146
mindset into filmmaking, translating 24–30; benefits 26–27; business model 29–30; competition 27, **27**; market 27–29; problem 25; solution 25–26
Minnesota Film Production Tax Credit program 126
Mirvish, Dan 93–94, 178, 191–196, *191*
MISSISSIPPI BURNING 72
MOONLIGHT 2
Morse, Emily 199
"Movies in the Park" 122
Murphy, Eddie 74
MUTED 54
MYSTIC PIZZA: pre-production 122

National Institute of Standards and Technology 125
Netflix 4, 5, 33

Nicole, Brandi 54–59, *54*; on career 54; on creative team leadership 58; on crowdfunding 56–57; on production 54–55, 58–59; on television experience 57; on working with casting director 55–56; on writer/producer 56
Nieto, Maria 184
Nixon, Richard *94*
Nolan, Christopher 15, 41, 72

OBVIOUS CHILD 2
OMAHA (THE MOVIE) 191, 192
open call, power of 113–115
OPEN HOUSE 191
OTHER GUYS, THE 11
OUT OF MY HAND 124

Palmer, Amanda 85
Parker, Alan 62
Patreon 6
Peterson, Megan 130–134, *130*; on GoFundMe campaign 131; on Hometown Heroes 132; on writing for *DROUGHT* 131
pizza, as microbudget feature 43–46
POOR AND HUNGRY, THE 72–73, 75, 76, 77
post-production 136–152; transparency in 139–140
Premiere Digital 189
pre-production 113–134; community and 116, 123–125; cultural enhancement 123; economic development 121–122; educational opportunities 118–119; open call, power of 113–115; planning of 127–129; promotional opportunities 119–121; research 116–117; strengths, knowing 117; symbiotic relationships 115–117; tax credits 125–127; workforce development 122–123
PRIDE AND PREJUDICE AND ZOMBIES 26, **27**, 68
problem solving 14–18
production 136–152
production manager: on clearance 68; on locations 66–67; on minor-aged actors 67–68; on schedules 67
promotional opportunities, in pre-production 119–121
PROTESTERS 119

PSYCHOSYNTHESIS 146, 149
publicity 50–51; *DEADBRAINS* 53
PURPLE RAIN 62

radical collaboration 7–8
Rae, Issa 32, 54
Ratzenberger, John 122
Reeder, Jennifer 36
ReelLife Entertainment pitch deck: ask slide *24*; benefit slide 18, *18*; business model slide 22–24, *22*; competition slide 18–19, *19*; market slide 19–21, *20*, *21*; problem slide 14–18, *14*; solution slide *15*, 16–18; title slide *13*
RISING STAR 6, 8, 11, 39–43, 46, 48–50, 78, 100, 103, 105, 113, 114, 198–200, 202; crowdfunding 79–82, 92, 94; distribution 187; film-adjacent content 145; marketing 154, 157; post-production 140, **140–143**; pre-production 116, 117, 119–122, *120*, *121*, 125, 129; press release 157–161, *162–174*; shooting 138–139
Robespierre, Gillian 2
Robinson, Mark 113
Roca, Michelle 134
ROCKY 62
ROCKY HORROR PICTURE SHOW 186

SAG-AFTRA *see* Screen Actors Guild-American Federation of Television & Radio Artists (SAG-AFTRA)
Sales, Soupy 121
Salt 'n Pepa 37
Sandberg, David F. 2
SATURDAY NIGHT FEVER 62
SAVE THE CAT! 61
SAVING PRIVATE RYAN: screenwriting 69
SAW 2
SCANDAL 57
scheduling: importance of 51–52
Scorsese, Martin 71
Screen Actors Guild-American Federation of Television & Radio Artists (SAG-AFTRA) 5, 6
screenwriting 60–77; carding 61–63; collective intelligence, harnessing 64; crowdsourcing 63–66; for *DEADBRAINS* 68–71; Long Tail, leveraging 65–66; perpetual beta 64–65; rich user experience 65; shelf 61–63; software 65
Screenwriting 2.0 64, 65, 69
Seattle True Independent Film Festival 80
Seed&Spark 6, 32–37, 78, 79, 81
Seimetz, Amy 122
SELENE HOLLOW 102
SHADOWS ON THE ROAD 146
shelf 61–63
SHE'S GOTTA HAVE IT 72
#ShortFilmSundays 54
Shove, Michael 200
"Show, Don't Tell" 146
Shults, Trey Edward 41
SKINAMARINK 96, 107; marketing 155
SLACKER 193, 194
Slate, Jenny 2
SMASH 11
Snyder, Blake 61
Snyder, Zack 28
Spacey, Kevin 69
SPIN 54, 56
startup business, film as 30–31
Startup Weekend 88
STAY WITH ME 8, 43, 44, 92, 99–100, 199; post-production 139; pre-production 114–115
Stevens, Wallace 42, 122
St. Louis County: Production Incentive Program 127
STORY SOLUTION, THE 61
studio filmmaking 5–6
Support Our Stories 78
Swift, Taylor 185, 186
symbiotic relationships 115–117

tax credits, pre-production and 125–127; city credit 127; county credit 127; state credit 126
TAYLOR SWIFT: THE ERAS TOUR 186
TCAF *see* Testicular Cancer Awareness Foundation (TCAF)
TCF *see* Testicular Cancer Foundation (TCF)
team building 50–51; *DEADBRAINS* 53
TENET 15

Testicular Cancer Awareness Foundation (TCAF) 103
Testicular Cancer Foundation (TCF) 103
THEATRE IS EVIL 85
TO DYE FOR 67
TOP GUN: MAVERICK 195
tracking 156
Turturro, John 2
Twain, Mark 116
Tyler, Mia 121

UNFORGIVEN 200
UNIBALL: community engagement 103–104; crowdfunding 81
UNICO 50
UPM 70
THE USUAL SUSPECTS: screenwriting 69

VANILLA PLOT 200
video on demand (VOD) 188
VOD *see* video on demand (VOD)

Walker, Brad 133
THE WALKING DEAD 146
Wan, James 2
WARM BODIES 26, **27**, 68
Web 2.0 64
West, Jen 54
WGA *see* Writers Guild of America (WGA)
"Where's Balldo" campaign 81, *82*
"Whoop That Trick" 62
Worden, Karen 84
workforce development, pre-production and 122–123
work/life balance, people struggling with 47
WORLD WAR Z 26, 68; screenwriting 69
Wrench, Sam 186
Writers Guild of America (WGA) 5

Yale Entrepreneurial Institute 88